A Guide to Effective School Leadership Theories

Educational administrators know that leadership requires hundreds of judgments each day that demand a sensitivity and understanding of various leadership strategies. Bridging the gap between the academic and practical world, *A Guide to Effective School Leadership Theories* provides an exploration of ten dominant leadership strategies to give school leaders a solid basis in theory and practical application. Demonstrating the advantages and drawbacks of each theory, readers are encouraged to discover the most appropriate strategy, or combination of strategies, that will best enable their school to achieve positive results. Each chapter includes:

- Introductory vignettes grounding the leadership theory in practice.
- Discussion of the history, development, and utility of the strategy.
- Research findings for further exploration of the theory.
- End-of-chapter questions and activities designed to connect theory to practice.

This book is essential reading for aspiring and practicing school leaders who wish to have a better understanding of their leadership role. Providing a focused, up-to-date introduction to the current themes and dimensions of educational leadership, *A Guide to Effective School Leadership Theories* presents all the tools necessary to analyze and implement effective leadership in readers' own settings.

Matthew Lynch is Assistant Professor of Education at Widener University.

A Guide to Effective School Leadership Theories

Matthew Lynch

Routledge
Taylor & Francis Group

NEW YORK AND LONDON

First published 2012
by Routledge
711 Third Avenue, New York, NY 10017

Simultaneously published in the UK
by Routledge
2 Park Square, Milton Park, Abingdon, Oxon OX14 4RN

Routledge is an imprint of the Taylor & Francis Group, an informa business

Library of Congress Cataloging in Publication Data
Lynch, Matthew, 1978-
A guide to effective school leadership theories / Matthew Lynch.—
1st ed.
p. cm.
Includes bibliographical references and index.
1. Educational leadership—United States. 2. School management and
organization—United States. I. Title.
LB2805.L96 2012
371.2—dc22
                                                                    2011034384

ISBN: 978–0–415–89950–5 (hbk)
ISBN: 978–0–415–89951–2 (pbk)
ISBN: 978–0–203–18101–0 (ebk)

Typeset in Bembo
by RefineCatch Limited, Bungay, Suffolk

This book is dedicated to the educators and educational administrators who work diligently to ensure that every child in the world receives a quality education. This dedication is your standing ovation! Take a bow!

Table of Contents

Preface

A number of studies over the past two decades have centered on leadership in the school setting. Though the studies varied in scope and focus, their conclusions, for the most part, agree: in the current environment of dramatically shifting educational policies and divisive, competing theories, the role of the school leader is more important than ever. School leaders today must have the tools to respond with alacrity and dexterity to emerging trends and policy changes, and must be trained not only in decision-making, but in effective communication, analysis, and networking.

Prior to 1960, schools in the United States, like most organizations and political institutions, were run on a strictly hierarchical basis, with the principal (usually a European American man) firmly in the driver's seat, and the teachers and other stakeholders given top-down commands and expected to follow through without questioning authority. Teachers, parents, and the community had little opportunity to express their opinions within the system, and dissatisfaction was rife.

In the last half-century, scholars in fields such as philosophy, psychology, and business management have focused their attention on schools, with dramatic results. While strong leadership is still warranted, most scholars now recommend that school leaders improve communication skills and implement strong bottom-up structures that allow the voices of all stakeholders to be heard.

As minorities and people of color within the U.S. swell in proportion to the European American majority, who are expected to become the minority by 2050, the ethnic, racial, and socioeconomic complexion of schools is also shifting dramatically. School leaders must take this new plurality into consideration. The presence of diverse voices, languages and cultures, means that the old methods aimed at a homogeneous student population will no longer work. In welcoming a more diverse community and creating a curriculum that appeals to a greater range of American experiences, school leaders must learn to create an expanded vision.

Political changes in the United States have created a shifting climate that is keeping school leaders on their toes. With the renewed emphasis on testing and accountability, school leaders must balance quality instructional time and the value of subjects such as art and music with the need to focus on test results. This is creating tensions and divisions within schools, and school leaders must use their diplomatic skills to deal with angry parents and disgruntled teachers.

The school leaders of tomorrow will, for the reasons outlined above, be very different creatures from those of the previous generation. *A Guide to Effective School Leadership Theories* aims to present an array of educational leadership styles/methods in a succinct and practical manner, in order to give the potential school leader a solid basis in theory and practical application. Theoretical background and philosophical discussion are grounded by case studies and vignettes demonstrating the advantages and drawbacks of each method. The various methods are presented positively, and the discussion questions and activities at the end of each chapter provide the reader with an opportunity to explore the ramifications of each method as it pertains to a variety of situations. In addition to the discussion questions and activities, a handful of selected readings is provided at the end of each chapter, allowing the reader to investigate each topic in more depth.

Let's take a look at the material covered in the various chapters.

Organization of the Book

Chapter 1: Transformational Leadership: The (Un)Disputed Champion of Leadership Strategies

Transformational leadership, which was developed by James Burns and Bernard Bass, places relationships at the center of educational leadership. It encourages leaders to develop tools and strategies that encourage all stakeholders to participate in creating the mission and commit to the purpose of the school. In the transformational model, school leaders must have the charisma to influence employees, the intelligence to create strong, sustainable participatory structures, and the ability to give individualized attention. Transformational leadership is compared and contrasted with three similar leadership styles: transactional leadership, emotional leadership, and servant leadership.

Chapter 2: Instructional Leadership: A Catalyst for the Promotion of Teaching and Learning

Instructional leadership is the traditional top-down, principal-as-dictator method of school leadership. This chapter looks at the history of school leadership, and the changes implemented in the 1970s and 1980s, when the focus shifted to "effectiveness." The three essential tasks of a school leader—defining the school's mission, managing the instructional program, and promoting a positive school learning climate—are examined through the lens of instructional leadership, and the positive and negative aspects of this method are elucidated. Finally, the Myers-Briggs personality evaluation test is used to determine the optimal personality traits of a school leader.

Chapter 3: Distributed Leadership: A Humanistic Approach to Shared Governance

Distributed leadership is rapidly becoming a prominent new model in schools across the United States. As it becomes clear that not all school leaders have the exceptional qualities needed to successfully enact transformation, distributed leadership, in which stakeholders share responsibility, is becoming more wide-spread. This method is highly flexible, and the chapter outlines some of the ways in which distributed leadership manifests itself, from "soft bureaucracy," to democracy in school politics. Some of the practical considerations of moving from an instructional to a distributed model are examined in the latter part of the chapter.

Chapter 4: Ethical Leadership: Using Your Moral Compass to Steer the Ship

Ethics is an area of growing concern in the educational sphere. New media allows for greater scrutiny of teachers and staff, and lawsuits are becoming commonplace. This chapter examines the historical basis of ethics, looking at the philosophical inquiries of Aristotle, Kant, and Mill, before turning to the neces-sity of a solid ethical structure in the school system, and the means of creating such a structure. Areas investigated include: creating a defined moral code; the use of ethics vocabulary; the necessity of empathy in administration; and the application of and monitoring of equal and fair approaches.

Chapter 5: Emotional Leadership: Using Your Heart to Lead

Emotional intelligence (EI) was first described by Salovey and Mayer as a distinct area of human intelligence. While intellectually brilliant people often rise to the top of organizations, it takes a degree of emotional intelligence to make an excel-lent manager. This chapter looks at the characteristics of emotional intelligence as they pertain to school leadership. The strong connections between emotional and transformational leadership are noted, and its impact on motivation and effectiveness are described. The chapter also examines the role of emotional intelligence in teaching, and the resulting impact on school leadership.

Chapter 6: Entrepreneurial Leadership: How Schools can Learn from Business Leaders

Studies of successful entrepreneurship have burgeoned in the past decade, with researchers intent on discovering the secrets of a thriving business. Many of the lessons learned have been co-opted by the educational sector, and more and more schools are operating on the "business model." This chapter examines the various aspects of an effective entrepreneur, including goals, objectives, structures, and work procedures, and makes connections with school leaders. The characteristics of a successful business leader are outlined, and the implications for school leaders are noted.

Chapter 7: Strategic Leadership: Those Who Fail to Plan, Plan to Fail

School leadership requires planning at the micro and macro levels. This chapter looks at three historic models of strategic leadership: internal, prevalent in the 1980s; interface, formed in the 1990s; and future leadership, which has been the primary model in the new millennium. The basic elements of strategic leader-ship are examined, and research stemming from interviews with leaders possessing high-level strategic skills is presented. The latter portion of the chapter outlines the qualities of a successful leader.

Chapter 8: Sustainable Leadership: The Race is Won by Those Who Endure

In this chapter, Hargreaves' vision of the "knowledge society," which encourages individuals to work in teams, uses problems as learning opportunities, includes everyone in the organizational vision, and develops "social capital" through relationship-building, is used as the template for sustainable leadership. At the forefront of the issues currently facing U.S. educational sustainability is the changing demographics. The chapter outlines these changes, and suggests ways of creating structures that give all entities a voice. Finally, the chapter looks at institutional "forgetting," discussing which elements of the past must be put aside in order to move on in a constructive manner.

Chapter 9: Invitational Leadership: Developing a School Culture of Trust, Respect, and Hope

Invitational leadership is a relatively new model, developed in 2002 by Purkey and Siegel. This chapter looks at the definition and background of the model, and goes on to show how invitational leadership manifests itself in the school setting. The model is based on four tenets: optimism, respect, trust, and intention. The chapter examines each of these as they relate to the school setting. It then compares and contrasts the model with other prominent leadership models, using recent research studies and interviews with school leaders and teachers.

Chapter 10: Constructivist Leadership: A Framework for Building Sustainable School Improvement

Finally, we look at constructivist leadership, one of the most promising of the new leadership models. The constructivist model, which is rooted in Kant's philosophy, acknowledges the changes in the educational climate that have occurred due to globalization and the rapid adoption of technology and the Internet. In constructivist learning, students actively and continuously construct their own meanings and understandings of reality. It is thus a highly adaptable model. The advantages of "participantship," as opposed to "followership" are examined in the last part of the chapter, with special emphasis placed on the role of school leaders in empowering all stakeholders.

A Guide to Effective School Leadership Theories provides school leaders, present and future, with a solid background in the history and praxis of school leadership. With an understanding of the various models in current operation, readers will have the tools needed to analyze and implement effective leadership in their own settings.

Acknowledgements

First, I would like to thank God for being my strength and my refuge. I would also like to acknowledge the collective unconscious of my ancestors. You paved the way for my ascendancy into the upper echelon of academia and served as a catalyst for my intellectual development.

Of course, I have to acknowledge my parents, Jessie and Patsy Lynch, for giving me their love and support. Also, I want to thank my sisters, Tammy Kemp and Angelina Lynch, for having my back. To their children, Adicuz, Kayla, Kerri, and Kelton: I hope my accomplishments will motivate each of you to live up to your limitless potential. No matter what, remember that your uncle loves you. I would like to also acknowledge my mentor, Dr. Rodney Washington, for his invaluable support, guidance, knowledge, and inspiration. Thanks for being the big brother that I never had! I also would like to acknowledge the invaluable support and guidance of my editor at Routledge, Heather Jarrow, and her editorial assistant, Allison Bush.

I would like to acknowledge the educators, administrators, parents, citizens, and politicians who work tirelessly to ensure that every child reaches their intellectual potential and receives a world-class education. Thank you for caring about our children. I would like to acknowledge and apologize to countless scores of children who were not properly educated by the U.S. education system. These children are the collateral damage that should spur us to create lasting change. I have dedicated my life to ensuring that every child in America receives a quality education, and I will not rest until it becomes a reality.

Chapter 1

Transformational Leadership

The (Un)Disputed Champion of Leadership Strategies

On a typical Tuesday afternoon at Parker Middle School, an observer might see a crowd of parents and grandparents, waiting for an escort to the auditorium to see the fifth-grade play. At the front desk, the school administrative assistant is explaining the afternoon assignment to a new substitute teacher. Across the hall, in a small examining room, the school nurse is listening to a parent who is concerned about her child's food allergies. Near the principal's office, a local policeman is waiting to speak with someone about a family situation involving a student. Two teachers are also waiting; they want permission to organize a field trip.

Any one of these situations might call for involvement from a senior school administrator. As it is, several people are acting simultaneously on the school's behalf, each making judgments about what school policy should be. What is the role of the administrator in each of these situations?

A school is complex. Other organizations can rely on a six-word advertising slogan, a skilled workforce, and knowledgeable customers. By contrast, a school must satisfy parents and other relatives, teachers and staff, students, and governments. The whole community has an interest in its school system and looks up to the school to set examples of leadership.

With its crucial role in the shaping of careers, lifestyles, and culture, the impact of a school is immeasurable. Research in psychology has shown that children pick up lifelong habits in childhood, and are hugely influenced by those to whom they are entrusted. Strong, dynamic leadership, especially in elementary school, is thus critical in creating solid students and citizens.

Managing a school is an arduous task. Individuals given this responsibility need to develop leadership that will be effective for the school and in the community. Recently, a new method called "transformational leadership" has proven highly effective in fostering staff loyalty and behavioral growth among students. This new approach has received worldwide acclaim and found its way into many complex organizations. However, despite its success in other types of organizations, transformational leadership has not yet been introduced into many school systems. This chapter explains transformational leadership, and describes how it can be applied in a school.

Direct Leadership vs. Community

Consciously or not, leaders make a choice between defining a school as a formal organization or as a community. Though both may be applicable, which definition is stressed can make an enormous difference.

A leader who assumes a school is a formal organization is bound to be control-driven. His or her focus is on the organizational need for rules and standards. In such a system, it is assumed that principals and supervisors are the "responsible" members of a school, and are better able to make day-to-day decisions than teachers or staff.

This form of leadership is called "direct leadership." An administrator tries to be in active control of all aspects of the school, including school activities, monitoring of teachers, analysis of curriculum, etc. Most principals assume they are responsible for everything that goes on in the school, and do not even recognize that alternatives to direct leadership exist.

Perception of a school as a community fosters a different approach to leadership. A community is not defined by evaluation and instructional leadership, but by the principles, beliefs, and values that bind it together. Sergiovanni (1992) referred to these principles and values as "centers." If new leadership styles were employed, teachers and staff would become self-managing, leaving the principal to deal with strategic issues of educational policy and community involvement, rather than day-to-day implementation. Once a school leader lets go of command and instructional leadership, he or she is spared the rituals of formal evaluations. Released from the strictures of command, teachers and staff are free to grow professionally. The outcome is not only more satisfied staff, but also improved quality control.

In the example of a typical day at Parker Middle School presented at the beginning of the chapter, situations of varying degrees of importance are presented. Some may be dealt with by the principal, but most are being taken care of by other members of the staff. Astute delegation of responsibility and empowerment of staff are key to transformational leadership, as we shall see.

What Is Transformational Leadership?

Transformational leadership is a concept that was formulated by James MacGregor Burns (1978) and Bernard Bass (1985). It focuses mostly on the achievement of organizational objectives through comprehensive approaches.

Bass (1985, 1990, 2003, 2005, & 2006) and Bruce Avolio (1990, 2003, & 2005) developed transformational leadership from its original theoretical concept into the formal ideology that it is today. Their work has since been improved by other scholars. According to Bass (1990), in transformational leadership, leaders broaden the interests of employees. They generate awareness and acceptance of the purposes and mission of the group, and stir employees to look beyond their own self-interest for the good of the group.

Bass and Riggio (2006) state that the essence of transformational leadership lies in developing employee commitment, which then leads to the achievement of the goals and objectives of the organization. Commitment to these goals is achieved through the empowerment and motivation of employees. Transformational leadership is concerned with relationship-building and the establishment of suitable working conditions between a leader and his or her followers. The leader must maintain an open-door policy and avoid bureaucracy. The development of a culture of trust is deemed more effective than the short-term benefits of meeting predetermined targets through coercion or rewards.

Bass and Riggio (2006) identify four attributes to describe transformational leadership: idealized/charismatic influence, inspirational motivation, intellectual stimulation, and individualized consideration.

Idealized/Charismatic Influence

This refers to a leader's ability to inspire others in such a positive manner that he or she becomes a role model. This trait is acquired through the leader's choice of lifestyle, language, etiquette, and mannerisms. This brand of charismatic leader usually achieves a high level of trust, since he or she leads by example and lives by his or her word.

Idealized influence involves the upholding of high moral values and integrity in a leader. By so doing, it becomes easier for the leader to encourage his or her followers to forsake their self-interests for the common good of the organization's success. A charismatic leader is also known to be adept at handling and sharing responsibility, thus making his or her leadership transformational (Avey et al., 2008).

Inspirational Motivation

A transformational leader's chief goal is to gain the support of his or her followers toward a common end. The leader must motivate and inspire these followers for support. According to Avey et al. (2008), this can be achieved through addressing work challenges, so as to give them meaning. Bass and Riggio (2006) state that team spirit must be aroused to attain set goals.

Communication and interaction are vital for effective transformational leadership. The leader must seek to develop a work culture that will instill a sense of belonging among the followers, which in turn will enable them to accept the organization's objectives as a shared vision. Charismatic-inspirational leadership is usually achieved when a transformational leader embraces both inspirational motivation and idealized influence (Bass & Riggio, 2006).

Intellectual Stimulation

Transformative leaders stimulate the minds of their followers to encourage them to be creative, a factor that quickens the realization of organizational objectives. Avolio, Bass, and Jung (1999) suggest that the best way to stimulate workers is to encourage them to be critical of old assumptions and to tackle problems in new ways. This emphasis on the need for employees to be rational in all their undertakings should increase their innovativeness and diligence. Effective transformational leaders also enlist the support of their followers when it comes to problem-solving and new conceptions.

Individualized Consideration

A transformational leader deals with his or her followers personally instead of in group settings. Though this might not always be possible in large organizations, the leader should still attempt to establish individual-level relationships with followers. The leader analyzes each follower for areas of strength as well as possibility for improvement. Individualized consideration also makes followers feel that their efforts are recognized and that their performances are crucial to the organization's goals and objectives.

Communication plays a key role in the personal relationship between the leader and the follower. A transformational leader will always ensure that communication is "two-way," and that he or she does as much listening as talking (Avolio, Bass, & Jung, 1999). Individualized communication also equips the transformational leader with information necessary for effective delegation. The leader learns when to delegate, and to whom, by noting the individuals' needs and capacity (Bass & Riggio, 2006).

Delegation by a transformational leader is unobtrusive and empowering to the follower, while the leader ensures that work is delegated and effectively carried out through monitoring.

Bass and Riggio (2006) define a transformational leader as one who:

- defines the reasons change is needed;
- creates solid visions and enlists commitment for them;
- focuses on long-term objectives;
- inspires others to depart from their self-interest in favor of organizational interests;
- mentors others to take initiative and accepts responsibility over their lives;
- restates organizational visions to make them more acceptable.

Transformational vs. Other Leadership Styles

Some forms of leadership appear similar to transformational leadership, but are in reality quite different. These are servant leadership, transactional leadership, and emotional leadership.

Servant Leadership

This popular form of school leadership is credited most often to Robert Greenleaf, though it has undergone several changes at the hands of various other theorists. A servant leader shifts focus from his or her own interests to the people he or she serves. The theory advocates for the complete severance of the leader's self-interest to shift all focus to the welfare of others under him or her.

The focus of servant leadership is not on the result, but on the means of achieving the result—primarily through articulation and handling of other people's needs. This assistance should be in the form of providing guidance in individual roles, empowering followers, and developing a culture of trust through which organizational goals can be met.

The concept of servant leadership, though popular and effective, has suffered tremendously from the lack of empirical support and the fact that it has remained largely undefined. Some scholars have recently taken an interest in servant leadership and have attempted to develop the theory to become more applicable at the organizational level. Russell and Stone (2002) have come up with a practical model that identifies both functional and building characteristics of servant leadership, and serves as a basis for identifying the similarities and differences between servant and transformational leadership. A side-by-side comparison between the two reveals relatively analogous attributes, because both styles of leadership are people-oriented.

Most notably, both types of leadership involve elements of integrity, trust, respect, delegation, vision, and influence on followers. Both leadership styles are keen on the appreciation, mentoring, recognition, and listening skills of the leader as empowerment tools for the followers.

However, there are certain points of departure between the two styles. While it emphasizes gaining trust and influencing followers, servant leadership calls for more sacrifice on the part of the leader. The pursuit of profits is peripheral for the servant leader. The objective for an organization is to develop society through constructive action. Followers are more likely to have greater freedom under a servant leader than under a transformational leader. Servant leadership is dependent on the leader's trust in his or her followers, rather than on the directive abilities of the leader.

Another principal difference is that of the leader's focus. Though both styles in one way or another call the leader to service, the servant leader's ultimate focus is the follower, while the transformational leader's greatest concern is to encourage followers to serve the organization diligently. The fundamental difference between the two styles is thus that the servant leader focuses on the followers' needs, while the transformational leader focuses on organizational goals.

The servant leader trusts in the process. His or her followers achieve organizational objectives because they become the leader's first priority. Bass (2005) adds that long-term objectives are met through the development of the people. This, he states, is different from transformational leadership, where all interests are aligned with that of the organization as the ultimate priority.

If we take the example of Parker Middle School presented at the beginning of the chapter, we can see that a substantial amount of trust has been placed in the hands of various stakeholders in the school: the nurse, an "escort" for family members, and the administrative assistant. Notice that even "minor" members of the school community have a role to play, but that all their roles are integrated into the organizational structure: they know their places within the well-oiled machine of the day-to-day running of the school.

Bass and Riggio (2006) and Yukl (2009) established that charisma is a key ingredient for transformational leadership. Charisma refers to charm and power to inspire, motivate, and excite others. It is thus notable that, while transformational leadership tends to rely on the leader's charismatic power to achieve effectiveness, servant leaders create the same motivation and influence through the act of service, without self-aggrandizement on the leader's part.

While both styles of leadership are effective, there are risks attached to each. Both may fall prey to manipulation and corruption, since, with these kinds of leadership, the leader eventually garners some authority or power over the followers, which can be used for negative purposes. Transformational leadership can be prone to manipulation. A charismatic leader may develop unquestioning followers. This can be a recipe for chaos if a leader's moral or ethical standards do not match his or her charisma.

Early research by Conger (1990) discovered the risks attached to charisma-based leadership, and argued that the possibility of negative influence is high. The leader may misrepresent his or her true vision in order to attract loyalty. Transformational leadership is especially criticized by Clements and Washbush (1999), who state that most studies advocating for transformational leadership do not attempt to include these negative attributes in their research work. This view has been echoed by Northouse (2009), who stated that transformational leadership is susceptible when the leader is unable to develop a strong rapport among his or her followers. He gives an example of narcissistic leaders who manipulate others because they enjoy being in control. He finds that some followers are too reliant on their leaders and establish strong links with them to satisfy their pressing dependency needs (Northouse, 2009).

While both transformational and servant leadership may have negative applications, their benefits far outweigh these negatives. Ideally, a charismatic transformational leader should be able to withstand the temptation to manipulate and engage in corrupt practices. Similarly, a servant leader should channel the feeling of reciprocation toward the meeting of common objectives and not for selfish ends. All in all, both servant and transformational leadership offer a leadership guide to contemporary needs in organizations.

Transactional Leadership

Another historical leadership style is transactional leadership, in which a leader offers some valuable thing in exchange for the follower's services. Most traditional relationships between leaders and followers are transactional, since most people believe "quid pro quo" ("something for something") to be the ultimate purpose of negotiation. In such an arrangement, everyone is happy and thus there is no harm done.

The contract between employer and employee is mostly transactional. The contractor knows what to do, and the contracting party keeps his or her end of the bargain. This leadership is applicable only to scenarios where both parties understand what takes priority (Aarons, 2006).

Transformational and transactional leadership are different, but can complement each other occasionally, depending on circumstances. Bass (2005) argues that the combination of transactional and transformational leadership is best. Though it may be easy to augment transactional relationships, it is not possible to replace it with transformational leadership, since transactional leadership is also an effective motivation technique.

A transformational leader who fails to charm his or her followers will often resort to transactional leadership. Transformational leadership calls for hard work and persistence. A leader without these characteristics would more easily use conventional strategies. Transactional leadership is a shortcut and is not as long-lasting as transformational leadership, because the reward promised may not always be available, but the charisma of the leader will never be depleted.

Transformational leadership calls for prudence. A leader finding himself or herself in a win–lose situation will often try to change it to a win–win, in which all parties are satisfied with the agreement. Where a leader cannot achieve the win–win situation, negotiation skills are called into play and transactional leadership becomes more viable. Here, the leader is often tempted to stay in transactional leadership. Transformational leadership transcends the transactional style. Motivation from within the follower produces powerful results.

Khunert and Lewis, in their examination of Kegan's Developmental Six-Stage Theory, found that leadership levels grow symmetrically with the maturity and experience of the leader. They found Stage 2 to be mostly transactional, Stage 3 to be a higher-level transactional style of leadership, while Stage 4 was transformational.

At Stage 2, everything a leader does for the organization is commensurate to the return he or she expects from it. The leader is new to the organization, and his or her responsibilities are not burdensome, since the leader has not deeply understood the organization's interests. He or she still holds personal interests above those of the organization. Since the leader has not had time to interact with other workers, his or her charisma may not be known, and loyalties cannot be immediately established. It is thus easier for the leader to employ a transactional style that works for everyone.

At Stage 3, a leader has interacted with the staff for some time. The leader at this stage feels some connection to the organization, and has begun to synchronize his or her interests to the organization's vision. The leader may still opt for transactional relationships, but will occasionally exercise charismatic or idealized influence. This is what Khunert and Lewis call "high-order transactional" leadership. At this stage, the followers have not yet accepted the organizational goals over their own.

Stage 4 brings about the feeling in a leader that he or she can no longer separate themself from the organization. The leader now accepts a role as custodian of the organization's culture, vision, and mission. Respect and trust increase, and the leader leads by setting an example, so that the staff accepts the organization's mission and vision as more powerful than their own interests. At this stage, all parties have integrated their goals and interests to conform. Bass (2005) identifies several dimensions inherent in transactional leadership. He starts by referring to "contingent rewards" as one of the key identifiers of this leadership. Contingent rewards are exchanges of valuables or the use of economic tools to influence followers to embrace organizational objectives.

Another trait of transactional leadership is "management by exception." The active form of this type of management involves assessing employee performance and taking corrective measures where needed. In the passive form, the leader only intervenes where things have gotten out of hand. The last of the transactional traits is the laissez faire leadership, in which the leader allows employees to do as they like.

Emotional Leadership

Emotional leadership is loosely related to transformational leadership. Here, leadership involves tapping the leader's emotional center to lead, where decisions are based on the feelings of the leader at the time. It is easy to confuse charisma with emotional attributes. Some may assert that transformational leadership also involves a level of emotional influence. However, the two types of leadership are structurally different, because transformational leadership is, in essence, a rational process.

Influence of Transformational Leadership on Behavior and Performance

It is well established that transformational leadership is a widespread and influential style of leadership that brings about a high level of effectiveness in almost all types of organizations.

Bass and Riggio (2006) attribute this success to certain behaviors of leaders that influence rational thought and motivation in their followers. The tapping of values, beliefs, and ideals of followers by transformational leaders to a higher vision is the most crucial part of leadership that brings about effectiveness. Their inspiration enables followers to discover novel means of problem-solving. Followers' reactions toward transformational leadership have been the subject of much research. It is quite common to find such tenets as trust, personal confidence, job satisfaction, identification, a feeling of belonging, and fairness being emphasized as indicators of the level of success of a transformational leader (Piccolo & Colquitt, 2006).

Another approach to transformational leadership has been the examination of followers' feelings about themselves in terms of input to their assigned jobs or groups. Indeed, it is most logical to gauge the success of leadership on the effects it has on the behavior of targeted followers. In the school setting, it is crucial that students, parents, staff, and other interested groups feel that their leadership values their input and that they are responsible for the success of the school in their individual capacities (Piccolo & Colquitt, 2006).

Perhaps the most important mechanism for gauging the efficacy of transformational leadership is a critical examination of the performance of individuals, rather than the identification of their feelings toward leadership. The rationale for transformational leadership, in contrast to other styles, is results-based.

"Management of meaning," a term first suggested by Smircich and Morgan (1982), is defined as the ability of a leader to structure and bring about "reality" in how work is done. This kind of reality is defined in Hackman and Oldham's (1980) research as being encompassed by four characteristics: identity, variety, autonomy, and feedback. A transformational leader should be able to bring out these characteristics in their followers.

- *Identity*: followers should be able to complete whole tasks while still adding value to them.
- *Variety*: a transformational leader should elicit an array of results by encouraging the use of different skills by followers.
- *Autonomy*: the leader allows for personal growth and freedom at work.
- *Feedback*: the tools of analysis by which the leader assesses the performance of the entire establishment and helps to decide what needs to be rectified. In a school, it is important that all students and staff, being the direct followers of school leadership, acquire these characteristics from the transformational leader.

Though the above characteristics may in one way or another involve the feelings of followers, their intended purpose is to bring about a higher synergistic level of performance. Using the above characteristics, a researcher is able to analyze the influence of transformational leadership on performance and behavior. The integration of all these aspects brings out the total synergy created by transformational leadership and an idealized and motivated following.

Judge and Piccolo (2004) find that transformational leaders enable followers to perceive organizational goals as being congruent to their own goals and interests. By so doing, they introduce a higher level of responsibility in followers, which results in better performance. The use of intellectual stimulation by bringing in new styles of solving problems and a higher tolerance for individual freedom may in fact inculcate autonomy and variety, named characteristics of good performance. Through inspirational motivation and charismatic influence, followers are actually more bound to feel that their roles in the organizational setting are significant.

Goal Commitment

The next step in recognizing the impact of transformational leadership on job performance is linking job characteristics with goal commitment. A study by Piccolo and Colquitt (2006) defines goal commitment as the determination to achieve a goal through persistence and constant nurturing.

Piccolo and Colquitt (2006) identify two key factors of goal commitment. The first is "volition," which they define as the independent decision by a person to attain a certain goal. This factor is consistent with the performance characteristic of autonomy. The other is "feedback," which is the self-motivating key to keep the individual optimistic that the goal is achievable.

In other studies, both volition and feedback have been found to be influential to goal commitment. The fact that they are closely linked to characteristics of job performance may be indicators of how the five listed characteristics are related to goal commitment. While it is not quite clear which leads to the other, it is generally accepted that goal commitment and job performance are closely related.

Piccolo and Colquitt (2006) found that follower perceptions and follower goal commitment are positively connected. In many goal-setting theories, commitment draws a line between goal difficulty and job performance. Piccolo and Colquitt also established in their model that goal commitment is directly linked to job performance. Commitment becomes a driver of performance as individuals choose to bind themselves to desirable behaviors.

Imagine yourself in the position of the "escort" for the parents and grandparents in the vignette at the beginning of the chapter. Simply being given that role, which an autocratic leader might have insisted on taking for him or herself, forces the escort to think in terms of the best interests of the school: How do I look? How does the auditorium look? What are these "outsiders" seeing as they enter the school? How do I want the other students to behave? Taking responsibility encourages even minor stakeholders to make a stronger commitment to the school.

In a school setting, commitment toward the school motto by students and staff can have a direct influence to their overall performance, be it academically or in co-curricular activities. For example, if a school's motto states "excellence through discipline," anyone who takes this line to heart would endeavor to succeed while maintaining a disciplined order. The link between commitment to the motto and success is self-evident.

In Lowell Elementary School, in Madison, Wisconsin, the students and staff participate in the recitation of an affirmation every morning at communal breakfast. "I am Somebody. I am capable and lovable . . . I can do anything when I try," they chant. This emphasis on individual accountability and performance has had a dramatic effect on the school, which had been floundering. The affirmation served as a foundation stone for the changes the school was starting to implement under new leadership. Teachers based art, music, and writing assignments on the new affirmation. Suddenly, children and teachers alike felt accountable for their actions, and were assured of their place and necessary role in the school (Gramling, 2010). This is transformational leadership at its best: the leader instigates a process that allows staff and students to take ownership of the school.

Adopting Transformational Leadership

Transformational leadership emphasizes perception. Results can only be achieved through intrinsic motivation (from within the follower). Transformational leadership will not flourish if it is unable to influence the core—the follower's feelings.

Transformational leadership requires training the leader in the use of language and imagery. This can be done by incorporating these "transformational characteristics" into training courses. However, the personal effort of the leader determines whether transformational leadership is achievable. Studies by Dvir et al. (2002) and Barling, Weber, and Kelloway (1996) have found that, compared to eclectic leadership training, training in transformational leadership produces the best results. The positive connection between transformational leadership and job characteristics suggests that we should expect an opposite result in organizations that do not employ transformational leadership. "Job enrichment" is often used to boost performance. However, it does not produce intended results, and is time-wasting and expensive. Rather, a leader should get involved in follower performance by using positive language, symbols, and imagery in communication in the organization. In the previous example of Lowell Elementary, the principal used the recited affirmation as a focal point and material for creating a positive self-image. Rather than focus on top-down dictates, she created a common theme, in which everyone, including the leader, could participate.

When switching to a transformational style of leadership, it is imperative for the leader to recognize the urgent need of skill and character in influencing how followers view his or her responsibilities. A principal or dean has to understand how he or she is to influence and shape task perception. Objective job characteristics and the individual's construction of what is to be done for the organization have the biggest impact on perception of tasks. Thus the shaping of day-to-day tasks in a transformational manner helps foster the perceptions of followers.

Transformational behaviors are encouraged as a continuous process. A school intending to convert to this style first needs to assess the departments where it is needed. Piccolo and Colquitt (2006) suggest that instead of a needs assessment, the organization should include transformational components in their yearly assessments, such as 360-degree feedback and managerial surveys. Transformation need not come immediately, but it is worthwhile for any school to build on these principles, since its long-term effects are enriching to the whole establishment. Students learn leadership from the school. Attempts to grow transformational leadership in student affairs would help ensure that students initiate this leadership later in life.

Combating Negativity Through Transformational Leadership

Meta-analytic research, like performance and follower satisfaction (Avey et al., 2008), has produced evidence of a positive relationship between transformational leadership and work-related results. Various suggestions for the above outcomes have either directly or indirectly related them to the fact that transformational leaders make work meaningful by providing autonomy. Studies such as Bono and Judge (2003) find that the followers of transformational leaders form strong opinions that their work is esteemed and self-congruent. Again, their research serves to support the widespread notion that followers of transformational leaders feel more empowered.

Transformational leaders motivate by increasing self-efficacy in followers, by facilitating social identification within a group, and by linking organizational values to follower values. This allows followers to feel more determined in their work and augments their perceived empowerment.

While cynicism and intentions to quit are widely considered pointers to employee negativity, initial research in organizational behaviors has considered them to be generalized traits. However, recent studies have found cynicism to be a specific construct. Cynicism can be seen as a reflection of the followers' perception of the leader. Avey et al. (2008) found that cynicism is a product of ineffective leadership and lack of participation and consultation in decision making.

Positive-minded or optimistic followers have been found to be less cynical and more resilient when faced with drawbacks at work. It is also evident that followers who can make an impact in their environment (empowerment) are less likely to be cynical toward change. The feeling of empowerment makes them believe that any situation can be remedied and that they have the power within them to effect the necessary changes. Transformational leadership brings about the same feeling of empowerment in all followers. There is an inverse relationship between cynicism and transformational leadership, because persons under a highly transformational leader are usually intellectually stimulated and are constantly challenged to be open-minded. With idealized influence, people generally identify with their leader.

The unique aspect of transformational leadership is its ability to inspire and motivate followers toward change in organizations, and, in the process, achieve performance beyond expectation. When a leader encompasses organizational dynamism, it is likely that followers will be less cynical, since they are witnesses to change.

Intention to quit (ITQ) is another form of employee negativity reaction to poor leadership. Factors that have been linked to ITQ include poor pay, and lack of job satisfaction and goal commitment. These aspects can be directly or indirectly linked to turnover intent. A higher sense of effectiveness is linked to higher self-worth. Avey et al. (2008) argue that individuals gravitate toward tasks where they are likely to feel effective. Employees are unlikely to have ITQ toward an organization where their need for efficacy is met in their respective job responsibilities. Highly resilient followers are more likely to adapt after setbacks at work that would lead to an intention to leave the organization.

Employees who have more responsibility and are more involved in direct decision-making and leadership will also be less inclined to quit. Glance back to the vignette at the beginning of the chapter. Would the escort for the parents or the school nurse feel more or less empowered if the principal had taken charge of the situation? Which would lead to greater job satisfaction?

Various studies have demonstrated relationships between follower empowerment and job satisfaction, between empowerment and decreased anger and frustration, and between empowerment and a sense of organizational attachment (Crossley et al., 2007; Judge & Ilies, 2004; Spreitzer & Mishra, 2002).

The basis of transformational leadership is to harmonize employees' follower goals with those of the organization. A concord between follower and organizational goals is paramount to fighting ITQ. An effective transformational leader reduces follower ITQs by showing how the values of the group are in agreement (Bass & Riggio, 2006). The followers decide to stay in the organization because their goals and values are intertwined with those of the organization. The idealized or charismatic influence of transformational leadership encourages followers to identify with and emulate their leader as a beacon of inspiration. They are thus compelled to stay with the leader to maintain their identities.

Inspirational motivation helps build emotional commitment to goals, which causes followers to feel appreciated and needed in the organization. They are less likely to leave the organization because their leader is meeting their needs.

Universality of Transformational Leadership

Is transformational leadership a universal style of leadership, or is it regional or culturally limited? Many sources have attempted to carry out cross-national studies to establish this.

Boehnke et al. (2002) investigated the existence of universally consistent behaviors. They sampled 145 senior executives in two divisions of a global petroleum company and its subsidiaries around the world. These executives were asked to state what they considered exceptional organizational performance and to identify key leadership behaviors they perceived as leading to extraordinary outcomes.

One of the major findings of the study was that the basic dimensions of leadership that produce extraordinary performance are universal, with little variation in the six different parts of the world sampled. However, some leadership differences were attributed to the different corporate cultures in the two company divisions.

The following characteristics of transformational leadership were gleaned from the coded data:

- Effective in producing more job satisfaction.
- Promoting followers frequently.

- Developing individuals to higher group or personal performance levels.
- Producing innovative products.
- Receiving patents for follower-produced work.
- Reducing burnout and job stress.
- Encouraging more volunteering from followers.
- Leading in units that work best under stress.
- Generating greater affinity for risk and creativity.
- Tolerating dissenting perspectives.

In the final result, transformational leadership is identified as consistent with a clear majority of sampled behaviors, as provided in the executives' descriptions of their version of exceptional organizational performance. 89% of descriptions include *visioning* as a key element of exceptional performance. *Intellectual stimulation* is cited in 80% of the reports, while *team building* and *coaching* are found in 73% of descriptions. Aspects of *inspiring behavior* appeared in 68% of reports.

All the italicized attributes above refer to a transformational style of leadership. It is intriguing to note that the only non-transformational characteristic in more than half of the reports was "recognizing and rewarding," at 62%, which is an element of the transactional style of leadership. Another pointer was that correcting or avoiding behavior as effective styles of leadership was named by only 15% and 3% of respondents, respectively. In fact, most reports showed them to be ineffective styles—73% did not even mention them.

It is apparent that transformational leadership is widely accepted as an exceptional leadership technique. It is applicable in all kinds of organizations, including the school setting.

Adopting Transformation Leadership in Schools

A study was carried out in Los Angeles at Griffin Elementary School. The school's principal, Yvonne Davis, converted the rationale of the school from a formal organization to a set of community norms (Bass & Riggio, 2006). The transformation was described as mind-changing. Teachers, who had viewed their role as an individual duty, to be commanded and supervised by higher authority, now found that when they shared responsibility among themselves, teaching and learning became intertwined and much easier. In the community setting, a principal becomes less of a planner, supervisor, and controller, and more of an affirmer, a "re-enforcer," and supporter.

Though community-building takes time, the research found that its impact was long-lasting, even after the principal had left: the metamorphosis was worth the wait. The building of a common vision was paramount to a school's change.

The most significant challenge for a school is that its leadership has to handle different kinds of people with different goals and interests. A school leader has to ensure that students are following curricula, excelling academically, and becoming outstanding members of society. In comparison, teachers' goals are to meet curricula deadlines and ensure that students are up-to-date with class work. The leader's task is to confront student deviance and teachers' possible cynicism and lack of motivation.

A transformational school leader will be adept at ensuring the focus of students in their studies through individual consideration, inspirational motivation, and charismatic influence. A leader will not have set problem-solving techniques at his or her disposal, but will involve students and teachers to come up with solutions to problems as they arise. For example, in the vignette presented at the beginning of this chapter, the leader might utilize the services of the administrative assistant and the school nurse to solve problems.

A transformational leader in a school setting will be quick to identify various aspects and areas deserving transformation. He or she is likely to seek out-of-the-box solutions for problems. Teacher issues will be best handled through consultation and individualized consideration. The leader identifies cynicism and intentions to quit among teachers, and reassures the affected individuals that they are needed in the school, thus realigning their values and goals to resonate with those of the school.

Transformational schools shift their emphasis from "leadership" to "professionalism." While most school administrators claim that their teachers are professional, studies show that professionalism cannot develop when stifled by leadership based on command and instruction. Direct leadership and professionalism are thus antithetical. Professionalism is more about competence than skill. It involves a higher degree of trust, and ensures a teacher's commitment to achieving a social end, including caring, a commitment to excellence, and a devotion to the practice itself as a norm. Virtue shapes the thought of a professional, while instructional leadership degrades the feeling of responsibility and shared values.

T. J. Sergiovanni, (1984) proposed five alternative approaches to full transformational leadership in schools. These are:

- Technical leadership, through sound management of school resources.
- Human leadership, through networking and establishing social and interpersonal bonds.
- Educational leadership, through expert knowledge on educational matters.
- Symbolic leadership, through role-modeling and behavior.
- Cultural leadership regarding the values, beliefs, and cultural identity of the school.

The first three approaches—the technical, human, and educational aspects of leadership—are the primary influences on a school's effectiveness. The symbolic and cultural aspects are the ones that add the most value and are responsible for the overall effectiveness and excellence of the school.

Summary

The traditional concept of direct leadership places an enormous burden on a school leader to run almost every aspect of leadership. Substituting command leadership with a community-based approach, coupled with professionalism and collegiality, can produce almost instant results. New tactics are warranted. Transformational leadership can change the mindset of staff and students. The leader appeals to their inner centers to foster a community, not just to serve the leader's interests.

Transformational leadership also brings about professionalism in the teaching staff by allowing them autonomy and room to improve their professionalism. Because a leader allows followers to face challenges and find solutions by themselves, teachers are more involved in school affairs. Collegiality is most likely to develop when challenges are faced and surmounted together, without supervision from the leader.

We have also seen how transformational leadership improves job performance through the four pillars of charismatic/idealized influence, individual consideration, inspirational motivation and intellectual stimulation. Studies have now shown that it also positively affects the psychological wellbeing of employees (Avey et al., 2008).

Transformational leadership also helps in individual goal-setting and goal commitment. The leader transfers responsibility by making the individual feel part of a whole. Bass (2005) states that, fundamentally, a transformational leader "attempts and succeeds in raising their colleagues, subordinates, followers, clients or constituencies to greater awareness about issues of consequence. A leader relies on vision, self-confidence, and inner strength to present the appropriate vision, be it popular or not."

Transformational leadership brings about a shift of focus. A leader no longer offers rewards, but empowers followers to become leaders through mutual responsibility and trust. Bass (1985) states that transformational leadership inspires staff performance beyond its leader's expectations. Transformational leaders enable their followers to maximize performance, harmonizing the interests of subordinates and shared values.

Although there have been few studies linking transformational leadership to student performance, various other research studies would suggest that a highly effective style of leadership would positively influence student performance. Transformational leadership can be said to bring about a wide range of results at a personal level (i.e., followers' empowerment and identity) and in a group or organizational level (cohesiveness and collective efficacy). It produces these positive effects primarily by shaping the followers' self-worth and promotes identification with their leader. Therefore, what distinguishes a transformational leader is the combination of head and heart, and ability to comprehend and apply emotions effectively as a mode of connection and influence.

Transformational leadership results in wide-ranging changes wherever it is introduced. It is effective in solving problems that are related to the school setup. It would be prudent for school leaders in the U.S. to utilize it in their running of the school community.

Discussion Questions

1. Sergiovanni referred to the principles, beliefs, and values that bind a community together as "centers." What are the centers in your community?
2. Bass and Riggio list six attributes of a transformational leader. Which do you feel is the most important? Which is the least important? Why?
3. What is one drawback of the transformational leadership model? What steps might be taken to reduce the negative effects of transformational leadership?
4. List two ways in which transformational leadership can help reduce ITQ.

5.   In the story at the beginning of this chapter, five situations are mentioned, involving parents and grandparents, the school nurse, the administrative assistant, a policeman, and teachers. Describe how a principal might use the transformational leadership model in dealing with each situation.

Activities

1.   Lowell Elementary School created an "affirmation," which students and staff recited every morning. Create your own affirmation, and then suggest ways in which it might be used in the school.
2.   Develop a role-play based on one of the five situations described in the story at the beginning of the chapter. Discuss the leadership technique used in the skit.

Selected Readings

Anderson, K. (2008). Transformational teacher leadership: Decentering the search for transformational leadership. *International Journal of Management in Education*, 2(2), 109–123.

Avey, J. B., Hughes, L. W., Norman, S. M., & Luthans, K. W. (2008). Using positivity, transformational leadership and empowerment to combat employee negativity. *Leadership & Organization Development Journal*, 29(2), 110–126.

Avolio, B. J., & Yammarino, F. (2007). *Transformational and charismatic leadership: The road ahead.* Boston: Elsevier Science.

Bass, B. M. (2008). *The Bass handbook of leadership: Theory, research, and managerial applications* (4th ed.). New York: Simon and Schuster.

Bennis, W. G. (2009). *On becoming a leader.* New York: Basic Books.

Hall, J., Johnson, S., Wysocki, A., & Kepner, K. (2008). *Transformational leadership: The transformation of managers and associates.* University of Florida IFAS Extension. Retrieved from http://edis.ifas.ufl.edu

Chapter 2

Instructional Leadership

A Catalyst for the Promotion of Teaching and Learning

Jane Ashley sat across the desk from Principal Stover, waiting for her post-observation review. A social studies teacher with two years' experience, Jane obviously enjoyed being in the classroom and the students seemed to like her.

However, Principal Stover was at a loss for words. Jane's teaching style was flat. Her observations about American history seldom departed from those already mentioned in the textbook. The students quietly took notes, discussed chapters, and created reports that reflected exactly what was in the book. This confused Principal Stover, because Jane had come from a strong academic background, and obviously knew a lot more about the subject than she was sharing. The students, the principal was sure, were more capable and creative than Jane was allowing them to be. But what could he say? How could he explain what she was missing?

In the U.S., most schools have always been run on an "instructional" model, where the principal is the dictator, the ultimate decision-maker, who supervises and gives direction on almost every aspect of school activities. This is the oldest method of leadership in the educational world, and research on instructional leadership is vast. However, it has reached few conclusions about what makes instructional leadership effective. As is evident in the vignette above, a principal might be aware of problems, but unless he or she is able to offer constructive advice toward solving the problems, that awareness is of little use.

In recent years, more than a hundred research studies have focused on issues concerning leadership in primary and secondary education, in attempts to find answers to broad questions about its effectiveness in areas like teacher morale and student performance. So far, this wealth of research has reached inconclusive and, at times, contradictory conclusions. Some findings support the need for vigorous instructional leadership, while others find negative results from direct administrative involvement in other school functions (Hallinger, 2005).

It is difficult to reach widely accepted conclusions about instructional leadership because many different concepts and behavioral models have been developed. This chapter will provide a summary of how instructional leadership developed, its changing faces, and its relevance to contemporary American schools.

Development of Instructional Leadership

The search for models of instructional leadership has identified several competencies that are often associated with administration. Cuban (1988) coins the term "principalship" to summarize the various political, managerial, social, and instructional roles that are vital to the principal's job description. He concludes that a principal's effectiveness is achieved by finding the correct balance among these roles.

During the 1970s and 1980s, extensive emphasis was placed on developing institutionally effective schools. Leadership centers became popular, promising to enhance the abilities of current and future school principals. This focus on leadership development was the result of external policy reforms aimed at school improvement through changing school leadership practices (Hallinger & Wimpelberg, 1992). From these efforts came the "effective schools model" (Marsh, 1992). These centers conclude that school leadership should be firmly rooted in curriculum development. Research on the effectiveness of this approach is not conclusive, and it is too soon to determine the long-term benefits of this emphasis on instructional leadership.

American society, especially after the implementation of No Child Left Behind, is now focused on performance standards. School principals are finding themselves at the center of arguments about accountability and school improvement. Policymakers expect that administrators will function effectively as instructional leaders. Government standards for education require that principals be instructional. These efforts have been linked explicitly to training curricula, occasioned by government policy in the United States (Gewirtz, 2003; Hallinger, 2003; Murphy & Shipman, 2003). Those principals who fail at improving school performance risk termination.

In light of the performance standards that take precedence in the world of instructional leadership, principals must adapt their leadership style to fit the needs of their school. A school with negative teacher morale, low test scores, and an unsupportive community will need a different leadership approach than a well-developed, high-performing school. It is the responsibility of the principal to identify and react to each circumstance with the appropriate leadership strategy. In developing these skills, an instructional leader needs to identify which type of leader he or she is.

Types of Instructional Leadership

Each instructional leader can be characterized as a visionary, a developer, or a rational scholar. A visionary is a "people person" with an open mind and a sharp intuition. Visionaries transfer ideas into goals. A developer effectively but empathetically motivates others to do their best. Developers are the leaders who make sure that the job not only gets done, but gets done in the most effective and logical manner. Developers transfer ideas into things. Rational scholars are leaders who set aside emotions to logically and pragmatically lead. Rational scholars transfer ideas into rules, procedures, and steps. All three types of leadership are needed. Visionaries, developers, and rational scholars working together and properly matched to the appropriate responsibility promote an environment that is conducive to learning. However, incorrectly matching these types of leadership can be disastrous.

Stages of Instructional Leadership

Instructional leadership is a process, and in order for a school to be an effective, well-developed institution, principals must lead the teachers and staff through the process. James MacGregor Burns (1978) described the first component of the process as being either transactional or transformational. Transactional leadership relies mainly on extrinsic motivations, while transformational leadership relies on intrinsic, psychological motivations. Transformational leadership takes place while the school is working to improve and become highly effective.

Additionally, Etzioni (1988) examined the moral dimension of leadership and motivation. Etzioni found that, while both intrinsic and extrinsic motivations were effective, what truly allowed for quality work and management were the beliefs, feelings, and cultural norms of the teacher. Both the intrinsic and extrinsic motivations, in addition to the moral dimension of the principal and teachers, are examined in each of the four stages of instructional leadership. The four stages are bartering, building, binding, and bonding.

The most rudimentary stage of leadership is that of bartering. Bartering refers to a situation in which the principal strikes a deal with the faculty or staff and is best used when the goals of the principal and the teachers are different. For example, the teachers may be uninterested in attending an after-school fall festival, so the principal may barter with teachers and staff and offer an off-campus lunch period in exchange for their attendance. The interest of the principal lies in the safety and morale of the school, while the teachers' interests lie in completing their job-related tasks and going home.

An effective principal builds trust and provides support to their faculty. Building is the stage of leadership that shifts the tangible, extrinsic rewards into psychological, intrinsic rewards such as achievement, responsibility, and competence. Building begins when a common effort is exerted in attaining the same goals. After reaching a level where each teacher possesses intrinsic motivation to improve and contribute to the school's betterment, the principal's leadership style then transfers to binding. Binding occurs when principals and teachers work together to create a set of values that fosters positive relationships and develops a sense of community.

Bonding is the highest level of leadership. Bonding occurs when the overwhelming sense of community is so prevalent that school improvement becomes an everyday way of life. All stakeholders work together as a unit with common values, goals, and desired outcomes. It engenders a school that is connected as a close-knit, functioning community (Blasé & Blasé, 2004).

Instructional Leadership Techniques

Various situations, people, and demeanors call for different leadership strategies during each stage of instructional leadership development. Typically, a school that isn't functioning at an optimal level requires bartering. The principal as an instructional leader must possess the ability to determine the type of leadership style needed and implement it in a manner that treats all subordinates with equal support and respect. The types of interaction, no matter the developmental stage, are traditional, human resources, and binding leadership.

Traditional leadership relies heavily on a managerial hierarchy, meaning the principal is the boss and the teachers are subordinates. Traditional leadership has its basis in teachers doing what they are supposed to do because the boss said to do it. Teachers seem to comply simply to avoid the consequences.

A human resources practice of leadership is the perspective that a leader must utilize "people skills" to get the desired response. In short, principals use their expertise and skills to motivate teachers to perform. While some may refer to the motivation as manipulation, principals are working to meet the needs of teachers. Issues with human resources leadership practices are evident. It is obvious that the teachers and the principal do not have the same goals. Teachers grow accustomed to only performing exceptionally if and when their needs are met.

Just as binding is the desired level of leadership, likewise it is the desired technique used by principals. Binding as a leadership technique relies heavily upon morals. The teachers complete the obligations and duties out of a sense of responsibility to the students, the school, and other teachers.

Each technique can be described as enacting either bureaucratic authority or personal authority. While bureaucratic authority has its place no matter what the level of leadership, it typically tends to foster negative morale among teachers. It suggests implicitly that principals know more than teachers and that teachers cannot be trusted. Teachers in this type of environment perform as expected and nothing more. As a result, they become separated from their work and start viewing teaching as "just a job" rather than a vocation (Friedkin & Slater, 1994).

The opposite of bureaucratic authority is personal authority. Personal authority focuses on interpersonal skills and human relations. Teachers feel a genuine need to help, do their part, and go the extra mile to reap the reward of being a part of a fully functional, outstanding school system.

Taking the opening vignette as an example, if Principal Stover would use bureaucratic authority to influence Jane Ashley to change her teaching style, he might call her into his office and deliver a grim report, listing her failings and showing exactly why she was not living up to the standards set by the school. He might have a prepared set of changes that she would have to make . . . "or else." Now, Principal Stover would certainly be able to defend his actions. He would be referring to pre-set standards that Ms. Ashley had read through. He could claim that he had provided detailed instructions for change. However, from Ms. Ashley's perspective, he might come across as threatening and intimidating, and that tension would certainly influence her teaching style.

On the other hand, if Principal Stover took the time to sit side by side and elicit from her several ideas for improvement, he could use those as building blocks to present some other options for enlivening the class. He might encourage Ms. Ashley to sit in on the classes of more motivational teachers, or offer to send her to a teacher in-service. The gentler, more human interaction of this "personal authority" is likely to generate a desire to go the extra mile.

Roles of the Instructional Leader

Although the roles of the instructional leader are too numerous to list, the roles can be grouped into categories of brief overview. First, the school leader must collaborate. Collaboration must take place among all stakeholders: the principal, the teachers, the parents, and the students. While it is commonplace for teachers, parents, and students to correspond and collaborate regarding instructions, principals must also collaborate with teachers to review student performance. A principal should attempt to be aware of the progress of each class, and to the greatest extent possible, each student.

Next, the instructional leader has the role of guiding teachers in content alignment. The instructional leader should be sure that teachers have access to the curriculum and have ample resources for aligning the content with the curriculum. Providing mentors for new teachers and allowing for collaboration among departments fosters school effectiveness.

The roles of collaboration and content alignment are directly related to the role of text and resource selection. Principals should encourage teachers to make decisions regarding the text and resource selection; however, it is the principal's duty to ensure that the resources are useful, reliable, and relevant (Copland, 2003).

Variables of Instructional Leadership

In the day to day lives of school principals, other variables come into play. They have to decide which tactic to implement during each stage. One variable is that of the principal's comfort level and experience with the strategy. Rarely will they use a strategy that they are not comfortable using. The teacher and principal's past relationship and encounters require the principal to adapt to each situation. There is no valid and reliable way of measuring the level of development of the teacher; therefore, the principal must take all variables into consideration in order to formulate the best approach.

After identifying the types, styles, techniques, and roles of instructional leadership, you should be ready to execute what you have learned. When all of the components of instructional leadership are evaluated and implemented, a school can move towards meeting the performance standards necessary and desired. There is no one right answer or approach, but rather a consideration of all the factors and variables that play a part in the decision making.

Concepts of Instructional Leadership

Several models of instructional leadership have been proposed. Studies by scholars such as Andrews and Soder (1987), Hallinger and Murphy (1985), Leithwood, Begley and Cousins (1990), and Leithwood and Montgomery (1982) have attempted to identify different dimensions of instructional leadership. Hallinger and Murphy's model (1985) is the most inclusive, and has recently been used by various other scholars. It suggests that there are three dimensions in instructional leadership, which accurately define what administrative leadership entails. These dimensions include:

- defining the school's mission;
- managing the instructional program;
- promoting a positive school learning climate.

From these three dimensions come ten instructional leadership functions.

Defining the School's Mission

In instructional leadership, the principal's role is deeply involved with direction-setting for the school. Hallinger (2005) explains this first function in part as "framing" and "communicating" the school's goals.

In-depth analysis of the "mission" dimension reveals that it focuses on the principal's role in cooperating with his or her staff, to ensure that the school continuously runs on clear, measurable, and time-based goals, whose result is the academic progress of students. Here, principals are chiefly responsible for communicating goals, which should be widely known and supported throughout the school.

One weakness of these models is that the process of goal development is not considered; its importance is less critical than simply meeting performance outcomes. The research simply accepts that goals should be set by the principal in collaboration with staff to achieve effectiveness (Hallinger, 2005).

Perhaps the most indispensable element in this instructional leadership is ensuring that the staff incorporates performance goals into their daily routines. Historically, many schools have had only vague, ill-defined goals, but today, a leader must communicate a clear demarcation between academically focused efforts and those implemented solely to succeed at externally generated standardized test measurements.

An excellent example of problems facing a school beset by standardized testing was recorded in a study by Hallinger and Murphy (1985). Teachers in "effective" California elementary schools were observed while teaching. In one case, a teacher had a unique activity center located at the back of the class. Researchers observed that students were not working at the center during the class period. When questioned, the teacher stated that, although she genuinely liked the activity center, she had no time to use it, since the class had not made the progress required in basic subjects. The teacher then reported that her principal expected teachers to spend more time on reading, spelling, writing, and math than were necessary to achieve the expected progress in basic subjects. When questioned, the principal restated this expectation almost verbatim.

This provides a compelling example of effective instructional leadership in defining a school's mission:

- The mission was academically focused, and deemed appropriate by the administrator for the needs of the school's students.
- The principal's objectives were expressed and modeled clearly, in writing, all around the school, such that the teacher and the principal used precisely the same language to discuss academic priorities.
- The mission was given priority status by teachers in their lesson planning and implementation.
- The goal was well-articulated, actively backed, and modeled by the school's principal.

Instructional leaders can apply this research to their mission-building strategies. The questions that this principal asked himself in the definition of the school's goals were:

- Are the goals clear and easily understandable?
- Are they written down and known by everyone in the school?
- Do the goals apply in the day-to-day activities at the school?
- Does the principal constantly and actively reinforce and articulate these goals?
- Do the goals have the support of the rest of the school?

Of course, in another situation, encouraging the use of the activity center might be warranted. For example, in the vignette at the beginning of this chapter, Principal Stover feels that Jane Ashley's teaching style lacks verve and interest. In this instance, the use of an activity center or other alternatives to conventional teaching styles might generate more excitement among the students.

Managing the Instructional Program

This second dimension focuses on coordination and control of the school's curriculum and all elements that involve instruction. This dimension incorporates three leadership functions, including supervising and evaluating instruction, coordinating the curriculum, and monitoring student progress. Managing the instructional program requires the principal's active participation in stimulating, supervising, guiding, and monitoring teaching and learning processes in the school. These functions demand expertise as well as a commitment by the principal. He or she is asked to be "neck-deep" in the school's instruction and curriculum (Cuban, 1984; Dwyer, 1986; Edmonds, 1979; Marshall, 1996).

   In the California school example noted previously, the teachers were questioned on how they monitored student progress. Several teachers responded that the principal knew the reading level and academic progress of almost all students in the elementary school (Hallinger & Murphy, 1986). This kind of personal engagement is not possible to achieve in every school, but the behavior reflects the degree of the principal's involvement in monitoring and managing the school's instructional program and curriculum.

Promoting a Positive School Learning Climate

This third dimension in instructional leadership supports several academic strategies for success:

- Protecting instructional time.
- Promoting professional development.
- Maintaining high visibility of administrators.
- Providing incentives for success to teachers.
- Developing high standards.
- Providing incentives for learning to students.

This dimension is the broadest in both scope and purpose. Promoting a positive school learning climate brings alive the widely held notion that effective schools create an "academic press" by developing high standards of learning and manifestly greater expectations from both students and teachers (Purkey &

Smith, 1983; Hallinger, 2005). These schools usually pursue a culture of continued improvement where rewards are well aligned with the aims and practices of the school. The principal must model those values and practices that create continuous development and improvement of both teaching and learning (Dwyer, 1986; Hallinger, 2005).

Common Findings from Research into Instructional Leadership

Scholars have conducted scores of research studies on instructional leadership since 1980. Most current research has focused on the qualities associated with the concept of "instructional" in nature (Hallinger & Heck, 1996a). We now have a significant knowledge base on this topic, including:

- Effects of so-called "personal antecedents," such as gender, experience, training, age, and school context.
- Effects of instructional leadership on the school's mission, goals, expectations, curriculum, teaching, learning, and motivation.
- Direct and indirect impact of instructional leadership on student achievement and other school outcomes.
- Instructional leadership and personality.
- School effectiveness and instructional leadership.
- Instructional leadership and other leadership styles.

Instructional Leadership and Student Performance

Research finds that schools that make a positive difference in the learning levels are led by principals who make a positive contribution to staff effectiveness and students under their charge (Hallinger, 2005). In the 1980s, instructional leadership was often depicted as "hands-on" leadership in classroom matters. Recent research by Hallinger (2005) reports that few studies find instructional leaders who are directly involved in the supervision of classroom instruction. Research by Hallinger and Heck (1996a, 1996b) finds that instructional supervision is most commonly found at the elementary school level. The majority of recent studies reports that the involvement of principals in classroom instruction are indirect and carried out through building a school culture and modeling (Hallinger, 2005).

However, most scholars now find that a principal's impact on student learning is statistically significant, but minimal. Even marginal impact is vital to desired outcomes, because policy makers still use these findings to justify their emphasis on the selection and training of school leaders as a strategy for school improvement. The role of the principal in shaping the school's vision and mission is described as the most influential "avenue of effects" (Marks & Printy, 2004).

School context has been found to have a significant effect on the success of instructional leadership exercised by its principals (Hallinger, 2005). Instructional leadership effectiveness should be viewed as an independent effort, but also as dependent on the learning environment.

Research by Rowe (2007) and Hallinger (2005) shows that successful instructional leaders work with other stakeholders to shape the school to fit its mission.

Instructional leaders directly influence the quality of school outcomes by aligning the school's structures, such as academic standards, timetables, and curriculum, with the school's mission (Rowe, 2007). Leaders are more effective when they lead by defining missions and managing activities that increase harmony with practices needed for effectiveness (Meier, 2010; Hallinger, 2005).

The instructional leadership behaviors of school principals are viewed as precursors to school effectiveness. Although some critics have questioned the empirical validity of this argument (Hallinger, 2005), the supporting evidence suggests its validity. Empirical evidence from 40 studies of American schools by Hallinger (2003) shows these effects of school leadership on student achievement.

Various models were found to produce different results:

- "Direct effect" models attempt to show a direct link between leaders' practices and school outcomes.
- "Mediated effect" models suggest that leaders' effects on school outcomes are conditioned by environmental factors like culture or organization.
- "Reciprocal effect" models assume that relationship between principals' behavior and the schools' environment are interactive.

While most studies have relied upon direct effect models, indirect effect models showed greater impact of instructional leadership on student performance. The study found that of 21 initial studies, 9 found no relationship between the two, 6 showed mixed effect, and only 6 showed a positive relationship.

The reason for the paucity of positive results is best explained by contextual differences in the school setting, variations in the role of principals, alternative models, and differences in methodology. Outcomes from past research on the effects of instructional leadership behavior on school outcomes may have introduced bias in the various research studies. While effective school research reveals correlations between instructional leadership behaviors and school outcomes, most research methods were either case or ethnographic studies; very few other studies were co-relational or supported the existence of an allowed-for causal relationship.

The ambiguity of the role of the principal in instructional leadership has been another problem. Instructional leadership has rarely defined practices and behaviors that are required to be initiated by the principal, thus making it unclear as to what needs to be considered for effective instructional leadership. The traits described as instructional leadership in past research have been isolated personal traits, such as "locus of control" and "leadership styles," that relate to effective schools without factoring in the school context. The problems associated with these studies have been put into question in their role as vital indicators of the important dimensions of instructional leadership (Hallinger, 2005).

Hallinger (2005) posited several qualities of instructional leadership behaviors. These traits appear to have the best effects on student achievement:

- The leader as resource provider.
- The leader as instructional resource.

- The leader as effective communicator.
- The leader as visibly present in the school.

The presence of these instructional leadership qualities is correlated to increase math and reading scores, especially among the low-achieving students (Hallinger, 2005).

Hallinger also explored, through a sample of 87 elementary schools, the extent to which principals play a role in the reading achievement of students. The result indicated a direct link between leadership and the existence of a well-articulated school mission. It was the mission that influenced the students' opportunity to learn and the teachers' expectations for student achievements. Principals influence student learning, but indirectly.

The research also found that principals in successful schools spent more time in direct liaising with teachers to draw up the school's instructional program. This finding is consistent with earlier research by Brewer (1993), which found that better academic results in high schools were obtained where principals framed and upheld high educational/academic goals.

Hallinger (2005) restates that higher achievement in school performance is feasible through coordinating school goals with the curriculum. The model suggests that goals are the instrumental agents to focus attention of staff and students in a whole range of relevant activities. The study offers the following research questions to provide insight on the leadership style in a school. These questions will also help an administrator determine whether he or she is practicing effective instructional leadership.

- Do principals frequently invest their time in the different instructional domains (i.e., through classroom supervision or monitoring of teaching)?
- What domains of instructional leadership behavior in the principal can be significantly associated with student achievement and academic performance?
- How do the contextual variables, such as students' socioeconomic background, school size, and student achievement, relate?
- What are the known mediated effects (if any) of the principal's instructional leadership behavior in predicting student achievement and performance?

In the opening story, Principal Stover's inability to come up with constructive criticism in response to Jane Ashley's lackluster teaching suggests that he is himself lacking in imagination. Creative modeling of leadership behavior from the top down can create a culture of innovation and adaptability that will be beneficial to teachers and students alike.

Personality and Its Influence on Instructional Leadership Behavior

Research into effective instructional leadership has often focused on the personal characteristics of leaders in education (Leithwood, Harris, & Hopkins, 2008). In much of this research, the Jungian personality theory stated in Myers-Briggs is used to study links between leadership and personality due to its utility (Bayne, 2005) and effectiveness with diverse audiences (Kise & Russell, 2008). Halverson,

Grigg, Prichett, and Thomas (2007) suggest that the ability to use data strategically is a successful leadership skill. Data manipulation appeals to a "Thinking" preference in Myers-Briggs. Stein and Spillane (2005) argue that increased teacher-to-teacher collaboration is a successful instructional model more appealing to Myers-Briggs "Extroverts." Research into successful instructional leadership by Drago-Severson (2007) concludes that principals need to focus on teachers' developmental diversity and other contextual variables. The levels of focus and attention needed for this would only be appealing to leaders with a Myers-Briggs "Feeling" preference. Beatty (2007) intimates that instructional leaders who are more "emotionally attuned" would be highly successful, while Bryk and Schneider (2002) also establishes that the development of relational trust between teachers and principals would be a potent recipe for success, which is appealing to leaders with a "Feeling" personality.

Leadership models can be predicted to appeal to some administrators more than others, based on their personality dimensions. A wider range of skills and styles cannot be accommodated by one person, because a leader already has his or her own preferences, influenced by personality (Kise & Russell, 2008; Reeves, 2006). The natural differences in personality among various leaders result in preferences that operate below the level of the leader's awareness. It is also not humanly possible for leaders to comply with such varied and complex requirements.

Some researchers have recognized the need to address the problem of inherent conflicts or preference, or opposition brought about by leadership expectations. Dwyer (2007) suggests a model, utilizing Myers-Briggs concepts, that consciously combines the head, heart, and hands, so as to balance cognitive (Thinking) and instrumental (Sensing) elements of available leadership models with intuition (Intuitive) and sensitivity to building working relationships (Feeling). This comprehensive leadership model is complemented by Sternberg's (2002) model of "successful intelligence," and Kise and Russell's (2008) model of "differentiated school leadership." These integrated models acknowledge the personality of the leader as a vital component in leadership.

As a result of personality differences, a leader develops judgments and responds to his or her environment by focusing on certain leadership aspects more than others (Firestone & Shipps, 2005). Variations caused by factors such as age, upbringing, and gender have been shown to affect personality development and formulation. Practices are also influenced by the interaction between personality and contextual aspects associated with the workplace. Examples of these contextual aspects include the perceived nature of work, the leadership experience, the school level, and the leader's position (Macdaid, McCaulley, & Kainz, 2007).

Leithwood and Jantzi (2005) analyzed the role of efficacy as related to leadership effectiveness, and found that there is a connection between belief in one's ability ("confidence") and effectiveness. Efficacy can be described as a leadership trait that takes into account the leader's personality characteristics. Hogan (2004) noted that many traits linked with leadership, such as efficacy, are closely associated with a leader's personality.

Reynolds (2006) reveals that there is no shared understanding of how schools or classrooms operate. He argues that, because of this lack of consensus on how schools should be run, principals and teachers fill the void through their own personal views and conceptions. Similarly, Meier (2010) suggests that the void caused by a lack of agreement is best filled by personality preferences influenced by certain variables, such as experience and the nature of the task. Heck and Hallinger (2005) note that the lack of harmony between conceptual and methodological schools of thought using the available research criteria has left room for researchers and leaders to rely on their individual conceptions of what is applicable and valid. This study has increased pressure on researchers to come up with models aimed at instructional effects that are most inclusive of leadership practices geared toward school improvement. The preferences of leaders are indicated by their attitudes toward certain practices in their job description. Kise and Russell (2008) identified key practices in all eight domains of instructional leadership.

Leadership practices are necessary even where there are opposing areas of preference. This requires that leaders have an unrealistic flexibility level in their instructional practices. In her study on personality and instructional leadership in schools, Meier (2010) offers support to those models that are considerate of the reality of personality differences.

So which is the best way forward? It would seem prudent that school leader and administrators first acknowledge their inborn, natural predispositions toward some practices over others. They should then reflect on whether these preferences affect their leadership practices. Honesty and transparency in acknowledging personality differences would motivate the leaders to consider ways to satisfy the various needs of their schools. As Kise and Russell (2008) note, self-awareness is a prerequisite to the development of tendencies in the leader that complement effective team-building.

Educational policy makers should be aware of the range and nature of current successful practices. The Meier (2010) study examines these "best practices" associated with successful instructional leadership. She notes that there are many best practices, and that educators have expressed concern about their abundance and contradictory nature.

In consideration of the above, leaders should study these practices before implementing research recommendations that purport to affect student performance. Reasonableness in implementation should begin with an acknowledgement of the breadth of research recommendations by policy makers. The Meier (2010) study finds that most leaders showed a preference for practices within their own personality type. These practices were also found to be closest to the instructional core of their schools. Leaders' preferences are often put into practice. Policy makers and researchers should explore whether these inclinations can be translated into behavioral changes that might positively impact on school outcomes.

Delegation is a pillar of leadership, considered by many researchers as a vital component for leadership success. Research has shown that delegation is dependent on personality preferences, which translates to predictability in leadership behavior (Ozer & Benet-Martínez, 2008) and (in)competence. The leader's preferences are heavily influenced by what is natural, comfortable, and enjoyable for the leader.

School leaders should consider reshaping their school leadership responsibilities in a manner considerate of administrators' preferences (Meier, 2010), thus attempting more modest implementations, based on sound research study. While this may be more supportive of a differentiated rather than instructional leadership style, the importance of incorporating varying human differences is vital for any leadership paradigm. Bolman and Deal (2003) point out that diversity improves a team's competitive advantage.

While the Meier (2010) research study does not recommend that personality type be considered while hiring school leaders, it calls for the positive use of personality preferences in a thoughtful and creative manner in team-building and task assignment.

As schools seek to redefine themselves as learning communities, its members must work together in a collegial fashion, by challenging and engaging with each other. Jungian theory finds that diversity generates synergy and innovation. Most leadership researchers and theorists have noted that human differences provide creative tension needed in the forward movement and growth of any institution (Fullan, 2007). Antonakis, Cianciolo, and Sternberg (2004) state categorically that models of leadership that ignore the nature of leaders do so at their own peril.

As school principals work to close the achievement gap in learning, they benefit from a conscious understanding of their own natural preferences in relation to instructional leadership. Acknowledging human differences that are often depicted as weaknesses can be a seed for success in educational leadership.

The New Instructional Leadership

It is becoming clearer that school leadership is going through a revolution. New policy formulations call for higher academic standards and accountability. So-called accountability systems capture a wider range of instruments to develop and monitor school change. Researchers have joined the fray of those who will reinvent instructional leadership in schools (Halverson et al., 2006).

Halverson et al. (2006) state that more focus on student results leads to local changes that align with the performance goals of the educational system. There is a general presumption that these changes will come automatically, since public reporting of school outcomes brings pressure for reform. However, part of this change will come from development of direct incentives that yield innovation, efficiency, and solutions to performance problems.

Halverson et al. (2006) state that accountability systems will provide the onus to develop standards required for improved instructional and assessment practices, while acting as incentives for participation in the process. This simple logic of an accountability system is compelling, and provides an irresistible rationale for educational reform.

This new vigor in instructional leadership has been mainly spurred by the provisions of the No Child Left Behind Act (2002). The recent debate in the U.S. on the legitimacy of using standardized tests to gauge student learning has led to new leadership efforts and spending to help schools achieve better test scores (Halverson et al., 2006). These efforts have pressured new instructional leadership, characterized by school analysts, researchers, and school leaders as data-driven decision-making. However, this new instructional paradigm had been envisioned earlier in research (Bernhardt, 1998; Holcomb, 1999; Johnson, 2002; Love, 2002).

This new instructional style has also been referred to as "learning-centered" leadership. The revolution began with a push by state education leaders to process student data from available achievement tests. Private companies enjoyed financial benefits from the sale of data reporting systems to schools to enable them to sort the data (Burch, 2005). State education leaders addressed the inability by local school leaders to use data effectively by hiring consultants, who created data analysis workshops and data retreats. School leaders adopted new comprehensive school reform plans and curricula coordinated with state learning standards, resulting in systemic changes in student learning.

Halverson et al. (2006) found that positive results from these school, district, and state efforts to meet accountability demands through data-driven decision-making can only be achieved through willingness by practitioners to change their instructional leadership practices to conform to these new structures.

From emerging results and observations, the most dominant problem in data-driven decision-making is the implementation of these new accountability practices. Most schools already had active and working internal accountability systems. Schools already made decisions through the use of data, such as class attendance, test scores, student discipline, available budgets, and teacher reputations. Administrative reliance on these old internal accountability systems has been the biggest contributor to resistance to reforms in school instructional practice. Early research studies such as Weick (1982) discovered that existing school organizational structures insulated current instructional practices from external pressure to change.

It is necessary to encourage data-driven decision making by challenging school leaders to reinvent their existing practices. Halverson et al. (2006) state that, "The heart of the new instructional leadership is the ability of leaders to shift schools from cultures of internal accountability to meet the demands of external accountability" (p. 8). Instructional leaders need knowledge and supporting frameworks to guide them in the use of accountability data to improve student performance.

For this goal to be accomplished, leaders need to factor in external accountability as a replacement for traditional methods. This new paradigm is an improvement over traditional practices such as teacher evaluation, professional development, curriculum design, and the formulation of new cultures of learning. These older techniques will have to be reframed so as to address the challenges of contemporary schools.

Wilson (2004) states that understandable accountability systems rely on two-way information flow that connects classroom practice with external accountability measures. This requires higher levels of teaching and leadership linkage, teacher collaboration, learning synchronized with existing instructional goals, and close monitoring of instructional outcomes. To achieve success in these, the leader must assist students in taking tests, avoid a reduction of learning in favor of test preparation, and justify changes in instructional practices to the community.

This new instructional leadership paradigm takes the debate on education standards beyond the familiar categories of instructional and transformational styles to a level that creates credible and accountable learning systems. In schools countrywide, there are increasing cases of school leaders who are engaging in new practices based on accountability shaped to improve student learning.

Halverson et al. (2006), in their "data-based decision making instructional system" (DDIS) model, made suggestions of what the model should include. They provided six functions that reflect a modern model of instructional leadership: data acquisition, data reflection, program alignment, program design, formative feedback, and test preparation.

Data Acquisition

Data acquisition refers to the collective processes that are meant to seek, collect, and prepare useful information for teaching and learning activities. The data gathered and processed at this stage are taken from standard student assessment test scores. However, there are other fields of information that are needed to inform teaching and learning. These are:

- Student placement and behavioral records.
- Student demographics.
- Classroom grades.
- Data on current teacher personnel.
- Community survey data.
- Budgetary information.
- Master schedule and calendar information.
- Curricular information.
- Technological capacity.

Data storage, also referred to as data warehousing and data reporting, is a vital element of data acquisition. There is a need to use local data systems, since the NCLB Act requires certain information on student performance. Schools have established a retail base for a wide variety of data storage and data analysis products.

Data Reflection

This refers to the processes by which acquired data are manipulated to transform student learning data into improved teaching and learning practices. DDIS data reflection is a structured opportunity for both teachers and leaders to make useful sense of data, rather than relying on guesses of "what works."

Data reflection can be done at a school-wide level, grade level, or even in subject-area meetings. One vital element of data reflection is problem framing. This part involves active consideration of data capability to improve outcomes. The conclusion of data reflection is a plan of action.

Program Alignment

This part of the DDIS model involves making the school's instructional program consistent with the content and performance standards in classrooms. Program alignment is an essential part of planning for instructional leadership, probably the most sensitive part of DDIS, in order to influence the outcome of the implementation of the model's recommendations.

Program Design

This refers to the process of the new instructional leadership style to adapt its instructional needs—including modification of curricula, student service programs, and instructional strategies—to improve student learning. It is through program design that the school's policies, plans, and procedures are defined in such a manner that reported problems are addressed. Program design also involves the inspection of the school's financial ability to procure and maintain new program through budgets and grants.

Formative Feedback

Feedback is always a crucial part of adoption of new strategies. The DDIS model creates a continuous and timely flow of information, designed to improve student outcomes. These structures provide vital information on student learning or teaching practices and are inculcated into the DDIS system when used in the improvement of program design.

This feedback is different from data acquisition and reflection. It applies to information gathered to measure the school's progress measured in terms of student performance.

Test Preparation

This last part of the DDIS model is a collection of activities that are designed to assess, motivate, and develop student academic capabilities. It also includes strategies to improve performance on state and district assessment tests. Test preparation covers a wide range of issues, such as test formats, testing skills, and teaching to deficiencies, as well as test preparation.

"Teaching to the test" refers to study content, called "formulaic instruction" by Halverson et al. (2006). In short, it is teaching students topics that are examinable without regard to holistic learning. Researchers found out that most leaders in schools across the U.S. have reformed multiple aspects of school life to link their instructional programs to test content. Halverson observed that schools where the DDIS mode was put into action did not narrow their curriculum to the structure and test content. The researchers noticed instead that, in schools with DDIS systems, there were rich instructional systems designed to help students meet standards in state exams.

A DDIS usually links the school system functions to a system that better facilitates information flow to improved student performance. Once school leaders understand this system, they can focus attention on the critical areas of instruction that need reform. This system of instructional leadership is insightful, innovative, and results-oriented. It increases precision in predicting student outcomes and developing key areas of study relevant to academic improvement.

Summary

Improvements and renovations in instructional leadership have kept instructional leadership relevant even in the face of transformational and distributed leadership. It is accepted that a school must practice some level of instructional leadership. Instructional leadership may be either transactional, meaning that it is based on extrinsic motivation, or transformational, meaning that it relies on psychological motivation to succeed. A key component of instructional leadership involves defining the school's mission. This entails "framing" and "communicating" the school's goals.

A leader may use bureaucratic authority, in which the hierarchical structures place binds on the stakeholders to achieve certain outcomes; or personal authority, which relies on the integrity and personal relationships with the stakeholders to achieve objectives. Personal authority is highly dependent on personality. We looked in depth at the Myers-Briggs personality assessment test, and discovered that certain personality traits are required for effective leadership. Key among these are the "Thinking," "Feeling," and "Extrovert" aspects included in Myers-Briggs.

The No Child Left Behind Act has ushered in a new era of data-driven school administration. Leaders have been forced to change their methods to suit the new focus on data acquisition, data reflection, program alignment, program design, formative feedback, and test preparation.

Though it has been forced to undergo a shift in focus, instructional leadership remains a crucial aspect of the school setting. If it can reinvent itself, it will remain a dynamic force well into the future.

Discussion Questions

1. What part does a leader's personality play in leadership? Is one personality type better than another? What are the drawbacks of certain personality types?
2. List three important qualities that school goals should have.
3. Use the Myers-Briggs categories (Thinking, Sensing, Intuitive, Feeling) to describe the ideal principal.
4. Think about the principal at a school you attended. How would you describe his or her personality? Do you think the principal's personality affected the operation of the school? List three ways.
5. The chapter maintains that a principal's involvement in instruction makes a difference in student outcomes. If you were Principal Stover in the opening vignette, what would you say to Jane? Prepare three statements of exactly what you as an instructional leader would say to encourage her to challenge herself and her students.

Activities

1. "Defining a school's mission," according to Hallinger and Murphy, is central to a principal's role. What is the best way to come up with this definition? In small groups, discuss this, and develop a method. Each small group should then use its method to come up with a mission statement and three associated goals.
2. Write attributes of a successful principal on sizeable strips of paper. Using sticky tack or double-sided tape, post these on a wall. Then move the strips up or down, depending on perceived importance. Once a consensus seems to have been achieved, discuss the attributes. Which rose to the top? Which sank? Why?

Selected Readings

Attewell, P., & Domina, T. (2008). Raising the bar: Curricular intensity and academic performance. *Educational Evaluation and Policy Analysis, 30*(1), 51–71.
Greenlee, B.J. (2007). Building teacher leadership capacity through educational leadership programs. *Journal of Research for Educational Leadership, 4*(1), 44–74.
Hoy, A. W., & Hoy, W. K. (2008). *Instructional leadership: A research-based guide to learning in schools.* (3rd ed.). Boston, MA: Pearson.
Reitzug, U. C., & West, D. L. (2007). *Problematizing instructional leadership: The voices of principals.* American Educational Research Association conference (AERA), Chicago, Ill.
Stronge, J. H. (2008). *Instructional leadership: Supporting best practice.* Alexandria, VA: Association for Supervision and Curriculum Development.

Chapter 3

Distributed Leadership

A Humanistic Approach to
Shared Governance

Amy Paquinette took over the principalship of Sequoia Middle School after the previous principal had left in the middle of the year, citing health issues. In the three months that the school had functioned under the assistant principal, things had fallen apart. On her very first day in the job, Ms. Paquinette was horrified to find two students sitting in a hallway, bent over a video game. They claimed that their teacher had given them permission to leave the room. When she confronted the teacher, she found that it was true—the students had been disrupting the class, and the teacher had sent them to the principal's office. But the acting principal told them he had no time to deal with them, and sent them into the hallway. There seemed to be no structures in place to deal with this type of situation.

The acting principal was sitting before a jagged mound of files. As Ms. Paquinette questioned him, trying to get a sense of the school's situation, his eyes filled with tears. It transpired that the former principal had worked ten to twelve hours a day, six days a week, and had done everything himself. He had made it a point to visit every classroom once a day. All paperwork had to be approved by him. Every test had to cross his desk. All disciplinary cases were referred to him. He'd been able to sustain that for seven years. But finally, high blood pressure and a nagging stomach ulcer had forced him into sudden retirement. The assistant principal, who felt he was expected to keep the same pace, was overwhelmed, and worried that his health would deteriorate as well.

Distributed Leadership and Sustainability

Having looked at transformational and instructional leadership, we can begin to see that the style of leadership that a school leader decides to use usually delivers concrete results—increased student performance, work ethic, or motivation for teaching staff. In this chapter, we will look at distributed leadership, another promising leadership style that could bring about positive outcomes in American schools.

Timperley (2005) states that, while expectations that transformation of schools depends on exceptional leaders have been found to be unrealistic and unsustainable, the idea of distributing leadership across people and situations has started to become the new framework for understanding the realities of the school setup and its improvement. However, as this is a fairly new concept, empirical studies on how leadership is distributed in successful and poorly performing schools are rare. Researchers have, however, found some risks and benefits attached to distributing leadership. Key concepts of distributed leadership presented in earlier theories have been challenged.

Though it is clear that strong leaders with exceptional vision do not always create lasting transformation, the reasons why this is so remain a matter of discussion. To some researchers, such leaders are not available in sufficient numbers to meet the demands of school leadership in today's world (Copland, 2003). Others have stated that this conceptualization of a "heroic" leader often does not appeal to potential leaders (Gronn & Rawlings-Sanaei, 2003).

Additionally, the number of administrative tasks that a principal undertakes daily leaves insufficient hours in the day to complete these activities, and the principal finds him or herself attempting to cope with more mundane responsibilities (Elmore, 2002; Gronn & Rawlings-Sanaei, 2003). Another problem arising from this type of "heroic" leadership is that the vitality of the school rests on the leader's shoulders. As we saw in the vignette, when the exceptional leader moves on, progress in the school often comes to a standstill. Past practices may also reemerge.

Therefore, a growing perception is that a more achievable and sustainable conceptualization of leadership has to replace the model of "a single 'heroic' leader standing atop a hierarchy, bending the school community to his or her purposes" (Camburn et al., 2003: 348). The alternative should involve thinking of leadership in terms of the range of activities and interactions that are distributed across multiple people and situations and also to involve role complementarities and network patterns of control.

Distributed leadership is thus a focus on how school leaders promote and sustain conditions that are successful for schooling and interaction with others, rather than on the structures and programs necessary for academic success (Spillane et al., 2004). This thinking on leadership has roots in the 1980s and early 1990s as ideas about the cultural and historical influences on individual cognition led to an understanding of this cognition being distributed through material and social artifacts in a certain environment.

Equally, earlier scholars such as Sergiovanni (1984) suggested that emphasis should be placed on changes in organizational thinking, particularly to developing organizational cultures involving many actors contributing to norms, beliefs, and principles from which the organization's members developed a shared purpose. However, the idea of distributed leadership only came into focus for the first time in the research literature of the mid–1990s.

Emergence of Distributed Leadership

Recent research has attributed distributed leadership to changes in perceptions in the modern setting. After its disappearance after a short stint in the mid-1990s, it reappeared as a movement of sorts after Gronn (2000) wrote his preliminary taxonomy of distributed leadership.

So vast is the movement now that even the National College for School Leadership (NCSL) of England now has a dedicated Distributed Leadership website. The U.S. has followed a similar trend. Examples include Spillane et al.'s (2004) five-year Distributed Leadership Study project at Northwestern University and the Distributed Leadership Model (DLM) developed by the Sloan School of Management.

Despite the craze, distributed leadership has not yet eliminated confusion due to its perceived conceptual elasticity. This lack of conceptual clarity has not provided ample room for a complete implementation of the concept in empirical research. Popularity aside, there is scant evidence showing a direct causal relationship between distributed leadership and school outcomes. Questions abound as to what is driving the emergence of distributed leadership as a genre within the field of educational management and leadership. Some scholars have purported that it is simply a remake of earlier leadership formulations, such as Etzioni's "dual leadership theory" (Etzioni, 1965). Hartley (2007) states that this should not be of much concern. Instead, scholars should be critical of its efficacy as a form of leadership practice and how to develop it as an inchoate theory and set it into practice within the leadership field. Therefore, we should endeavor to look at converging political, economic, and cultural conditions, to allow for the expression of distributed leadership as both rhetoric and practice.

To achieve this goal, we should first attempt to gain a clearer understanding of what distributed leadership really is. Spillane (2006) states that a comprehensive definition is elusive, since the appeal of distributed leadership lies in the ease with which it can become all things to all people (Spillane, 2006). Bennett et al. (2003) refer to this leadership style as "disparate," with multiple and differing definitions.

Some scholars, such as MacBeath (2005), have generated an empirical taxonomy of distribution into categories, such as distribution formally, and distribution as pragmatic, strategic, incremental, opportunistic, or cultural. Hartley (2007) states that distributed leadership is not a new idea, but has been around for a long time in the form of delegated or shared leadership. Nevertheless, it is well known that attempts to show a direct causal relationship between leader behavior and pupil achievement have yielded little that is definitive (Levacic, 2005). A study by Leithwood et al. (2006) states that there is cause for optimism, but the researchers admit that their claims are not robust. However, they all find support in varying amounts of fairly sound empirical evidence. They claim that school leadership has a greater influence on schools and students when it is widely distributed, but admit that, despite the popularity of this claim, evidence of its support is less extensive, and in some cases less direct, than that in support of the other claims made.

It becomes clear, then, that the policy on distributed leadership is ahead of the evidence. Therefore, much of the available research on distributed leadership is technical, since it purports to enhance prediction and control, or practical, since it focuses on "interpretation of symbolic communication" (Hartley, 2007). We are therefore left to question the positioning of distributed leadership in the broad topic of organizational theory.

Scholars have differing opinions on this issue. Some find that distributed leadership associates with the normative rhetoric and stands abreast of human relations management in schools, loosely coupled systems and with organizational culture (Ogawa, 2005). Others have found that it occurs within a "soft bureaucracy", i.e., an organization where processes of flexibility and decentralization exist side by side with more rigid constraints and structures of domination.

Hartley (2007) states that, as is common with other discourses of legitimating authority such as "empowerment" and "ownership," the notion of distributed leadership also appears to incorporate democratic procedures. However, research such as Woods (2004) has found that this type of leadership is not as democratic as might be assumed, because distributed leaders are appointees and do not hold office as a result of an election.

The presumed harmony and consensus often associated with distributed leadership has also been questioned, since some researchers have found that distribution tends to underestimate the micro-political aspects of leadership practice, e.g., in Hatcher (2005) and Storey (2004), and completely ignoring the distribution of wealth beyond the school and the link of such distribution to school achievement.

However, supporters of distributed leadership have countered this criticism by stating that it does inculcate micro-political aspects and is not a completely consensual creation. They draw support from the fact that leading theorists responsible for the emergence of the genre, such as Gronn (2000) and Spillane et al. (2004), draw upon Engeström's (2001) socio-cultural activity theory, which does not ignore the micro-political aspects of an activity system.

There is scarcely any research on distributed leadership focusing on domination and exploitation in leadership. Therefore, the analysis of distributed leadership as a type of designer leadership customized to deliver government policy. This criticism has been restated as,

> The knowledge base that was fashioned in the political process of creation remains truncated, historical, decontextualized and most important, immobile. The construction of a static, fixed platform upon which to construct a system of licensure and accreditation to evaluate a graduate educational program amounts to intellectual sacrifice of progress for permanency.
>
> (English, 2006: 465)

In the U.S., most commentators have not seen anything wrong with the NCSL's endorsement of an untested leadership style and have in fact approvingly referred to it as having growing international visibility and a reputation for stellar leadership development programs through its support of a distributed leadership philosophy (Dean, 2006).

The earlier concerns by Grace (2000) and English (2006) point to the growing political imperative that currently informs the education and training of school leaders. Through their research, we are therefore left with the question: If the emergence of distributed leadership is not supported by a reliable theoretical evidence-base, then what are the political considerations giving it prominence?

Reasons for the Emergence of Distributed Leadership

Two explanations have been offered for the emergence of distributed leadership. The first is the failure of the "charismatic hero" associated with transformational leadership, for reasons illustrated by the vignette at the beginning of this chapter. The second is the greater complexity of the tasks now handled by school leaders. Ingvarson et al. (2006) argue that it is not the heroic leader who makes an organization function well, but rather the "mundane" matters. What makes an organization efficient, they say, are the following:

- the *competence* of its members;
- the quick use of *initiatives*;
- an *identification* with a shared destiny based on trust;
- a *collective endeavor*;
- *unobtrusive coordination.*

Others regard distributed leadership as a pragmatic response to the demands of contemporary policy shifts. In its *Independent Study into School Leadership*, Pricewaterhouse-Coopers (2007) alludes to the growing range of new government policies that would reasonably require greater partnerships and collaborations among different professional cultures. In the U.S., they cite the *Every Child Matters* agenda, the 14–19 agenda and workforce remodeling as examples of new requirements for school leaders.

According to Pricewaterhouse-Coopers (2007), distributed leadership is well within the broader policy spectrum for public services. In a government's emerging model of governance for public services, we see the three modes of governance that the government favors. These are hierarchy, market, and network. If we superimpose the school setup on the government model, then we see the correspondence of the schools' "capability and capacity" maps onto a network regime of governance where distributed leadership is positioned.

Distributed leadership can therefore be said to be isomorphic to the broader policy process, since government will construct a need, goal, or objective that would require both school actors and non-school actors to distribute their efforts intra-organizationally and/or inter-organizationally to achieve this end. It is also a cultural complement to the formalized structural union of hitherto separate organizations (Hartley, 2007).

Distributed leadership resonates with the merging or networking of work-based activities according to current trends on inter-agency working in schools; with the joint production of personalized needs and solutions (Leadbeater, 2004); and finally with workforce remodeling (Tabberer, 2005). All these efforts seek to merge the professional cultures of hitherto disparate groups.

With the above in mind, the emergence of distributed leadership is not only a reaction to the recent policy shifts; it also reflects changes in contemporary culture. Hartley (2007) states that organizations can no longer control their workers through the so-called rational or bureaucratic structures of the past. Such structures inhibit the kind of independent work that relies on solidarity, respect, or mutual trust, since all they end up doing is bringing about authority differences.

Hartley (2007) suggests that the present focus on distributed leadership is not so much related to the cultural turn toward emotionality, like transformational leadership, but is more of an example of management theory resonating with a contemporary cultural shift toward the general weakening of traditional rationality. Organized social structure is consequently giving way to a "network culture" (Page, 2006).

These new changes also indicate a change in the knowledge economy (Hartley, 2007). We have begun to see a species of "socialism" in education, evidenced by the use of terms such as "universal education" to symbolize the effective declassification of education as a market commodity in this age. Governments around the world are now keen to set up policies that ensure literacy is achieved by all, irrespective of social status. The role of the school leader is therefore shifting from economic management to social management.

Distributed leadership, even when implemented diligently, does not always proceed smoothly. One principal comments, "In the morning as soon as I open my door teachers are waiting for me. Most of the time they want me to confirm or okay what it is they want to do. I give them (teachers) the authority to make decisions, but they are afraid to, so as a result, are always checking with me to be sure every decision is all right with me. I feel frustrated being the 'confirmer' or 'okay person.' I never have time to get to my desk at all . . . It's like they (teachers) don't trust me to support them or their decisions" (O'Hair & Bastian, 1993: 18).

However, if positively conceived and integrated with the existing school structure, distributed leadership can have profound results. One principal encouraged his teachers to create a two-day workshop to help each other through recurrent issues. The organizers used positive questions, such as, "How would you like to have a class size of 20 students?" and "How would you like to see every child in your class successful?" to tempt teachers into attending the workshop. Following the workshop, the principal noted, "the staff could hardly wait for school to get started. We sent wonderful letters to parents telling them what a great year we had planned. Never had the work been so exciting or so rewarding. In many ways the staff worked harder than ever before" (Sergiovanni, 1993: 23).

The distributed leadership movement continues to gather pace, with more commentators alluding to its replacement of the previous "heroic" leadership phase. It has been argued that:

> the emergence of distributed leadership is very much a sign of the times: it resonates with contemporary culture, with all of its loose affiliations and ephemeralities; and it is yet another sign of an institutional isomorphism whereby the public sector purports to legitimate its policies by appeals to the new organizational forms within the private sector.
>
> (Alvesson & Thompson, 2005: 488)

Nature of Distributed Leadership

Most of the theories on relational leadership place emphasis on the process and context of leader-led relations (Uhl-bien, 2006). Distributed leadership, being such a theory, therefore focuses on the fact that leadership is relational and cannot be captured by an examination of individual attributes on their own (Kempster, Cope, & Parry, 2010). This assertion is supported in earlier research by Hosking (1988) and Bennett et al. (2003), who state that leadership is an "emergent property of a group or network of interacting individuals working with an openness of boundaries and the varieties of expertise are distributed across the many, not the few."

We therefore tend to see a systemic perspective operating at the heart of distributed leadership, where individual action only makes sense when viewed as part of a pattern of relationships forming a collective activity. This school of thought has been reiterated persuasively in a recent study by Thorpe, Gold, Anderson, Burgoyne, Wilkinson, and Malby (2008), which sought to build on Gronn's (2000) argument that no one is an expert on everything in an organization.

The opening vignette presented the classic example of a pyramid-shaped leadership structure, in which the former principal, perhaps with the best of intentions, insisted that every decision be channeled through his desk. He was not open to the above-mentioned "varieties of expertise" or interactions: he considered himself the expert on everything. And, as became obvious, this took a toll on his own health and on the future health of the school.

Parry and Bryman (2006) suggest that there are five strands of development in distributed leadership that point to its nature. The first strand is an improvement of earlier works by Manz and Sims (1991), and Sims and Lorenzi (1992), which suggests that distributed leadership as a form of leadership supersedes the individual heroic model and is more inclined toward "super leadership," a new leadership paradigm that emphasizes "leading others to lead themselves." In super leadership, followers are stimulated to become leaders in their own right.

The second strand is drawn from the work of Kouzes and Posner (1998) and acts as a corollary to the first. It places more emphasis on the leaders' ability to develop capacity in others and turn their constituents into leaders (Parry & Bryman, 2006). Under this phase, the issue is not about handing down leadership to others, but more to do with liberating them so that they can use their abilities to lead themselves and others. According to Parry and Bryman (2009), these two themes bring about change away from the "heroic" leaders, and toward social influence anchored on teams as sources of leadership.

"Leadership as a social process" is the third aspect of distributed leadership. This aspect primarily focuses on leadership processes and skills that encapsulate a perspective beyond the traditional formal roles of designated leaders. It draws on the earlier work of Hosking (1988; 1991) to build leadership in terms of an "organizing" activity based on a holistic process of social influence that cannot be said to be the exclusive function of the traditional leader. This focus on leadership practices is influenced by the notions of communities of practice and the learning capability leading to the development of tacit knowledge of entrepreneurial leadership practice tailored to particular situations (Kempster, Cope, & Parry, 2010).

What is of importance here is how the everyday activities of leaders fuse social processes, roles, and identities (Kempster, 2009). This suggestion implies that we cannot see distributed leadership in practice as separate from people's socially learned implicit theories of leadership (Kempster, Cope, & Parry, 2010).

The fourth expression of distributed leadership draws on the work of Gordon (2002). It is characterized by its critical stance of drawing a distinction between distributed and traditional leadership by examining the power structures of organizations. These power structures, which affect leader–follower relationships, maintain traditional notions of differentiation between leaders and followers in all power and information asymmetries. These asymmetries are made clearer upon contrasting the empowerment encapsulated in flattening hierarchies and the act of delegation. However, we find that the power structures always reinforce preexisting leadership characteristics, in spite of the rhetoric on the alleged distribution of power by those in senior positions (Parry & Bryman, 2006).

The fifth strand of distributed leadership is that of leadership defined within the context of e-commerce or an advanced information technology environment (Avolio et al., 2001). According to Parry and Bryman (2006), certain challenges to leadership arise from the advancement of communication technology. While new modes of communication, such as texting and emailing, allow leaders to pass information to large groups of followers quickly and in large volumes, followers can easily access the same information independently. Thus leaders lose control over information flow and its consequent power.

Technology thus forms part of the organizational transformation, and part of the leadership process as well (Avolio et al., 2001). Parry and Bryman (2006) state that,

> Leadership is not solely a set of characteristics possessed by an individual, but an emergent property of a social system, in which "leaders" and "followers" share in the process of enacting leadership. The notion here is very clear that effective leadership depends upon multiple leaders for decision-making and action-taking. "Collective effort" with "mental and organizational agility" would describe their interactions and leadership style.
>
> (Parry & Bryman, 2006: 455)

It is in this fifth perspective that we encounter the emergence of new structures of the "Internet culture." Here, the expectations, requirements, and necessities are for multiple leaders taking myriads of decisions through coordinated action-taking; consequently, leadership is widely dispersed or distributed. Kempster, Cope, and Parry (2010) state that the tensions described in the large organizational context are very real, since they have an effect on the control of leader-follower structures, experiences, and expectations. The impact that these tensions have on the school setting in distributed leadership remains to be seen.

Testing Distributed Leadership

As stated earlier, research on distributed leadership has not been tightly focused on student outcomes. Of the myriads of published studies on educational leadership, less than 30 have empirically tested the relationship between leadership and student outcomes, both academic and non-academic (Robinson, 2008). Because distributed leadership is quite young compared to other leadership styles, the number of such studies is understandably fewer.

There has been a call by several researchers for more research on student outcomes and their relation to distributed leadership. Nevertheless, studies by Camburn et al. (2003) and Harris (2005) have questioned why schools with a distributed pattern of leadership should have a greater density of instructional leadership, more innovation, and better student outcomes than those utilizing other leadership styles. One of the arguments raised is that better outcomes are achievable under distributed leadership because more of the expertise and talent of staff will be identified, developed, and utilized than under a traditional hierarchical style.

The above argument is particularly compelling when one considers the breadth and depth of pedagogical expertise required to enable all students to perform successfully with challenging curricula (Robinson, 2008). The second argument relates to the sustainability of efforts required to improve teaching and learning. It is much more likely that schools with more distributed leadership will have more knowledgeable staff, who take personal responsibility for the improvement of student outcomes. The nature of distributed leadership thus reveals two basic concepts: "distributed leadership as task distribution" and "distributed leadership as distributed influence processes" (Robinson, 2008). We will look at these separately.

Distributed Leadership as Task Distribution

Most of the recent works on distributed leadership have framed this kind of leadership as the performance of particular tasks. Spillane et al. (2004) define leadership as,

> The activities engaged in by leaders, in interaction with others in particular contexts around specific tasks . . . identification, acquisition, allocation, co-ordination, and use of the social, material, and cultural resources necessary to establish the conditions for the possibility of teaching and learning.
> (Spillane et al., 2004: 11)

Robinson (2008) defines the above-named tasks as the "what" of leadership, and goes on to state that the "how" involves mobilizing school personnel to identify and take on the tasks of changing instruction as well as harnessing and mobilizing resources needed to support the overall transformation. This explanation introduces a second dimension to leadership in the form of influencing others to make changes in their environment.

Spillane et al.'s (2004) theoretical description of distributed leadership can thus be said to be situated in the performance of certain tasks and interactions between shifting combinations of leaders and followers in the course of task performance. Leadership is therefore distributed across the three constitutive elements of leader, follower, and task.

A good case study of task distribution is evident in a series of studies of distributed leadership by Spillane, Camburn, and Pareja (2007). They analyzed certain patterns of distributed leadership by using the electronic logs of 52 school principals. These logs were created by the principals upon prompting by electronic beeps set at random intervals throughout the day. After hearing the beeps, the principals were supposed to record whether they were engaged in particular leadership tasks, and whether they were the ones leading or co-leading those tasks or whether others were doing it for them.

The "how" part of leadership was obtained by prompting them to record their primary intentions at the time by choosing from a list of intentions that included increasing knowledge, monitoring teaching and curricula, developing common goals, motivating or developing others, or redesigning the teaching and learning. Through these options, the researchers captured the principals' intention to exercise direct or indirect influence over their staff.

In their earlier study of distributed leadership, Camburn et al. (2003) also took leadership as a task performance approach in the sample of schools participating in a comprehensive school reform program. At first, they defined leadership as,

A set of organizational functions that leaders might be expected to perform—including not only instructional leadership functions, but also functions related to broader school and building management, as well as boundary-spanning functions entailing the acquisition of resources and the establishment or maintenance of relationship with external constituents.

(Camburn et al., 2003: 349).

Both authors evaluated distributed leadership by asking all those with formally designated leadership roles to report the priority and/or the amount of time they devoted to a variety of leadership activities in the current year. However, these studies differ in that Camburn et al. (2003) did not explore the intended or actual influence of these leaders.

The results of this kind of approach in distributed leadership as relates to its impact on student outcomes are more readily apparent if the logic of the possible relationship is made explicit. Simply put, leadership is clearly seen in the performance of certain functions or tasks. When this view of distributed leadership is adopted, it becomes clear that some patterns of the leadership of these tasks, such as wider distribution, have more visible effects on student outcomes than others if, for example, there is more hierarchical distribution (Robinson, 2008).

The question therefore becomes how to establish what counts as a leadership task. Camburn et al. (2003) use organizational theories as their reference point when making such decisions. They state that they follow "A long line of research and theory that conceptualizes leadership in terms of organizational functions and then examines who within an organization performs these functions" (Camburn et al., 2003: 349).

The problem with this approach is the likelihood that the leadership tasks required for this purpose might be different from those required for the narrower purpose of achieving particular goals in a specific type of organization. This is because most organizational theories cannot discriminate between leadership tasks that have more or less direct and indirect impact on outcomes (Robinson, 2008).

A better resource for this purpose of selection is the existing evidence base, which links certain types of leadership and student outcomes. As research has shown, the leadership tasks that deliver more results for students are those that are involved in instructional leadership. This was confirmed in a meta-analysis of 27 published studies of the impact of instructional leadership on student outcomes. The studies showed that the actual impact of instructional leadership was two to three times greater than that of transformational leadership (Robinson, 2008).

The five different sets of leadership practices measured demonstrated different relative impacts. It was found that there were fewer relative effects in the tasks of establishing goals, strategic resourcing, and establishing an orderly and supportive environment. The effects were average for planning, coordinating, and evaluating teaching and the curriculum, but were huge when it came to promoting and participating in teacher learning and development (Robinson, 2008).

Clearly, use of an evidence base is better than using generic organizational theory, but further specification of these instructional leadership tasks is required to show a connection between distributed leadership and student outcomes. For example, if we take the leadership dimension with the strongest impact on student outcomes, which is leaders' promotion of and participation in teacher learning and development, we can establish its applicability in distributed leadership (Robinson, 2008).

Since research on the impact of learning opportunities on the students of participating teachers has shown that various aspects of the context, content, learning activities, and learning processes that are associated with these opportunities make a discernible difference to their effectiveness for students, we can begin to relate them to distributed leadership (Timperley & Alton-Lee, 2008). For example, we find that what is crucial to achieving effectiveness is not whether the teachers volunteer for the learning opportunity, but whether they engage with the ideas at some point in the process (Robinson, 2008).

In summary, evidence suggests that, when testing the links between distributed leadership and student outcomes, researchers should go beyond measures of density and distribution of leadership activities, and also assess the leaders' ability to shape professional development opportunities in a way that ensures they have qualities strongly associated with more positive outcomes for students.

After selection of leadership tasks inherent for distributed leadership, the second step is collecting evidence on the patterns of responsibility for the selected tasks. This involves critical analysis regarding who is involved and the extent to which those with responsibility are knowledgeable about the task characteristics. It also entails looking at the extent to which those with responsibility ensure that those task characteristics influence task performance (Robinson, 2008).

The third step investigates the links of these tasks to student outcomes. This is usually the most complex and expensive part of the study, since it involves modeling and measuring the impact of variables, especially those concerning student background, which would otherwise confound the impacts of distributed leadership (Leithwood & Levin, 2005; Levacic, 2005). This explains why there are so few multivariate studies on leadership impacts.

Since testing of the relationship between leadership and student outcomes is costly and complex, valuable contributions can be made by researchers who study the leadership of teachers and teacher learning practices, especially where there is prior evidence of their impact on student outcomes. Careful analysis of descriptive studies of leadership practices, provided they are measured in ways that capture their association with student impacts, enables us to know a great deal about the distribution of leadership practices that are most likely to make a difference to students. However, subsequent descriptive or intervention studies would provide more direct tests of the leadership to student outcome relationship.

The consequences of not studying the various influence practices are that little is learnt about the change process, which is at the core of leadership. This presents problems, since the rationale for the current emphasis on distributed leadership is based on the belief that widely distributed instructional leadership fosters more sustained improvement of learning and teaching (Elmore, 2004). This process obviously requires skilled change agents, who may be principals, faculty or department heads, curriculum leaders, coaches, professional developers and facilitators, or even classroom teachers.

When we look at the influence process itself, we learn more about the shifts in school and teacher culture that are generally needed to support the wider distribution of those leadership tasks that are vital for sustained improvement in learning and teaching (Harris, 2005). Literature on the requirements for the facilitation or inhibition of teacher influence over their peers is quite considerable, and if distributed leadership is to fulfill its objectives, then it should focus on how those in senior leadership positions authorize and develop a more distributed leadership approach.

In the vignette, Amy Paquinette discovers two students playing a video game in the hallway. As became obvious when she questioned them, they had fallen through the cracks of the leadership structure. Distributing leadership among many stakeholders not only relieves some of the pressure on the principal; it also casts a broader net. If other teachers or staff members felt responsible for the well-being of the students, they would likely have stopped to question the students before Ms. Paquinette got to them, or the acting principal would have had someone—the guidance counselor or the school nurse—to whom he could have entrusted the students.

Distributed Leadership as Distributed Influence Processes

Researchers have often characterized leadership as an influence process that changes how others act or think (Fay, 1987; Leithwood & Riehl, 2005; Yukl, 1994). Therefore, one way of determining leadership is by examining its consequences. There are many ways of exercising influence that do not qualify as leadership, such as force, coercion, and manipulation, which must be distinguished from leadership. The distinction, however, between all these influence processes is based upon the source of influence (Robinson, 2008).

These sources of influence—namely, positional authority, personal qualities, and rational persuasion—often distinguish leadership from any other form of power relationship.

Robinson (2008) outlines a process that can link this view of leadership with student outcomes:

a)   Tracking influence attempts that cause changes in the thoughts and or actions of followers;
b)   Distinguishing those that are based on those influence processes associated with leadership rather than with manipulation, coercion or force; and
c)   Tracking the impact of change in followers in the form of student outcomes.

This kind of research, however, poses several conceptual and measurement challenges. Research measures to establish those who engage in particular tasks do not qualify as measures of leadership, since it is assumed that the consequences of the influence attempt are constitutive of leadership. Gronn (2000) plainly states that the aggregation of individual acts of leadership does not quite capture the idea of leadership as a conjoint activity. Where leadership is involved in the performance of certain tasks by interdependent and reciprocally influencing agents, the unit of analysis may be the pattern of interaction and not the frequency of leadership acts by a particular agent.

Spillane, Camburn, and Pareja (2007) capture the influence process by asking principals to record their intention to influence. However, we need to also ascertain the outcome of such intentions if we are to understand the complete influence process. Robinson (2008) suggests that if researchers were to link leader actions and teacher reactions more tightly, then they would open up the "black box" between leadership and student outcomes. Though she admits that there is still considerable research required to link teacher reactions to student outcomes, she applauds the shift in the majority of studies from the study of isolated individual acts to the study of interacting units of leaders and followers in an attempt to come up with coherent results.

Robinson (2008) further recommends another way of identifying the consequences of leadership attempts. This method involves focus on followership rather than leadership, and consequently seeking more information about sources of influence through phrasing questions such as "Where did you learn that?" or "What led you to make that change?" In this way, the research on distributed leadership will shift from telling us who does what to whether the completed acts influence the intended recipients.

As earlier mentioned, the second phase in establishing the link between distributed leadership and student outcomes in this approach of "distributed leadership as distributed influence processes" is identifying whether the particular influence process used is of the type that qualifies as leadership. Robinson (2008) suggests that we should again focus on followers and why they appear to accept certain influence attempts. However, she suggests that caution is necessary when using such data to determine the distinction between coercive, manipulative, or leadership influence processes, since more emphasis should lie on analysis of the interaction rather than follower judgment.

Earlier research by Friedkin and Slater (1994) assessed expertise as a source of leadership, by asking teaching staff in a sample of 20 California elementary schools to nominate those persons in the school who they turn to for advice on events or issues that arise in the school. Most teachers reported that they turn to other teachers for advice, but this is not a good indicator that they are influenced by them. Nevertheless, it is probably an indicator of the sources of leadership influence in a school. The authors argued in their analysis of the research that the professional orientation of most school cultures stipulate that it must be the leader's competence rather than his or her formal office that legitimates the leader's power.

It is clear that the first and second steps establish that the interactions of interest constitute leadership. The third step involves establishing the actual impact of distributed leadership on student outcomes. Again, we look at the work of Friedkin and Slater, who asked teachers to nominate their sources of advice and proceeded to test the relationships between nominations of principals and of teaching colleagues with schools' average performance over a four-year period, based on standardized tests of reading, language, and mathematics.

The researchers found that there was a strong link between a principal's role in teachers' advice networks and school performance. It was also found that there was no independent link between the school's performance and the extent to which teachers referred to other teachers as sources of advice. Though it is outdated (the research was completed in 1994), the importance of this study cannot be overemphasized. Because its measure of leadership is derived from followers' reaction to it, it investigates perhaps the most important source of leadership influence in schools, which is attributed expertise. It also links leadership to student outcomes, which puts it in a category on its own in the assessment of the influence process of distributed leadership.

The approach toward distributed leadership as an influence process is positive, since it embraces the social dimension of leadership through an elaboration of the particular influence processes that distinguish it from other types of influence, such as force, coercion, and manipulation. It utilizes influence processes that make use of the power of ideas, reasoning, and argument. This is particularly important in schools, since the professional culture of most schools typically constrains any form of reliance on positional authority (Robinson, 2008).

There are some negative aspects of this concept, such as its lack of any educational content, and consequently, it provides little or no guidance to the types of leadership practices that are likely to influence teachers in ways that make a difference to students (Robinson, 2008). Also, this leadership conceptualization has been criticized for not identifying particular leadership traits that are most likely to improve student outcomes, and instead focusing on distribution of leadership. Most of the research available shows that the knowledge needed to identify and specify the types of leadership tasks that deliver these credible benefits are found in educational and not in leadership literature (Robinson, 2008).

Yet another limitation of this concept of distributed leadership is that it overlooks some of the ways in which leadership is exercised indirectly, since not all interaction is through direct interpersonal communication. The three sources of leadership influence suggested—acceptance of positional authority, response to requisite personal characteristics, and acceptance of reasonableness of requests and ideas—assume that all leadership influence is exercised through direct face-to-face interaction. However, this conception ignores the more indirect ways in which educational leaders contribute to teaching and learning, such as the creation of the conditions that enable others to think or act differently and independently. This leadership practice is known as empowerment, and plays a huge role in the influence process. Empowerment was the central element lacking in Sequoia Middle School, as described in the vignette. The former principal was able to perform the tasks on his own: to visit every classroom once a day, approve all paperwork and tests, and oversee every disciplinary case. However, the vacuum created when he departed left the school in dire straits. No one had been empowered to take over the tasks that had been his domain.

A more powerful normative framework is needed for evaluating educational merits if analyses of distributed leadership are to contribute to a greater understanding of its role in improving teaching and learning processes. In summary, the concept of "distributed leadership as distributed influence" helps us distinguish between leader-follower interactions and how they produce change, which is a determining feature of what qualifies as leadership. Recent research into distributed leadership has extended the unit of analysis from that of leader–follower to include the interactions among leader, follower, and other aspects of the situation, including the tools that guide and regulate teachers' work (Robinson, 2008).

Distributed Leadership: Descriptive or Normative?

In order to discover the character of leadership required for to actually implement this type of leadership in the school setting, we need to know whether it is descriptive or normative. Robinson (2008) argues that if distributed leadership research is to make stronger links with student outcomes, it needs to be normative, grounded in the knowledge of the conditions that teachers require for them to improve learning and teaching.

Since leadership in one way or another takes a distributed form, descriptive research has much to do with studying how it is distributed in particular contexts and the consequences of its distribution. Researchers have provided certain descriptive questions that enable us ascertain the kind of leadership distribution needed (Robinson, 2008). These questions include:

- To what extent does the pattern of distribution follow the contours of task relevant expertise?
- What do teachers report about the sources of in-school influence on selected aspects of their practice?
- To what extent do tools feature in those reports?
- Are the influential tools smart tools?

For school leaders who are committed to creating stronger links between their form of distributed leadership and the improvement of schooling and teaching practices, particular qualities of distributed leadership that promote such improvement need to be looked into to achieve effectiveness.

A good example of distributed leadership in action was in seven New Zealand elementary schools participating in a literacy initiative. Timperley (2005) looked into the qualities of distributed leadership that separated high- and low-gain schools. In the two high-gain schools, teacher leaders communicated their expectations to the teachers that they would work with to reduce the gap between the set national benchmarks and each student's current reading achievement. In contrast, the expectations of the school leaders in the five low-gain schools were that the teachers would implement the literacy program without further instructions.

There was also a difference in the use of data. The successful leaders relied more on disaggregated data to assist teachers to make connections between how they taught and the achievement of their students. In the low-gain schools, however, data was aggregated in such a way as to protect the privacy of each teacher's class results.

Another significant distinction involved the problem-solving strategies employed by the leaders through the evaluation of the transcripts of their meetings. The successful leaders of the high-gain schools were found to be more willing to identify problematic teaching practices and challenge the teaching staff group to come up with alternatives. In contrast, leaders in low-gain schools completely avoided the discussion of teaching effectiveness, since they were reluctant to accept teacher-led change.

Using the study, we see how identical structures of leadership distribution can produce varied consequences for students depending on the cultural norms adopted by the group and the knowledge and skills of those assuming leadership roles. Timperley (2005) summarizes this by stating that:

> Distributing leadership over more people is a risky business and may result in the greater distribution of incompetence. I suggest that increasing the distribution of leadership is only desirable if the quality of the leadership activities contributes to assisting teachers to provide more effective instruction to their students, and it is on these qualities that we should focus. If researchers did focus on these qualities, then we would have stronger task-specific normative theories about how distributed leadership could make a greater impact on student outcomes.
>
> (p. 417)

It is unfortunate that many of the normative claims made for distributed leadership are grounded in theories of power rather than in teaching and learning. However, distributed leadership is still seen as desirable to many theorists because it decentralizes the power and authority normally vested in the principal or senior management team. In an empirical study of a mandatory shift to peer-assisted summative teacher evaluation in a district, Goldstein (2003) states that wider distribution of power is the normative justification for a more distributed format of teacher evaluation. She describes how the peer evaluators collaborated with school principals in making the final judgment on evaluated staff, but is critical of the failure to fully transfer power to the peer evaluators.

Harris (2005) advocates the use of distributed leadership in power equalization and focuses more on the features of school culture and micro-politics that may impede its achievement. Other supporters of distributed leadership provide justification for it in terms of its potential to make more expertise available to staff in areas of instruction. Robinson (2008) looks at the implications of these normative arguments in learning more about the relationship between distributed leadership and student outcomes. She starts by stating that arguments for more democratic forms of school leadership and teacher empowerment are, in themselves, inappropriate grounds for calling for greater distribution of leadership in schools. This is because they are unethical, since the imperative of school leadership is to do what is in the best interest of students, not staff. Therefore, a democratic staff room, or one that provides multiple opportunities for collaboration or teacher leadership, is not an end in itself, since the overall goal of the school is to develop and sustain the type of leadership that delivers improved learning and better student outcomes.

Putting Theory into Practice

Timperley (2005) argues against a transformational view of leadership and advocates for the operationalization of distributed leadership in the school setting. She uses the normative position to examine the differential effectiveness of leadership. However, she states that her normative position is different from that of most researchers, who adopt the normative position that greater distribution is more desirable than containing leadership within formally specified roles such as

Day and Harris (2002) and Camburn et al.(2003). Contrary to those researchers, Timperley argues that distributing leadership among more people is risky and may result in greater distribution of incompetence. She suggests that increasing distribution of leadership is only desirable if the quality of the leadership activities assists teachers in providing more effective instruction to the students, a view supported by Robinson (2008).

The quality of leadership activities is only discerned in the context of leadership exercise, and not in isolation. This is because leadership naturally involves others who are situated in the same cultural, historical, or institutional setting (Spillane et al., 2004). Followers' reactions also influence how leaders think and act. Timperley (2005) states that the way some artifacts in the school setting are constructed and presented to followers also shapes different social interactions and outcomes, yet research rarely identifies these artifacts as being an influential part of leadership activity.

Timperley also states that the methodology used to investigate distribution of leadership is a determining factor on whether such distribution is effective or not. She therefore suggests that, where extent of distribution is the focus, survey reports can be used adequately to measure results, but if quality of activity and its consequences are required, direct observation is needed to understand the situation as it unfolds. In her study, observed leadership activities were restricted to team meetings for observational purposes.

Timperley alludes to some of the most observable phenomena, such as the power of leadership activities to shape teachers' visions and their expectations of student achievement in the various schools. The impact of changed activities was that different visions were harmonized in tackling the problems of student underachievement. Through meetings, teachers' beliefs and preferences on the issue of tackling the problem of underachievement changed to concerns about the achievement of individual students. Through these lenses, solutions became manageable and made sense to teachers within their sphere of knowledge and experience (Spillane et al., 2002). Teachers then learned about teaching individual students, and received assistance to improve student outcomes.

By structuring meetings in a manner conducive to dialogue, teachers stopped blaming the problems and started looking for solutions outside the classroom. Timperley states that this vision-in-action, evidenced in the meetings, became a more powerful tool than any other written statements. However, she also notes that some challenges were encountered during this process of trying to put distributed leadership into practice. The first challenge was the use of student achievement data, since teachers needed it to be in a form that allowed them to integrate the data into their instructional practice. The data was also too detailed to be useful in the principals' macro-functions.

Another challenge was the achievement of coherence across the school in ways that promoted student achievement. Here, Timperley states that though coherence was accomplished in all schools in the early stages of the study, it did not necessarily promote student achievement. The development of teacher leadership in a manner that promoted better student outcomes also presented challenges. This is because teacher–leaders who were highly acceptable among their colleagues were not necessarily those with the most expertise. Micro-politics within the school was an inhibiting factor to acceptability of most teachers with expertise. In light of the above, Timperley calls for more research into issues and dilemmas related to teacher leadership and their solutions, instead of simply assuming that distributing leadership among teachers will develop their instructional capacity.

Summary

As we have seen, distributed leadership is a relatively new concept, and one that needs development. Distributed leadership tends to promote and sustain conditions that are successful for schooling and interaction with others, rather than concentrate on the structures and programs necessary for academic success. It is focused on strengthening and empowering stakeholders within the school environment.

We looked at five aspects distributed leadership in the modern setting: leading others to lead themselves; develop capacity in others; develop leadership as a social process (increasing communities of practice and the learning capability); reexamining the power structures of organizations; and reevaluating communication in the current environment of e-commerce and advanced information technology.

Finally, we looked at Timperley's investigations into the quality and influence of distributed leadership. Many researchers now maintain that leadership has always been distributed to some extent within organizations, and express surprise that it has taken so long to develop conceptual frameworks. Since many researchers have now embarked on this end, it is possible that distributed leadership could be the preferred style in the near future. However, it is important that we do not become blind to the limitations of the concept itself and our ability to think about it and outside of it.

Discussion Questions

1. In the vignette at the beginning of this chapter, the previous principal had required that all paperwork, tests, and disciplinary cases pass through him. What are the advantages of this type of leadership? What are the disadvantages?
2. Timperley notes that "Distributing leadership over more people is a risky business and may result in the greater distribution of incompetence." Provide two ways in which a school might lessen the risk of "distributing incompetence".
3. Empowerment and ownership are key concepts in creating a healthy school climate. How can the distributed leadership model enable schools to employ these concepts?
4. Name one advantage and one disadvantage of advanced information technology (e.g., email) in creating a system of distributed leadership.
5. Imagine you are Amy Paquinette, the new principal in the vignette at the beginning of this chapter. What three concrete steps could you take to promote a distributed leadership model?

Activities

1. Two groups of class-members play the following roles: principal, teacher, and tardy student. One group presents a situation in which all authority is centered in the principal. How do they deal with the tardy student? The second group acts out the same situation, but in their presentation, authority is delegated. Is there more than one way to delegate authority? When is a strong central authority necessary? Discuss.

2. In this chapter, we found that creating an evidence base is better than using generic organizational theory. Design a tool that will create a solid evidence base for a school.

Selected Readings

Coldren, A. F. (2007). Spanning the boundary between school leadership and classroom instruction at elementary school. In J. Spillane & J. Diamond (Eds.), *Distributed leadership in practice*. New York: Teachers College Press.

Gronn, P. (2008). The future of distributed leadership. *Journal of Educational Administration, 46*(2), 141–58.

Hallinger, P. & Heck, R. (2010). Collaborative leadership and school improvement: understanding the impact on school capacity and student learning. *School Leadership and Management, 30*(2), 95–110.

Harris, A., & Spillane, J. (2008). Distributed leadership through the looking glass. *Management in Education, 22*(1), 31–34.

Harris, A. (2009). Distributed knowledge and knowledge creation. In K. Leithwood, B. Mascall & T. Strauss (Eds.), *Distributed leadership according to the evidence* (pp. 253–266). New York, NY: Routledge.

Mascall, B., Leithwood, K., Straus, T., & Sacks, R. (2008). The relationship between distributed leadership and teachers' academic optimism. *Journal of Educational Administration, 46* (2), 214–228.

Sherer, J. Z. (2007). The practice of leadership in mathematics and language arts: The Adams Case. In J. Spillane & J. Diamond (Eds.), *Distributed leadership in practice*. New York: Teachers College Press.

Spillane, J., Camburn, E., & Pareja, A. (2007). Taking a distributed perspective to the school principal's work day. *Leadership and Policy in Schools, 6*(1), 103–125.

cal Leadership

Using Your Moral Compass to Steer the Ship

Mr. Fisher had been one of the most prominent and creative teachers at Rosston Elementary for over a decade. He had a devoted following of students, and was renowned county-wide for taking "problem cases" under his wing and getting them hooked on learning. His methods were unorthodox, and involved closer attention and more one-on-one sessions than was the norm, but there was no question that they worked.

Now, however, a student had come to the principal, Mr. Allen, with the story that Mr. Fisher had met her one evening near her house, and had touched her inappropriately. The student, Gretchen, was a known liar and a petty thief, and had been suspended twice already this year.

Mr. Allen called Mr. Fisher into his office and presented the allegations. Mr. Fisher acknowledged that he'd met Gretchen near her house one evening. He said she'd called him in distress, saying her father had beaten her and she needed to talk. They'd talked for nearly an hour, sitting in his car. Mr. Fisher admitted that he'd given Gretchen a hug, but strenuously denied that there was any inappropriate behavior.

Mr. Allen knew he had to deal with the situation impartially. However, his gut feeling was that Mr. Fisher was in the right, and that Gretchen was taking advantage of him. Losing Mr. Fisher would be a calamity for the school, but a scandal that wasn't dealt with correctly would be even more damaging.

The Six Principles of Ethical Leadership

Ethics has always been a primary requirement for leadership, but in the twenty-first century, there has been a call for a new ethical leadership paradigm. More and more actors, both in the school setting and outside of it, are asking for a form of leadership based on morals and ethically grounded virtues. The challenge is to ascertain the kind of leadership that qualifies as ethical, the character traits associated with it, and its applicability to the U.S. school setting.

Ethics has been a major issue in the domain of public administration, and the amount of information on the subject is a testament to its importance. In an article examining the impact of New Public Management (NPM), Maesschalck (2004) found that its framework is reliant on the ethical decisions of administrators. Ethics thus remains a key aspect of public administration and to a large extent, the school.

According to Patton (2008), there are six principles that school leaders must conform to when implementing an ethical decision-making process on their campuses. These principles are:

1. The recognition of ethical issues and creation of possible solutions utilizing an inquiry approach (empirics).
2. Commitment to a defined moral code (ethics).
3. The understanding and use of ethics vocabulary to communicate with all stakeholders (symbolics).
4. The creation of a visual representation of the process to aid in understanding (aesthetics).
5. Involvement and empathizing with the team (synoptic).
6. Application, monitoring, and reflection on equal and fair approaches (synoptic).

I. Inquiry Approach

Patton (2008) states that school leaders must always recognize ethical issues when they arise, and be prepared to react decisively. The issues that school administrators face range from matters such as a parent's concern about the choice of a certain teacher, to providing a conducive environment for a special education student, to implementation of a zero tolerance policy for behavior-related issues, to teacher evaluations. However, as the vignette at the beginning of the chapter showed, the lines are not always clear-cut. Situations may appear similar on the surface, but there are always innumerable factors that make each one unique. It is the job of the school administrator to use discerning judgment in dealing with each decision.

According to the Josephson Institute of Ethics (2006), one of the most crucial steps in making decisions is thinking ahead. To achieve this, one must slow the momentum of events enough to permit calm analysis. This requires discipline, but is a good remedy for poor choices, since it prevents rash decisions and prepares school leaders for more thoughtful discernment.

In making decisions, school leaders must utilize the inquiry approach to ensure that solutions are based on facts (referred to by Patton as "empirics"). This is because facts serve to tell us about the present situation and help us draw conclusions about what ought to be. Utilizing facts in discussions about decision-making promotes a positive disposition in all parties. However, there must be a concise system in place for recording the facts, which guides the decision to create outcomes that are positive and situation-specific.

When this approach is used, Patton (2008) adds, what he terms a "cookie-cutter approach" is discarded. Consequently, decisions are based solely on ethical guidelines. This approach is not only a necessary part of the decision-making process, but also a crucial necessity in every other aspect of the school's plan, from teaching to learning to extracurricular and strategic planning activities.

According to the Josephson Institute of Ethics (2006), the first step when tackling an ethics-related issue is to consider the reliability and credibility of the person providing the facts and the basis of the supposed facts. In a case where the person giving the information states that he or she personally heard or saw someone say or do something, that person should be evaluated in terms of honesty, accuracy, and memory, while always ignoring assumptions, gossip, and hearsay. Thus, in the opening example, Principal Allen should first weigh the credibility of both Mr. Fisher and Gretchen. However, in a complex situation such as the one described, this is not enough to make a decision.

The school leader should consider all perspectives possible, while also being careful to consider the source's personal values, or whether the source has a personal interest that could influence the perception of facts. Where possible, the leaders should seek out the opinions of people whose judgment and character they respect, while distinguishing between the well-grounded opinions of well-informed people and casual speculation, conjecture, and guesswork. The final part should be the evaluation of the information in hand for completeness and reliability, to create a sense of certainty regarding the final decision (Patton, 2008).

2. A Defined Moral Code

In practicing ethical leadership, school administrators and stakeholders must always conform to a well-defined moral code. Morals may not just be about discerning between right and wrong, but may also be concerned with the development of virtues. Virtues are attitudes or character traits that enable leaders to act in ways that develop their highest potential by pursuing admirable ideals they have adopted. Examples of virtues include courage, compassion, generosity, honesty, justice, self-control, and prudence. Properly adopted virtues are habits and, once acquired, they define a person's character. Moreover, virtuous persons are naturally disposed to act in ways consistent with moral principles, and are thus more likely to be viewed as ethical persons (Santa Clara University, Markkula Center for Applied Ethics, 2006).

The setting of moral standards in a school is thus a crucial aspect. Once the standards are created, all stakeholders should align their behaviors and expectations with them (with "stakeholders" in this context meaning anyone who is affected by decisions made by school leaders). Ethical conduct should be clearly seen in making decisions in an equitable, honest, and empathetic manner. Ethical behavior should be consistent with the leader's words. The leader should take responsibility for his or her actions while treating each member of the school fairly and with respect.

3. Ethics Vocabulary

While school administrators and setters of education programs all agree that certain core values should be taught in our schools, there is greater pressure to ensure that the teaching profession is keen on a broader and deeper implementation of these values (Benninga, 2003). The need for values touches on all stakeholders. This is why school leaders should always consider their choices from the point of view of all stakeholders while making decisions. Good decisions are thus considerate of the impact they make in terms of actions and words. Because much of a leader's role is delineated by language, a leader striving for ethical rectitude must choose his or her vocabulary with care. In the ethical context, words like trustworthiness, honesty, truthfulness, sincerity, candor, integrity, reliability, loyalty, fidelity, devotion, respect, responsibility, fairness, equality, impartiality, proportionality, openness, due process, care, and law-abiding citizenship keep cropping up. The Josephson Institute of Ethics (2006) embodies them as pillars of character and suggests that every stakeholder in the school system should be familiar with them.

4. Visual Representation

The ethical decision-making process requires that school leaders are not merely fluent in the spoken word, but are also adept at other means of information transfer. For many people, a visual element is crucial to taking in information. Visual representations, such as video and flowcharts, should be used along with words and actions to convey the ethical message (Patton, 2008).

5. Involvement of the School Community

There is a growing necessity for school leaders to involve all stakeholders, so as to make ethical decisions that are broadly accepted. It is crucial for school leaders to start taking parent concerns seriously and to invite them into the decision-making process. This is because the more involved parents, businesses, and the community become, the more responsive decisions will be to existing needs. It has also been found that open exchanges through dialogue allow school community stakeholders to participate in the creative process of "shaping future directions and moving forward with important work" (Ghere et al., 2006). It is thus imperative that school leaders do all they can to promote collaborative decision-making. Special attention must be given to individual needs, growth, and self-development.

6. Equal and Fair Approaches

The application of fair and equal practices by those in leadership in the school setting is paramount in ethical decision-making. All actions by school leaders must be seen to be just, equitable, and humane. After application, thorough and honestly implemented monitoring is crucial to assuring that the practices are successful.

In addition, good decision-making aimed at improving academic achievement requires that the school and its stakeholders engage in school-wide reflective practices, which Patton refers to as "synoptic." Hindsight is vital, since it enables better decisions to be taken through thorough analysis of situations. Ghere et al. (2006) developed a reflection mnemonic that captures the essence of lessons learned on reflective practices. Relationships are first: Expand your options through dialogue; Focus more on learning; Leadership accelerates reflective practice; Energy is a vital element required for any system to grow; Courage is necessary to reflect and act; Trust takes time to build; Inside-out; Outside-in; and Nurture people and their ideas. Though their work basically deals with reflective practices and their impact on school improvement and student achievement, the phrases form an ideal description of reflection as an attribute of ethical decision-making.

In early 2010, a story from a small school in eastern Pennsylvania made international news headlines. The school, Harriton High School, had issued laptops to a number of its students. Unbeknownst to the students or parents, however, the school had activated the webcams and was using them to spy on the activities of students while at home. The spying became apparent when an assistant principal called a student in and told him that he was engaged in "improper behavior in his home and cited as evidence a photograph from the webcam embedded in the minor plaintiff's personal laptop issued by the school district" (Ilgenfritz, 2010). The students and their parents took the school to court, claiming that the spying was illegal and tantamount to entering a home without a warrant. After eight months, the case was decided in favor of the students, and the school paid a settlement of $610,000 (Martin, 2010).

The case raised interesting ethical questions. On the one hand, school officials were almost certainly operating under the impression that they were doing the best thing for the students. The spying was a genuine attempt to cut down on illegal activities. On the other hand, the officials clearly went too far in spying on the students in their own homes. In this case, more emphasis by school leaders on the aspects of trust and relationship-building, as outlined above, would have shown them that spying on the students was inadvisable.

Ethical Qualities of Leaders

Most ethicists and philosophers agree that there are three major theoretical fields in applied ethics. The theoretical fields are:

- Character-based ethics, such as Aristotle's (340 BC) concept of virtue ethics.
- Rule-based ethics, such as Kant's (1785) deontology.
- Results-based ethics, such as Mill's (1863) utilitarianism concept (Savra, 2007).

Recently, there has been a resurgent interest in Aristotle's virtue ethics. Aristotle stated that good traits of character are known as virtues. Virtue ethics thus focuses on what makes a good person and not what makes a good action. This distinction separates virtue ethics from the earlier-mentioned work of Patton (2008).

The advantage of virtue ethics as compared to other types of ethics is that they are intuitive and personal. However, the weaknesses of virtue ethics lie precisely in their personal nature, which often makes it difficult to obtain a consensus and resolve ethical conflict. A good example of this is an elected or appointed official who holds truth as a virtue and would not lie, despite the fact that lying could bring about great good for the society in question (Vance & Trani, 2008).

Rule-based ethics, on the other hand, focus on the action of decision-making and not necessarily the decision-maker, who in this case is the school leader. In this type of ethics, what is considered right action is that which is allowed by the rules, while the wrong is that which is forbidden. According to Kant (1785), these ethical rules have more weight than mere compliance with policies. The rules can be universalized, since they apply to people across the board and are extremely demanding.

Rule-based ethics are advantageous in the sense that they are clear and help to coordinate behavior, an important element required in school leadership. However, their weaknesses are that they can be quite complex and demanding, such that they could be unattractive to a large section of leaders. A school leader might be so strongly obedient to rules that he or she remains indifferent to an obvious situation of suffering or need by staff or students. For example, a principal who adheres rigidly to the rule that there is no talking in the hallway might punish a student who is weeping on another student's shoulder. In this instance, a more flexible attitude might seek to discover why the student is distraught, and result in better relationships. A lack of flexibility can be problematic in today's highly complex leadership scene, where leaders are expected to immediately address issues and adapt to various changes in a dynamic manner.

Vance and Trani (2008) state that consequential, or results-based, ethics, are a major part of any type of ethical leadership. Results-based thinking, also referred to as teleology, has two schools of thought: "Ends Justify the Means" and Utilitarianism. In both, the consequences of actions inform the basis for determining the right action. Classic utilitarianism was pioneered by Jeremy Bentham and John Stuart Mill, who laid down a framework of moral insight, teaching that consequences count. In the Harriton High School example given previously, the school officials were clearly operating from a position of results-based ethics: in their view, the ends (sniffing out immoral activity) justified the means (using webcams to spy on students).

In the concept of utilitarianism, the amount of happiness or unhappiness produced by an action should inform a person's decision on whether or not to perform an action. In this framework, every person's happiness and welfare is equally as important as everyone else's. Therefore, the right actions are those that produce the best balance of happiness over unhappiness (Rachels, 2007).

From the above stance is derived the "Principle of Utility," which advocates for the greatest good for the greatest number. This requires measuring the relative benefits and burdens of all stakeholders in a community at all times. Therefore, for every situation, the leader should identify all possible consequences of his or her action in light of happiness produced, weigh the total impact of each decision on happiness, and choose the option that best satisfies the principle of utility. One essential aspect of Utilitarianism is its level of inclusiveness, which distinguishes it from the other form of teleological reasoning, "The Ends Justify the Means" (Vance & Trani, 2008).

In "The Ends Justify the Means" reasoning, a "noble end" can be used to justify any means, no matter how unethical or unreasonable. In "The Ends Justify the Means," there is often an aspect that places the decision-maker as the biggest beneficiary. This produces even more parochial ethics.

Taking the opening vignette as an example, a Utilitarian solution would probably require a much greater amount of work. An independent investigatory panel would probably be set up, and the voices of each party would be heard in depth. The outcome might involve quite a bit of pain on all sides, as past behavior and true feelings are exposed. However, the end result would probably be more objectively just. If Principal Allen used "The Ends Justify the Means," on the other hand, he might easily decide in favor of Mr. Fisher, based on his personal interactions with both teacher and student. The outcome would be speedier, and would probably benefit the school in the long run, but may not reflect the truth of the situation.

Consequently, the concept of "The Ends Justify the Means" can easily be turned into a form of ethical egoism where self-absorption, gratification, and justification are the underlying reasons for consequential reasoning. It is notable that in Utilitarianism, the requirement of thinking about the greatest good for the greatest number discourages ethical egoism (Hinman, 2003).

However, Utilitarianism has a weakness in that it can be overly demanding. For example, a utilitarian school principal might be required to resign over a scandal that he is totally innocent of, in the interest of the school's image. On the other hand, the greatest advantage of Utilitarianism is the requirement that all avenues should at least be considered. This would certainly influence the decisions of the leadership, even where deontological and virtue ethics form part of the moral reasoning (Singer, 2006).

In this chapter, we review the ethical leadership qualities that are required of a successful school leader. As earlier stated, the emphasis in recent times is on virtue ethics, and we will focus on this area. Research on the impact of ethics on student outcomes is somewhat scanty. However, researchers and scholars who support this paradigm state that virtues usually have an inspiring trait, encouraging them to instill discipline that directly influences school outcomes.

Another factor that we have to consider is that ethical leadership is in itself a leadership style, though it would probably work well with transformational and instructional leadership, where there is so much emphasis on the individual traits of school leaders. It goes without saying that any type of leadership that does not recognize or base itself on solid virtues is bound to fail.

In the next part of this chapter, we look at two influential models of ethical leadership: Alexandre Harvard's model of virtuous leadership, and the leadership of George Marshall.

Harvard's Model of Virtuous Leadership

Ethical leadership is at times referred to as "virtuous leadership," particularly where virtue ethics inform the basis of that leadership paradigm. Harvard (2010) has come up with a model of leadership that takes into account the day-to-day application of virtue ethics in the leadership context. The methodology of virtuous leadership, according to Harvard, stems from two essential truths that form its basis:

1. Leadership is based on character, which is virtue in action.
2. Every person is capable of acquiring and developing virtue.

The concept of virtuous leadership is formulated for all leaders who seek to grow in their ability to lead and make effective decisions. It is rooted in classical teachings, and its applicability is universal and timeless, since it is based on the nature of the human being. Virtuous leadership is therefore relevant to all leaders, regardless of their sector of professional activity. Harvard (2010) summarizes his model in 10 simple points, as follows:

1. Truly authentic leadership training must be founded on an informed understanding of the nature of man. Such an understanding or anthropology must include the study of the science of virtue for it to be deemed authentic. Virtue is defined as a sound habit housed in a person's mind, will, and heart, which

is aimed at the good. Leadership should be virtuous, since virtues nurture personal excellence while at the same time build professional effectiveness. Virtues instill trust, which Harvard believes is the *sine qua non* of leadership.

2. Magnanimity and humility are the pillars of leadership and are therefore very important virtues. Magnanimity is defined as the character of striving toward a better dispensation, and one with greater symbolic appeal. Leaders should therefore be magnanimous in their dreams and visions, and in their ability to challenge themselves and their followers toward a greater future. Humility is then defined as honest self-appraisal and willingness to serve others. Inspired by humility, leaders should learn to pull rather than push, teach rather than command, and inspire rather than berate.

    Harvard states that leadership should be less about displays of personal power and more about the empowerment of others. Magnanimity and humility cannot be separated, since they both constitute a unique ideal of respecting the dignity and greatness of humanity. While magnanimity makes one conscious of personal dignity and potential for greatness, humility makes a person conscious of the dignity and greatness of others. Both magnanimity and humility are fruits of a proper appreciation of a person's value against pusillanimity, which inhibits self-knowledge, and pride, which prevents someone from understanding others. Both of these are derivations from a false depreciation of the value of a human being.

3. Prudence, courage, self-control, and justice are, according to Harvard, operational virtues of leadership. Prudence, which means practical wisdom, enhances the leader's ability to make correct decisions, while courage enables him or her to stay the course, face challenges, and resist pressures of all kinds. Self-control and self-discipline subordinate the leader's passions to the spirit and direct them toward the fulfillment of the school's mission. Justice, on the other hand, enables the leader to give every individual his or her due.

4. Harvard holds that leaders are trained, not born. His reason for this is that virtues are acquired through practice, and also because leadership is a question of character and not temperament. While temperament may aid in the development of certain virtues, virtues liberate individuals from temperament by imprinting character traits on it. Temperament is therefore not the major obstacle to leadership, but lack of character can be an obstacle, since it leaves one at the mercy of instincts and drained of moral energy, and thus incapable of leading.

5. Leaders, as Harvard emphasizes, do not lead effectively through their exercise of their *potestas* or power, which is inherent in their position. Instead, leaders practice effective leadership through their *auctoritas*, which is authority that stems from character. Harvard adds that those who lack *auctoritas* succumb to the temptation to exercise unalloyed power, and are therefore leaders in name only. He refers to a vicious circle in which low authority leads to abuse of power, leading to further erosion of authority. The path to authentic leadership is consequently blocked.

6. For a person to grow in virtue, he or she must first contemplate virtue, so as to appreciate its intrinsic worth and desire it. Second, the person must strive to practice all the virtues simultaneously, with special attention afforded to prudence.

7.   With constant practice of virtues, leaders become mature in all aspects, and especially those that involve judgment, emotion, and behavior. Maturity can be identified through the leader's unmistakable self-confidence, consistency, psychological stability, joy, optimism, naturalness, sense of freedom supported by responsibility, and interior peace. This maturity is also linked to realism, and thus good leaders are neither skeptical nor cynical. Realism is then defined as the ability to maintain the noblest aspirations, even as one is held back by personal weaknesses. Therefore, the mature leader does not give in to weaknesses, but transcends them through the practice of virtues.

8.   Harvard states that, in virtuous leadership, leaders have to reject a utilitarian approach to virtue, which he defines as the feigning of virtue to get a better reaction from one's followers. He adds that the leader's motive in his struggle toward virtuous leadership is not just to be better at what he does or to build his self-esteem, but rather to respond to an "inner calling," which pushes the leader to recognize him or herself as a human being capable of great achievement. In summary, greater effectiveness is not the objective of self-improvement, but rather one of its many good results. Therefore, the need for excellence precedes effectiveness.

9.   Virtue ethics, not rule-based ethics, should be the true code of the leader. This is because most leaders have a tendency to pay lip-service to so-called professional ethics, while the real test for a leader is to live the underlying virtues of justice, service, respect, and honesty. Virtue ethics do not, however, deny the rules' validity. Rather, they emphasize that rules cannot be the basic foundation of ethics. Instead, the rules should be at the service of virtue, thus augmenting virtue ethics to build original and creative leadership.

10. Often, Harvard notes, a believer in Christianity who ardently practices Christian life finds that it has a formidable impact on leadership, since the virtues of faith, hope, and charity are at the heart of Christian life. These virtues have the ability to elevate, strengthen, and transfigure natural virtues, which are at the base of leadership. Harvard concludes by stating that leaders cannot ignore these "Christian" virtues in their practice of leadership.

George Marshall and Ethical Leadership

George Catlett Marshall is a popular American hero, and an excellent exemplar of ethical leadership in public administration. Marshall's leadership philosophy and managerial style have much to teach school leaders about the nature of ethical leadership and its correlation to school effectiveness and outcomes.

Marshall is best known for the formulation and implementation of the European Recovery Program, popularly known as the "Marshall Plan," though he also served as a negotiator, war preparedness advocate, educational innovator, and government reorganizer.

Marshall's Attributes of Ethical Leadership

In his biographical work, Gerald Pops (2006) draws out the various attributes of George Marshall that are relevant to ethical leadership and which the school leader can learn from:

- Personal courage.
- Putting the interest of the public ahead of selfish interests.
- Integrity, self-control, and self-discipline.
- Task-centeredness and employee-centeredness.
- Recognition of other people's talents.
- Demanding high ethical standards from followers.
- Sensitivity and understanding of the political/social/economic environment.
- Inclusiveness.

The above-stated attributes enable us to develop a working model for the school leader. This is because these ethics-laden attributes can be logically and causally linked to organizational effectiveness. We will look at each of these attributes in turn and see how they relate to the school leader:

1. Personal courage: The situation in most American schools today shows that the challenges of school leadership are increasing by the day. The policy changes set by government toward education, the increasing diversity of culture, and the erosion of ethics call for bold and courageous leadership. Just as George Marshall confronted his superiors, school principals should not be afraid to present their dissenting opinions in light of changing state and district policy.
2. Putting the interest of the public ahead of selfish interests: Within the context of a school as a community, public interest in this case refers to doing what is best for the students, staff, and other stakeholders. Factoring in their opinions and implementing policy that favors them should always precede the school leader's interests.
3. Integrity, self-control, and self-discipline: The qualities of integrity and self-discipline cannot be divorced from any kind of leadership, let alone school leadership. This is because followers and the community at large look up to leaders in all capacities to maintain the highest ethical standards. Another reason for this is that leadership success and effectiveness rely too much on trust, which is hard to build upon in a situation where the leader has no integrity or self-discipline.
4. Task-centeredness and employee-centeredness: Effective school leadership, as shown in research such as that by Robinson & Harvey (2008), shows that school leaders should build on the needs of their staff to achieve better student outcomes. A successful school leader focuses on the needs of students and teaching staff alike as they make their decisions. The concentration on the task at hand through enhancing unity of purpose in the school is a likely recipe for success in the school setting.
5. Recognition of other people's talents: This involves the school leader's ability to reward staff and students who perform well. In this manner, the leader ensures that both teachers and students remain motivated. It is important also that school leaders identify those students and teachers with exemplary skills and place them in positions where their potential can be fully maximized (e.g., promoting a consistently successful mathematics teacher to head the mathematics department).
6. Demanding high ethical standards from followers: School principals should require that teachers follow a written code of ethics at all times. School rules

that reflect ethical practices should also be formulated so as to bring about a high commitment to ethics by students. Meanwhile, school leaders should also maintain high standards of ethical conduct that inspire students and teachers to emulate them.

7. Sensitivity and understanding of the political/social/economic environment: This applies in the school setting through the school leaders' understanding of education policy. It can also be extended to mean development of instructional capacity that can enhance the leader's knowledge of the actual requirements for ensuring better performance (e.g., through the use of data).

8. Inclusiveness: This can be as a characteristic of distributed leadership, or the leaders can embrace it as an ethical requirement. Inclusiveness in this sense means bringing on board all the stakeholders in decision-making and implementation. The need for people to feel considered has been shown to boost morale and motivate followers to a higher level of performance, which can yield better school effectiveness (Hallinger & Heck, 2005).

School leaders who follow the above model are more likely to achieve a higher degree of success in their running of the school, since ethics inspires followers to follow the leader's example and respect instructional authority.

An Ethical Framework for Leadership Practice

The framework referred to here is that developed by Shapiro and Stefkovich (2005), based on ethical reasoning in educational leadership aimed at guiding the decision-making of principals as they confront unfamiliar and complex situations in their schools. They suggest four approaches to ethical analysis that are known to influence the practice of school leaders. These include the perspectives of justice, care, critique, and the ethics of the profession. These four perspectives reflect the considerations taken into account by administrators as they make decisions. In order to illustrate these perspectives, we will describe each ethical stance and the problems related to the delivery of education by administrators in public schools.

The first ethic, justice, concerns issues related to individual rights and laws. In decision-making based on this perspective, administrators should pose the following questions: Does a law, right, or policy that relates to this particular case exist? If it does exist, should it be enforced? And finally, if there is no law, right, or policy, should there be one? (Shapiro & Stefkovich, 2005).

The story at the beginning of this chapter presents a good example of the gray areas inherent in ethical decisions. The principal is certainly aware that there are laws and policies in place to deal with claims of sexual harassment. However, he is also aware of other factors in this particular situation that might make pursuing a strict legal course unadvisable.

The critique ethic is responsible for sensitizing educators to the inequities of social class, race, disability, gender, and other differences, as they occur in the school community. When making decisions based on this perspective, school administrators should consider the following: Who makes the rules, laws or policies? Who benefits from them? Who has power to enforce? Lastly, he or she should find out who the silenced voices are.

The care ethic challenges school decision-makers to address certain values such as loyalty and trust. It calls for school leaders to show care, concern, and connection with stakeholders in solving moral dilemmas. The questions to be asked in this perspective are: Who is likely to benefit from what I decide? Who will I hurt by my actions? What are the overall long-term effects of the decision I make today? Finally, if someone helps me now, what should I do in the future to give back to this person or to society in general?

Shapiro and Stefkovich (2005) state that the ethic of the profession considers "the moral aspects unique to a profession and the questions thereof that arise from educational leaders becoming more aware of their own personal and professional codes of ethics." In decision-making by school leaders from this perspective, they should ask the following questions: What does the profession expect me to do? What would my community expect me to do? What should I do that serves the best interests of the students, who are diverse in their composition and needs? Utilizing this professional ethics perspective enables school leaders to become critical pragmatists who consider practical outcomes and the effects of their decisions beforehand.

The questions posed above are relevant to school leaders in addressing issues related to social justice, education of students with special needs, and to performance and resource inequities in their schools.

Applying the Ethical Framework to Principal Leadership

In this part, we apply Shapiro and Stefkovich's (2005) framework to decision-making in two situations that principals typically face in their running of schools: conducting an Individualized Education Program (IEP) team meeting as required by the Individuals with Disabilities Education Improvement Act (IDEA, 2004), and in disaggregating student performance data so as to monitor their school's advancement toward the Adequate Yearly Progress (AYP) provisions of the NCLB Act.

We then revisit the essential questions derived from each ethical perspective and consider their application in administrative practice. The questions are important for leaders at the district level, since they relate to the school's compliance with federal law and resource distribution required to educate all students to high standards. However, these questions are more relevant in the exercise of ethical leadership by those principals directly responsible for the academic performance of all students within the school. We then analyze the framework question by question in light of the IDEA and NCLB provisions.

I. The Ethic of Justice

In this ethic, we first posed the question: "Does a law, right, or policy that relates to a particular case exist?" (Shapiro & Stefkovich, 2005). We will look specifically at the area of special needs education. Here we find that the IDEA is quite specific about the conduct of IEP team meetings, especially on matters such as the information that should be considered and attendance (Crockett, 2005). School principals should know the procedures that govern team meetings. It is also crucial that they understand the issues of democracy and liberty that are involved in special education law. Lashley (2007) states that while the IEP team meeting assures that the student's interest and right to a free and appropriate education are granted by the school, the procedures to implement these issues may not be sufficient or effective in assuring the protection of student's interests, unless the principal, acting as the school district's representative, understands the rights inherent in the IDEA and the reason they are in place.

The principal must also know the legal and policy requirements of the Act and appreciate the historical and educational contexts that lead to those requirements. Therefore, the conducting of an IEP team meeting requires understanding of the rights and requirements therein and the ability to translate those rights into an educational program that meets the disabled students' needs.

In the NCLB Act, there is a requirement that school performance be reported annually to the public and that sanctions be imposed for those schools that do not meet AYP status. The sanctions are mainly in the form of funding cuts. As we learned in Chapter 2, principals now, more than ever, must become proficient at using data on student performance to improve instruction in their schools. One emerging issue is whether a student's IEP forms part of the general education curriculum, which is used in statewide NCLB assessments (McLaughlin & Nolet, 2004). This is an ethical issue challenging principals, since they have to critically analyze how a disabled student might benefit from standardized approaches while still meeting NCLB targets.

2. The Ethic of Critique

Here, we consider the essential question: "Who benefits from the law, rule, or policy?" (Shapiro & Stefkovich, 2005). From the IDEA, we learn that the IEP developed at team meetings is intended to benefit the disabled and the challenge is thus in developing an individually appropriate IEP that can reasonably benefit the student's educational wellbeing (Board of Education vs. Rowley, 1982). To achieve this, the principal must familiarize him or herself with the legal context of the IEP, but must also understand the student's educational needs. However, such an understanding has been made more complicated by requirements that students with disabilities be provided access to the general education curriculum.

In light of these requirements, many educators are of the opinion that the requirement for provision of general education for disabled students is a form of circular reasoning, since the IEP team must come up with a program that provides access to the general education curriculum for a student whose difficulties with the general education curriculum caused him or her to be termed disabled in the first place. This view of disability from a deficit perspective and special education as a place where problems of school failure are addressed can cause the IEP team to fail in its mandate. Since principals are school representatives and instructional leaders, they should be prepared to face the challenges brought about by the various contradictions and inconsistencies that arise from the convergence of the NCLB and the IDEA.

Through the NCLB, principals are faced with the question of which students should receive the focus of the school's performance improvement efforts and that of distributing the instructional resources to accomplish the same. Since students with disabilities are often members of the subgroup that has difficulty meeting the AYP expectations, it would seem prudent to allocate more resources for their benefit. However, in truth, most of the schools that do not meet AYP goals comprise several subgroups that are struggling academically, as well as students with disabilities who already obtain additional support through their IEPs.

Therefore, as school administrators prepare lists of students not meeting expectations, they will most likely find individual students represented in more than one group. Lashley (2007) gives an example of an African-American male student who has a disability and is from a family living below the poverty level. Since such a student is also counted in the whole school subgroup, he has a five-fold impact on the school's progress if he fails to meet performance standards. While some principals may look at this situation as an insurmountable problem, others may see it as an opportunity five times over, since improving that student's performance increases the AYP in five groups. Consequently, principals are being placed in a position where they have to decide who should benefit from the limited resources available and allocating resources to students who are likely to benefit the most.

Shapiro and Stefkovich (2005) raised the question: "Who are the silenced voices?" Since the IEP team is primarily designed to bring together the voices of parents and professionals on behalf of the disabled student, it is the principal's duty to ensure that parents are partners in their child's education. So far, research has found that parental attendance at IEP team meetings is usually problematic and their participation is mostly passive, since they find themselves receivers of professional information (McLaughlin & Nolet, 2004).

Lashley (2007) states that the lack of active engagement of parents is not surprising, since they may be from families whose experiences with schools have not been positive and inviting. It is therefore an important part of ethical leadership for the principal to consider ways in which IEP team meetings can be conducted such that the voices of parents are not silenced.

Upon the analysis of performance data under NCLB requirements, issues arise, especially concerning students who had been under-considered in school decision-making. This is because the use of data to inform principals' decisions brings to the fore various achievement gaps in the school. Addressing these gaps requires that principals engage the many stakeholders who may have interests in improved performance. In this way, the often muffled voices within these constituencies present fresh opportunities for principals to address not only the issue of student performance but also other related issues of educational and social inequity impact.

3. The Ethic of Care

As previously noted, the question: "What are the long-term effects of a decision I make today?" is essential to this ethic (Shapiro & Stefkovich, 2005). In answering this, we find that the IEP team makes important decisions affecting the lives of children and their families. While decisions as to eligibility and instructional programming may be routine for educators, they are in no way routine for students and their parents. The responsibility of making considerations about the future falls on the principal, since the other IEP team members may be focused on the student's immediate problems. It is thus part of their duties to ensure that the long-term effects are discussed during the IEP team's deliberations.

Additionally, principals in their organization of resources toward achieving AYP goals need to think about how those resources affect the holistic education of all students, not just with regard to their academic learning, but also on matters regarding their social growth and independent living.

They should also consider what aspects of caring, concern, and connection they might not have inculcated in the curriculum. Lashley (2007) states that the focus on academic performance should not undermine other roles of the principal, such as enabling students to develop socially and emotionally and become good citizens.

Professional Ethics

In this section, we look into the question: "What should I do in the best interests of the students who may be diverse in their composition and needs?" Lashley (2007) suggests that the IEP team should always plan and provide specific and intensive instructional practices that are in the best interests of student education. The policies in the IDEA and NCLB focus attention on the performance of individual students, including those with disabilities and those struggling academically.

Disaggregated student performance data finds that African-American and Latino students, especially males from poor families, often do not perform to standards in schools. In many cases, these students are also among the majority in special education programs, mainly because these programs have been associated with poorly performing students. Lashley adds that identifying this particular group of students as being eligible for special services points out the inequities in school funding, social expectations, and teacher quality in schools serving the poor, who are mostly minority students.

While both the IDEA and NCLB bring these problems to the fore, they do not offer direct solutions. This means that school leaders now have an additional responsibility to consider what constitutes the best interests of a diverse student body. Questions arise as to whether the same standards should be expected from all students, especially those who are disabled. There is also an issue as to comparison of performance. Should the performance of such students be compared with typically developing classmates? Making decisions such as these, which involve consideration of the best interests of students, raises issues about the provision of effective instruction and equitable allocation of funds, time, and personnel. A good example of this is the decision by a principal to spend money in hiring additional personnel to serve just a few students or even a single one, while such money could be used to benefit many students.

Lashley states that these and other concerns about preferential treatment, especially when it comes to disabled students, continue to arise from principals in various schools in the U.S. However, he states that the best interests of all students can only be served when school leaders come to terms with the ethical demands of their responsibilities. This comes with a new understanding of the accountability of the school leader for the education of all students. Such an understanding is derived from the knowledge traditions of specialized and general education, the legal provisions of the IDEA and the NCLB, and the wisdom that comes with practice. It is only through such understanding that a school leader can properly focus on school improvement, taking into consideration the vital elements of democracy, social justice, and equity in schools.

Reflections on Ethical Leadership

The U.S. media has been awash with cases of "ethical lapses" of judgment on the part of K-12 and university staff and stakeholders—including lapses by teachers, professors, school administrators, and board members. Such lapses range from inappropriate relationships between staff and students to falsification of test scores (Reilly, 2006). Reinhartz and Beach (2004) found in a study that, with the greater scrutiny given to leaders' actions, especially those who hold the public trust, the issue of ethical behavior has become an area of great focus.

While these unethical and illegal behaviors bring to the fore the ills in our society, Reilly (2006) states that our fixation with the impact of such behavior on students can distract us from the larger issue, which is that of producing leaders for our schools who can combine personal morality with professional will. Ethical schools can only come from ethical leadership provided by ethical leaders. Bolman and Deal (2003) were of the opinion that ethics must rest in the "soul," where there is a sense of identity that defines the individuals or organization's core values and beliefs.

Reilly (2006) attempts to find out what resides in the souls of ethical leaders. She states that the first is wisdom, which is borne out of a combination of an internal moral compass and the life experiences that have tested the leader's mettle in the past. Reilly (2006) states that the next "soul content" is embracing and adhering to one's vision. She poses the question, "Do you do things right or do the right thing?" She answers this by stating that the path of least resistance or that most frequented is often not the path aligned with the organization's vision. According to Beckner (2004), when we "see things whole," we recognize that it is not that which constitutes the landscape that is important. In education, higher test scores as a goal of schooling are just like increased profit as a goal in a corporation: they lack heart and soul and are not the fundamental purpose of schooling. Through wisdom, and embracing and adhering to the school's vision, school leaders are able to apply ethics in assessing each challenge and success that comes their way.

Reilly first asks that school leaders be mindful of and consider deeply the moral imperative of ethical leadership, which lies in addressing the most sensitive issues in our society. These include access to the basic human rights of freedom, justice, and equity (Beckner, 2004). Second, she asks us to recognize that, by taking action, school leaders fulfill the responsibility entrusted to them as educators—alleviation of suffering and initiation of healing processes within various spheres of influence.

Fullan (2003) was of the opinion that it is not enough for one to be a moral or ethical leader within oneself or within one's community, but the imperative should move from individual, to local, then to regional, and finally to societal levels. Reilly suggests that a model of moral imperative should always consider wisdom and adherence to vision.

Summary

From the above assessments of ethical leadership we see a common trend: an appeal to principles that shape the moral compass of people, especially those that involve justice and equity. Though the various models may be far apart, they appeal to an inner aspect of the school leader or to some acceptable form of behavior. This is the basis of ethical leadership.

We have also considered the impact of ethical leadership on certain aspects of school leadership, such as the adherence to the provisions of the NCLB and the IDEA, both of which have highly influenced the clamor for viable leadership models. We see the applicability of ethical behavior in decision-making and challenges that principals face in the day-to-day running of schools. These challenges are not limited to the K-12 system, but also extend into post-high school institutions.

Pops (2006) states that the ongoing research and theory-building on ethical leadership by scholars and researchers in the domain of public administration and leadership studies will help us understand its nature more clearly. Research models, as we have seen, are also based on the exemplary leadership of certain leaders in the public domain, such as George Marshall. We also need to assess the practical consequences of ethical leadership in the light of contemporary leadership problems.

Ethical leadership is a basic requirement in every institution, including schools. Though research linking ethical leadership to school achievements is scanty, we have seen that ethics is linked to the development of bonds especially of trust between leaders and followers, which have to be logically present for any type of leadership to be successful. Therefore, we can conclusively state that, though ethical leadership seems weak and unsupported on its own, it is a vital component in all other leadership paradigms, which would be fundamentally flawed without it.

Discussion Questions

1. When ascertaining facts, a leader should evaluate a witness for "honesty, accuracy, and memory." Think of a recent situation involving personal ethics, either one that occurred in your school setting or one that took place in the public sphere. How were the witnesses evaluated? Who made the evaluations? Did you agree with the conclusions?
2. Harvard defines utilitarian virtue as the "feigning of virtue to get a better reaction from one's followers." Is feigning virtue ever warranted? How can a leader ensure that his or her virtue is genuine?
3. In Shapiro and Stefkovich's "critique ethic," leaders are encouraged to ask the following questions: Who makes the rules, laws or policies? Who benefits from them? Who has power to enforce? Who are the silenced voices? Think about and answer each of these questions in relation to your school setting.
4. Imagine that you are a principal. You are given a one-time lump sum of $30,000. You can choose to use this money to fund assistance for two students with disabilities,

or to enhance a learning center that will be used by all 450 students in the school. What do you choose to do? What factors went into making your decision?

5. In the Harriton High School case, school officials were almost certainly operating under the impression that spying on the students was for their own moral good. Yet the court decided that the school officials were in the wrong. Can you think of another instance in which a "morally correct" stance might ultimately be the wrong one?

Activities

1. Act out how the situation in the vignette would be dealt with using rule-based ethics. How would it be dealt with using results-based ethics? Which one is the better choice in this instance?

2. George Marshall exemplified sound ethical leadership. In small groups, decide on which three of his leadership attributes best relates to school leadership. Explain how these might be put into practice in the school setting.

Selected Readings

Bogotch, I., Beachum, F., Blount, J., Brooks, J. S., & English, F. W. (2008). *Radicalizing educational leadership: Toward a theory of social justice*. Netherlands: Sense.

Brookfield, S., & Preskill, S. (2009). *Learning as a way of leading: Lessons from the struggle for social justice*. San Francisco: Jossey-Bass.

Chaleff, I. (2009). *The courageous follower: Standing up to & for our leaders*. San Francisco: Berrett-Koehler.

Easley, J. (2008). Moral school building leadership. *Journal of Educational Administration*,

Mendonca, M. & Kanungo, R. N. (2007). *Ethical leadership*. New York: Open University Press.

Shapiro, J. P., & Gross, S. J. (2007). *Ethical leadership in turbulent times: (Re) solving moral dilemmas*. Mahwah, NJ: Lawrence Erlbaum.

Chapter 5

Emotional Leadership
Using Your Heart to Lead

Jeremy Raffles was a physics and chemistry teacher at Elton Park High School. He had graduated with top honors from one of the most prestigious universities in the country, and the principal, Laura Cho, felt honored that he had chosen to teach at Elton. In his first two years, he'd transformed the science lab, bringing in new equipment and creating elaborate experiments, and he dazzled the staff with his impromptu lectures on new techniques in teaching chemistry.

Ms. Cho always gave teachers a bye their first year—she figured that it took a year to settle in and find their style. After the second year, she would evaluate their performance. When she looked at the grades of the older science students after Mr. Raffles' second year at Elton Park, she was dismayed: nearly all of the grades, except for those of the extremely gifted students, had dropped since Mr. Raffles had begun teaching.

Ms. Cho called some of the students into her office and asked them to describe their learning experiences with Mr. Raffles. It emerged that, while they respected his intelligence, he had an off-putting, and at times wooden, manner. He would occasionally ignore or mock questioners if he felt he'd already covered the material. One student complained that when she went to the lab after school for assistance, he'd shouted at her to leave, because he was in the middle of an experiment. He seemed to talk only to the top two students in the class, and they were the only ones who could understand him.

Following the conversation, Ms. Cho realized that she would have to confront Mr. Raffles, and talk to him about the need to connect emotionally with his students. A brilliant academic pedigree was excellent, but it needed to be accompanied by empathy and good manners if learning was to take place.

Emotional leadership has been described as the leadership of the future. Beatty (2007) states that knowing the score intellectually is not sufficient; we need to feel the future, too. She gives the example of former presidential candidate Al Gore, who traveled the world, spreading his message about global warming. At first, he assumed that when everyone learned the truth, they would immediately want to do something about it. However, to his dismay, he found out that a mere intellectual grasp of the truth is not sufficient. It needs to be augmented by emotional engagement and a sense of relationship and connectedness for it to translate into action.

Beatty is simply telling us what we already know—for us to act, we must be moved. In fact, the word "emotion" comes from Latin word *emovere*, which means move out, remove, agitate, or move. Beatty emphasizes that the lessons acquired in the development of social cohesion and the act of learning go hand in hand, with a possibility of greater social capital for the society and the world at large emanating from leaders' choices. In the opening vignette, Mr. Raffles possesses ample academic clout and tools, but lacks the emotional intelligence to effectively deliver his lessons. And because of this lack, he is failing in the central purpose of his career—helping students to learn.

Beatty warns that school leaders who choose to ignore the emotion factor, often because of its perceived inconvenience or difficulty, risk alienating their students and society's collective future. She adds that leadership preparation approaches should be grounded in "inner leadership," which acknowledges and puts emotions directly on the professional agenda. These approaches foster integrated mental and emotional capabilities coupled with resilient lifelong learners of all ages. These kinds of learners are better prepared to address future challenges with curiosity and enthusiasm, and in collaboration with others. They offer an assured presence that puts their followers at ease (Friedman, 1985). Beatty states that recognition of the value of emotion in leadership is a great place to start in facing the tough realities of leadership and thus enable leaders and followers to grow together. In research studies, one skill has been frequently cited as being crucial in a variety of leadership styles, and especially those involving intrapersonal and interpersonal skills: emotional intelligence (Downey, Papageorgiou, & Stough, 2006; Dulewicz & Higgs, 2003; Rosete & Ciarrochi, 2005). Some studies (Coetzee & Schaap, 2004; Kerr, Garvin, Heaton, & Boyle, 2006; Leban & Zulauf, 2004; Srivastava & Bharamanaikar, 2004; Wong & Law, 2002) provide empirical evidence that emotional intelligence has a positive effect on leadership effectiveness. Others find that emotional intelligence bears no statistical significance in leadership effectiveness (Barbuto & Burbach, 2006; Barchard, 2003; Brown, 2005; Brown, Bryant, & Reilly, 2006; Schulte, 2002; Weinberger, 2003).

However, Mills (2009) is of the opinion that emotional intelligence is a vital ingredient of leadership effectiveness and thus some changes need to be considered in the preparation for and practice of educational leadership. Those who specialize in leadership training need to ensure that the leaders develop skills linked to emotional intelligence not just as a "soft skill," but as a leadership style which is in practice.

In future, more and more educational leadership preparations will include the role of emotions and emotional intelligence in their coursework and training guidance. Ashkanasy and Dasborough (2003) favor the view that emotions are necessary in the understanding of organizations and also in leadership training. In addition, the skilful handling of challenging situations and people at work requires that leaders become aware of emotional intelligence. This requirement should thus be given the same kind of attention as the more traditional leadership tasks such as budgeting, finance management, and operational skills. Another probable outcome of this discovery is its incorporation into formal evaluations of emotional intelligence in current educational leadership.

In the wake of several models of emotional intelligence floated by researchers, a thorough examination of their effectiveness and impact on educational leadership is warranted. We need to know whether the specific and unique components of the various models offer different levels of impact on leadership effectiveness. Since the study by Mills (2009), from which we draw our inferences, focused exclusively on correlational studies of emotional intelligence and leadership effectiveness, there is need for further meta-analytic research that incorporates different methodological procedures.

Emotional Intelligence

The concept of emotional intelligence (EI) was first introduced by Salovey and Mayer (1990). It refers to a type of social intelligence that is separable from general or common intelligence. In their analysis, the researchers described EI as "the ability to monitor one's own and others' emotions, to discriminate among them, and use the information to guide one's thinking and actions." They later expanded their model to include the definition that EI is "the ability of individuals to perceive accurately, appraise, and express emotion; the ability to access and generate feelings when they facilitate thought; the ability to understand emotion and emotional knowledge; and the ability to regulate emotions to promote emotional and intellectual growth."

EI, as we saw with Mr. Raffles, has been found to make the difference between "just brilliant" people and brilliant managers and teachers. EI has also been found to influence the way people handle each other and understand emotions. It is thus a crucial component for leaders (Mills, 2009).

In Turner's (2004) opinion, EI is the "softer" component of wholesome intelligence, which directly contributes to both the professional and personal lives of people. Traditionally, IQ was defined as the ability to learn, understand, and reason. Currently, it is thought to only contribute 20% to a person's success, while emotional quotient (EQ), defined as the ability to understand oneself and interact with people, contributes a massive 80%. While EQ is vital for effective leadership, IQ is necessary for job performance, and is usually a key determinant in recruitment. Nevertheless, it is now clear that EQ is a crucial component in the ability of leaders to retain their positions and become successful in their tasks. Most firms hire for IQ and sack because of lack of EQ.

According to Barling, Slater, and Kelloway (2000), EI is comprised of five characteristics:

- Understanding one's emotions.
- Knowing how to manage one's emotions.
- Emotional self-control, which includes the ability to delay gratification.
- Understanding others' emotions (empathy).
- Managing relationships.

Another researcher, Lubit (2004), divides EI into two basic components: personal and social competence. Personal competence is defined as self-awareness and self-management (the ability to manage one's feelings effectively). Self-awareness is basically the knowledge of emotions and their impact, coupled with an individual's awareness of his or her strengths and weaknesses. Self-management comprises emotional self-control, adaptability (flexibility in changing according to situations and obstacles), honesty, trustworthiness, self-drive for growth and achievement, achievement orientation, continuous learning, willingness to take initiatives, and optimism.

Social competence, on the other hand, is made up of social awareness, which is the ability to understand what others feel; and relationship management, which is defined as the skills required to work effectively in teams. Therefore, the ability to understand other people's emotions, persuasions, motivation, conflict resolution mechanisms, and reasons for cooperation are probably the skills most essential for leaders and successful managers.

Social awareness includes empathy, insight, understanding of others' perspectives and emotions, appreciation of people's strengths and weaknesses, political awareness, respect for others and their opinions, conflict management skills, a collaborative/cooperative approach, sense of humor, persuasiveness/good negotiation skills, and ability to handle diversity prudently. Social competence can be developed through paying attention to others' emotions and behavior, seeking to understand others through deep reflection and discussions with third parties, broader thinking on the various ways to handle challenging situations, and the observation of the consequences of one's actions. Additionally, social competence can be built through observing others, thinking deeply as to why people behave and react as they do, and consequently identifying those types of behavior that are seemingly helpful in challenging situations (Lubit, 2004).

Another researcher, Goleman (2002), divides the 18 requirements of EI into four main groups: self-awareness, self-management, social awareness, and relationship management. When operating within the dynamic of a team, EI is built not only on the collective EI of the individuals, but also on their collective competency. The social skills required of people in emotionally intelligent teams and focused training methodologies can be divided into six areas: influence, empathy, adaptability, assertiveness, empathy, and inclusiveness.

These four groups could provide Principal Cho, in the opening vignette, with a framework to assist Jeremy Raffles to connect emotionally with his students. She might consider creating a list of areas for improvement that would include academic skills and lab organization (at which he excels) as well as self-awareness, social awareness, and relationship management, three areas where he lacks skills. In evaluating his responses to the list, she might start by emphasizing his intellect and lab skills, and then move on to a detailed, point-by-point explanation of what social awareness entails. This method would appeal to his rigorous scientific nature, and would allow him to work through the issues intellectually.

In their research, Caruso, Mayer, and Salovey (2002) suggested that there are two alternative conceptualizations of EI: the ability model and the mixed model. The ability model places EI in the same sphere as intelligence, where aspects such as emotion and thought interact in meaningful and creative ways. In this concept, EI is like verbal or spatial intelligence, except that it operates in the emotional context.

In the mixed model, the various aspects of personality are blended in a theoretical manner, resulting in a group of skills, capacities, traits, dispositions, abilities, and competencies rolled into one. These varied models have brought forth different methods of measuring EI. EI equips people with an ability to confront any situation with balance and maturity. This is why emotionally intelligent people usually have a deep-rooted sense of self-esteem, which enables them to understand other people, keep things in proportion, and maintain focus on what is important. These people also have a positive viewpoint of situations almost all the time, generally enjoy success in whatever they choose to undertake, have higher work performance and personal productivity levels, and enjoy greater job satisfaction.

Bardzill and Slaski (2003) noted the need for organizational leaders to recognize the importance of emotionally intelligent behavior and reward it. This is because the positive reinforcement of an emotionally intelligent environment usually enhances the development of a service-orientated climate. Consequently, emotional elements underlie the dynamics of many important aspects of the modern organization, and the role of EI should be considered while formulating policies, processes, and procedures.

Welch's (2003) study showing that EI enables teams to boost their performance makes it clear that it is essential to figure out what makes successful teams work. In the study, the requirement that the individual be emotionally intelligent is extended to teams. According to the study, which compared teams with identical aggregate, it was found that teams with high levels of EI performed better than teams with low levels by a margin of two to one. EI in teams is a significant factor and that it can be developed. The five EI team competencies necessary for success were: inclusiveness, assertiveness, adaptability, empathy, and influence. However, these competencies aren't enough on their own. Trust also proved to be a requirement, as it allows team members to examine where they can improve without being self-critical or defensive.

Three researchers, Vakola, Tsaousis, and Nikolaou (2004), proposed that EI contributes to a better understanding of the implications of change in policy by an organization. They asserted that employees with low emotional control react negatively toward proposed changes, since they are not well-suited to deal effectively with what they term the "demands and the resultant effects of emotionally stressful procedures." On the other hand, employees who are able to use emotions controllably are optimistic and take initiatives, and thus are able to reframe their perceptions of a newly introduced change to an exciting challenge. The attitudes toward organizational change reflect the positive relationship between the use of emotions for problem solving and the control of reactions.

Relationship Between Transformational and Emotional Leadership

In Chapter 1, we found that transformational leadership (TL) was a paradigm that stimulates purposeful activity in others by changing their view of the world around them and how they relate to one another. It is a leadership style that affects people's personal beliefs by touching their hearts and minds. According to Gardner and Stough (2002), the two most important competencies of effective leadership are the ability to monitor one's emotions and those of others. Their research found a very strong relationship between TL and EI. This was because EI correlated with all components of TL. In fact, the components of understanding emotions and emotional management were seen to be the best predictors of TL. This is because leaders who considered themselves transformational and not transactional reported that they could identify their own feelings and emotions, express those feelings to others, use their emotional knowledge when solving problems, understand others' emotions in the workplace, manage positive and negative emotions first in themselves and then others, and effectively control their emotions.

Barling et al. (2000) found that EI is mainly associated with TL in their study. They also found that active/passive management and laissez faire management styles were least associated with EI. Sivanathan and Fekken (2002) also found that followers usually perceived leaders with high EI as being more effective and transformational. Additionally, EI could be conceptually and empirically linked to TL behaviors. They concluded that having high EI increased the leader's TL behaviors.

Barling et al. (2000) in the same research study found that EI is associated with three aspects of TL, namely, idealized influence, inspirational motivation, and individualized consideration. When controlling for attribution style, they found that the three aspects of TL varied according to the level of EI. In idealized influence, leaders who identify and manage their emotions, display self-control, and delay self-gratification serve as role models for their followers and therefore earn their followers' trust and respect.

For inspirational motivation, Gardner and Stough (2002) found that leaders with the EI component of understanding emotions are able to perceive in an accurate manner the extent to which their followers' expectations can be raised. Gardner and Stough (2002) also found that a vital component of the TL behavior of individualized consideration is the capacity to understand followers' needs and interact with them accordingly. Empathy and the ability to manage relationships positively, both of which are characteristics of leaders with high EI, are the main requirements for individualized consideration. This view is supported by Palmer et al. (2001), who also found that inspirational motivation and individualized consideration are largely correlated with the leader's ability to monitor and manage emotions in him or herself and others. Finally, Barling et al. (2000) found that individuals with high EI engage frequently in transformational behaviors. When we put all these facts together, we find that transformational leadership and emotional intelligence are closely related.

The Impact of Emotional Leadership on Effectiveness

According to Modassir and Singh (2008), EI in leaders enhances conscientiousness and altruism in their followers. Consequently, leaders who are able to identify and manage their emotions and those of others develop sincerity and helpfulness among their followers. The study also demonstrated the impact that the EI of a leader has on the behavior of followers at the workplace. Riggio and Reichard (2008) state that, though preliminary research on understanding the crucial role emotional and social skills play in achieving leadership effectiveness is promising, much still needs to be done to develop emotional leadership as a paradigm in the ranks of transformational or instructional leadership. They find that most of the models of emotional and social skills have been used in an almost exclusive manner by social and clinical psychologists concerned with understanding effective interpersonal communication. However, the extension of emotional and social skill research into the domain of school leadership will enable a deeper understanding of the specific processes leaders use to influence and affect followers.

As earlier seen, emotional expressiveness is a vital component in charismatic leadership, and is linked to the leader's ability to inspire and motivate followers through the emotional contagion process (Groves, 2006; Reichard & Riggio, 2008). It has also been shown that the expression of positive emotions has a positive impact on groups (Bono & Ilies, 2006). However, there is a lack of research on how leaders express negative emotions such as disapproval, anger, and disappointment, and how this expression affects group performance. One practical suggestion is that skilled and controlled expression of so-called negative emotions is important for leaders, so as to avoid "demotivating" workers or building up resentment and resistance.

Since skilled emotional expressiveness is necessary, effective expression of the leader's negative emotions requires skills in expression, emotional control, and emotional sensitivity so as to gauge how these negativities are received by followers. Rubin et al. (2005) state that there has recently been considerable interest in the role of emotional sensitivity, which is the capacity to "decode" emotions in the work setting. In some of the research studies, measures of emotional decoding skills have been used as a surrogate for emotional intelligence. Other studies have examined the notion of emotional "eavesdropping," where leaders decode followers' emotions even when they are not intending to convey them directly (Elfenbein & Ambady, 2002).

The reason there has been so much interest in emotional decoding is that there are a number of measures available to researchers to study. Also, it is sensible to study the ability to "read" others' emotions in the workplace. Riggio and Reichard (2008) note that, though effective leaders must possess good skills in emotional control, especially during crises, their research shows that individuals who are particularly good at controlling and masking their emotional expressions usually seem distant and aloof. They add that any imbalance in the possession of emotional and social skills is linked to poorer psychosocial adjustment in teams and, consequently, to poor leadership. In summary, we find that emotional intelligence improves effectiveness across most of the research (Riggio & Reichard, 2008).

Improving Leaders' Emotional and Social Skills

As seen earlier, both emotional and social skills can be learned. However, the first step in improving leaders' emotional and social skills is to assess their current skill level. Riggio and Reichard suggest that there are two broad approaches for measuring emotional and social skills—performance-based assessments and self-report measures. Performance-based measures include the Profile of Nonverbal Sensitivity (PONS) by Rosenthal et al. (1979), the Brief Affect Recognition Test (BART) by Ekman and Friesen (1974), and the Diagnostic Analysis of Nonverbal Accuracy (DANVA) by Nowicki and Duke (1994, 2001). These measures usually involve a series of videos or photographs with an emotional content being shown to individuals who pose basic facial expressions in reaction to them. The judges then decode their responses. The measurements of emotional expressiveness are determined by the percentage of judges who correctly identify the expressed emotions.

There are no standardized performance measures of emotional expressiveness and emotional control, and thus most researchers rely on self-report instruments for reviews (Riggio, 2008; Riggio & Riggio, 2005). The measurement of emotional intelligence therefore tends to be self-reporting in nature, with the exception of MSCEIT, which is a performance-based test.

The assessment of social skills and social intelligence is also reliant on performance-based and self-reporting measures. The performance-based measures used here include that of O'Sullivan and Guilford (1976) and the Interpersonal Perception Task by Costanzo and Archer (1989), which measure the ability to read social situations and emotional (nonverbal) cues. Social skills, on the other hand, are measured through the use of trained observers, who usually assess these skills by watching individuals interact in social circumstances. The Social Skills Inventory (SSI) method formulated by Riggio and Carney (2003) is a 90-item self-reporting evaluation that measures the three basic emotional skills of expressiveness, sensitivity, and control, alongside the corresponding social skills. It is a study that has been used extensively in research to measure basic emotional and social skills, especially those of leaders.

The SSI is also a useful tool in measuring the intelligences of effective leadership and the extent to which possession of emotional and social skills relate to leader effectiveness. The Social Skills Inventory is used in research as a rudimentary assessment of each of the six skills (emotional and social) in comparison to norms (Riggio & Reichard, 2008). Through this comparison, one is able to ascertain the leader's skill strengths and the areas that need improvement (e.g., low expressiveness and high sensitivity may indicate that one is shy and perhaps hypersensitive to others' emotions). In the same capacity, high emotional expressiveness and low emotional control may indicate a person who is emotionally "out of control."

Through the above analysis, we are able to see that a balance of the various skills is important (Perez et al., 2007). Another likely evaluation is the bolstering of self-reporting assessment using performance-based measurement instruments such as the Interpersonal Perception Task (IPT), which is designed to measure sensitivity to emotional, nonverbal, and social cues. Participants provide feedback on correct and incorrect responses. They also receive instruction on the cues they should work on and on the role of common biases and stereotypes in the accurate analysis of social situations. Those who use the IPT show improvement in emotional and social sensitivity (Costanzo, 1992). This means that the IPT is not just an evaluation measure, but also an improvement technique.

Feedback is vital for developing emotional skills, since nonverbal cues of emotion, unlike verbal ones, are subtle and occur outside the common spheres of awareness. Therefore, Riggio and Reichard suggest that workshops to develop emotional and social skills use videotaped performances, role-playing sessions, and other training interventions to help leaders achieve optimal levels of emotional and social skills.

While social skill training is normally effective in overcoming problems in social interaction and overcoming social reticence and shyness, research shows that emotional skills, especially expressiveness, can be improved in a multi-week training session (Taylor, 2002). In conclusion, we find that targeted training, use of accurate assessments, and constructive use of feedback can be used to improve the emotional and social skills of leaders.

Emotions and the Teaching Profession

Leithwood and Beatty (2007) tell us that most school leaders live in what they term "emotionally hot climates." This is because their teaching staff has strong commitments to their work. Most of them feel passionately about teaching and see it as a "calling." The emotions that teachers undergo include love for (most) students, hate for the paperwork, the feeling of being "knocked out" when they see a student finally understand a concept, the dread of filling out report cards, the feeling of burn-out in December, and the "stomach churning" feeling associated with the first day of school every year. These emotions affect teachers across the board, irrespective of experience.

The ability to manage emotions has a profound impact on learning. Angelika Rinderle-Tessa tells the story of her son, in second grade, who was suddenly unable to solve easy math problems, though he'd previously loved math. After discussion, it turned out that his teacher had gotten frustrated one day and told him, "Nobody could do worse at math than you do." Rinderle-Tessa's son had clearly taken the statement to heart, and was unable to do math at all until the situation was dealt with (Rinderle-Tessa, 1999).

In this era of CCTV cameras, when most people have a cell phone with a camera on hand, teachers are less able to get away with emotional outbursts. In one particularly alarming situation, an irate algebra teacher at McGavock High School in Nashville, Donald Wood, was captured on camera hurling tables and smashing a window, while students tried to flee the classroom. He was later suspended for his actions (Daily Mail, 2010). While this kind of behavior is at the extreme end of the scale, it is not that distant from Mr. Raffles' emotional "woodenness" as described in the opening story. The outcome, in fact, is rather similar: the students are unable to learn because their teacher lacks the emotional intelligence to effectively deliver the lesson.

For the most part, school principals are implicitly discouraged from taking serious consideration of these teaching emotions as part of their job description. Actually, teachers' emotions are often seen as a troublesome distraction from other important, "rational" considerations, such as annual goals, budgets, and schedules. Leithwood and Beatty argue that the emotions at play in schools should figure prominently in the school leaders' views of their work. They claim that successful implementation of seemingly rational decisions depends on the leaders' sensitive interactions with the emotional realities of everyone involved, including themselves.

Leithwood and Beatty also claim that teachers' emotions have been largely neglected by educational researchers, policymakers, and other reformers. However, there has been a recent effort to refocus research in school leadership, especially on the important role of principals' pedagogical knowledge and its use in changing teachers' instructional practices (Stein & Spillane, 2005). When leaders neglect the emotional aspect of teachers' work in their attempts to influence it, the consequences can be disappointing. Oatley, Keltner, and Jenkins (2006) give a compelling explanation of the effects that emotions have on perception and human interaction. They argue that emotions have systematic effects on cognitive processes and lead to reasonable judgments from people about the world. The first step in confronting a teacher who, like

Jeremy Raffles or Donald Wood, is unable to effectively communicate with the students, is explaining the importance of emotional interaction. Because of the above-mentioned neglect of this area, many teachers have no idea how they are coming across to the students. If Principal Cho in the vignette spent some time with Mr. Raffles, demonstrating the use of emotional intelligence in the classroom, simply that realization might be enough to allow him to alter his teaching style.

Leithwood and Beatty state that emotions shape perception and attention, and accord preferential access to certain memories and bias an individual's judgment in ways that help him or her to respond to the environment. Recent brain research indicates that emotions have a profound effect on the decisions people make and the morality behind their judgments.

Emotions That Influence Teaching and Learning

Leithwood and Beatty (2007) draw evidence for their study from a large number of original empirical studies in the primary/elementary school context. They find that there are eight sets of teacher emotions that have significant influence in teaching and learning in schools. These are individual and collective teacher efficacy, stress/burnout, organizational commitment, job satisfaction, morale, trust, and engagement in the teaching profession. While they state that these are not the only teacher emotions that matter, they are supported by ample evidence worth recommending to school leaders for consideration in their decisions, actions, and communication with teachers. The two researchers summarize evidence on three of these eight sets of emotions: namely, individual efficacy, commitment, and stress/burnout, to illustrate the link between teachers' emotions and the quality of teaching and learning in schools.

Individual Sense of Self-Efficacy

Self-efficacy may be defined as "the extent to which the teacher believes he or she has the capacity to affect student performance" (Leithwood & Beatty, 2008). It is a belief about the teacher's ability to perform a task or achieve a goal. A sense of self-efficacy may be general, when we are referring to the teacher's belief about his or her instructional capacities when dealing with all children and curricula; or specific, when the teacher's belief is about his or her ability to teach a certain specific concept to a particular type of student. These beliefs are often associated with other thoughts and feelings: e.g., low levels of teacher self-efficacy are linked to feelings of anxiety and higher stress levels (Parkay et al., 1988). On the contrary, high levels of self-efficacy are linked to the teacher's feelings of optimism, confidence, and ability to solve problems.

These teacher emotions often have a direct impact on the interaction between teachers and students. An example of this is where higher levels of teacher self-efficacy bring about positive teacher behaviors, such as a decreased criticism of students' incorrect answers, persistence in helping the struggling students arrive at correct answers, and development of warmer interpersonal relationships in classrooms (Goddard & Goddard, 2001). These higher levels of teacher self-efficacy are also linked to better student results, especially in mathematics, reading in the elementary grades, and in diverse student populations (Anderson, Greene, & Loewen, 1988; Ross, 1992), while also causing positive student attitudes toward school, subjects, and teachers. This leads to lower rates of suspensions, expulsions, and dropouts (Esselman & Moore 1992).

Teacher Stress and Burnout

Burnout refers to extreme stress experienced by those who work in intense occupations, especially in offering services that are susceptible to chronic tension levels. It usually signifies the inability to function fully in one's job due to the prolonged stress related to these jobs (Byrne, 1991). Both stress and burnout are linked closely to an individual's state of mind. Dworkin (1997), holds that the greater the level of stress, the greater the burnout level.

According to Maslach and Jackson (1981), burnout is three-dimensional and includes feelings of emotional exhaustion or tiredness; "depersonalization" of teachers, in which they develop a negative and cynical attitude towards their students, parents, and their colleagues; and a reduced sense of accomplishment and self-esteem. It also brings about other negative effects, such as increased absenteeism, decline in classroom performance, and poor interpersonal relationships with colleagues and students. Burned-out teachers are usually less sympathetic toward the plight of students, and are less committed in their jobs. They develop lower tolerance for classroom disruptions, are less prepared for class, and are generally less productive (Farber & Miller, 1981; Blasé & Greenfield, 1985). As a result, burned-out teachers can have a negative influence on the morale of new teachers.

More research unearths the fact that burned-out teachers are more dogmatic about their practices and resistant to changes in those practices. They resort to blaming others for low achievement or failure. According to Dworkin (1987), high-achieving students that are placed under burned-out teachers achieve 20% less than those placed with other teachers. Burnout has also been linked to higher rates of student dropouts. In addition, as we saw with Donald Wood, burnout can lead to irrational and even dangerous behavior.

How Leaders Indirectly Influence Teachers' Emotions

Leithwood and Beatty (2008) summarize the indirect influences of leaders on teacher emotions as having much to do with teachers' working conditions in the classroom and in the school. They state that leaders are in a position to influence many of the working conditions in significant ways so as to have an indirect form of influence on teachers' emotions through their efforts.

Classroom Conditions

At this level, the volume and complexity of the teachers' workloads has a substantial effect on their emotions. Leithwood and Beatty state that their overall attitude about the workload volume is dependent on their perceptions of five features in their environments. Commitments to the school and morale are eroded, and feelings of stress/burnout are heightened when teachers perceive their workload volume as unfair when compared to the workload of other teachers in their school or district level.

Excessive paperwork and other burdensome non-teaching demands, such as hall monitoring, bus duty, and lunchroom supervision contribute to teachers' feelings of stress, lowering of morale and commitment to the school, and increased likelihood of moving on to other schools or other lines of work.

Apart from volume, the complexity/intensity of teachers' workloads produces the same negative perceptions. Complexity erodes job satisfaction, especially when teachers are required to teach in uncertified areas or when they are ill-prepared or students are uncooperative and achieve poor results. Complexity can, however, become manageable when teachers are given autonomy over classroom decisions so that they can do their job as best they know how. Manageability can also be increased through the creation of an atmosphere that encourages learning throughout the school and where instructional resources are made readily available.

Evidence from the teachers' point of view suggests that complexity or difficulty in teaching is significantly increased through insufficient preparation time, unreasonably large classes, and class composition (e.g., grouping high-performing students with those with special needs) (Harvey & Spinney, 2000; Naylor & Schaefer, 2003; Dibbon, 2004). Workload complexity is also increased by disruptive students and unmet student needs.

Students' aspirations, behavior, and their readiness to learn are influenced negatively by dysfunctional family environments, and this also influences teachers' emotions. Just as split or multi-grade classes affect elementary teachers, inadequate learning resources and unnecessary assignments can elicit negative feelings on the part of teachers. Complexity is increased by uneven patterns of demand on the teacher's time. Leithwood and Beatty summarize this situation as follows:

> At one extreme, holiday periods afford the relative luxury of time for planning and preparing for instruction without many other work demands to be juggled at the same time. At the other extreme many teachers spend from 24 to 28 extra hours preparing for and reporting to parents during each two to three-week reporting period every term on top of their other regular duties. In between these two extremes are teachers' "normal" weeks, of approximately 50 hours, about half of which time is spent in intense interpersonal interaction with a classroom of highly diverse children.

In summary, this core function of teaching (involving time) is probably the highest producer of stress for teachers, due to the sheer number of specific tasks that are entailed in the proper performance of effective teaching (Harvey & Spinney, 2000).

School Conditions

According to Leithwood and Beatty (2007), there are four sets of working conditions that have a significant influence on the emotions of teachers—school cultures, structures, relations with the wider community, and operating procedures.

School cultures have a significant effect on almost all teacher emotion sets. Positive contributions that affect the work of teachers influenced by school cultures are those where the goals and expectations for teachers' work are clear, explicit, shared, and meaningful. This means that there is little conflict or doubt in the teachers' minds about their roles. In such cultures, collaboration among teachers is encouraged and highly supported. The positive feelings by teachers about work are engendered in a culture that is genuinely collegial.

Management of student behavior is an important factor, since it has significant positive effects on the time required of individual teachers for the task of instruction. It also has an impact on student performance. This is because more time devoted to instruction leads to better student performance. Alternatively, time-consuming efforts to handle student misbehavior have direct effects on the teacher's job satisfaction, stress, absenteeism, and attrition. These negative results are, however, ameliorated when school leaders and teachers collectively set and consistently enforce rules for student behavior in the school. This assessment is supported by the 2003 PISA data in a large number of developed nations, the U.S. included, indicating that a school's disciplinary climate is among the four strongest predictors of effective student learning.

Teachers are also more likely to respond positively when their leaders value and support their safety and that of their students, and where high standards are required of students.

When it comes to school structures, the primary purpose is to enhance the development and maintenance of cultures that support teaching and learning. However, not all school structures can be altered easily or within a short time. Such alterations are dependent on size or location. For example, positive teacher emotions are associated more strongly with relatively smaller schools in suburban rather than urban locations. However, there is not much that school leaders can do about their school size or location, though there is now a "schools-within-schools" program, which is a popular response to large schools. Organizations such as the Gates Foundation are spending huge resources in order to reduce the number of large high schools.

However, all the other structural aspects of schools that affect teachers' emotions are quite malleable and can easily outweigh the negativities of large school sizes and urban locations. These include positive contributions to teachers' internal states of efficacy, satisfaction, commitment, reduced stress/burnout, morale, engagement, and other overt practices that provide teachers with opportunities to work together, such as common planning times. These positive effects are also associated with adequate time to prepare for classroom instruction.

Teachers also associate their positive feelings about teaching with access to quality development of professionalism (Hirsch 2004a; 2004b). While teacher learning opportunities can be found outside the school setting, the school is still a rich source of professional learning that is dependent on its structure and culture. In addition, the school's goals are a legitimate source of direction for teachers' professional learning. The students provide the teacher with challenges that stimulate learning, and the school's resources act as boundary conditions for the expression of learning. The forms of professional development that are known to contribute most to sustained teacher learning are study groups, coaching, mentoring arrangements, network linking with other teachers to explore challenges of mutual concern, and engaging in inquiry activities with students (Loucks-Horsley, Hewson, Love, & Stiles, 1998).

Empowerment and substantial participation in school decision-making is also important for teachers. According to the workplace performance theories of Hackman and Oldham (1975) and Gecas and Schwalbe (1983), autonomy and discretion enhance commitment in staff by making them the main causal agents of their own performance.

There is also a need for physical facilities that allow teachers to use the instruction type they deem to be most effective, so as to increase their engagement in their schools and their desire to remain in the profession (Hirsch 2004a; 2004b). Teacher engagement and retention is also increased where the school has stable and sustainable programs on which to build when faced by new challenges.

Community relations form part of school conditions that influence the teachers' job satisfaction, and also the probability of school and professional commitment. However, positive contributions only occur when the school's reputation in the local community is good and therefore is supported by parents and the extended community (Naylor & Schaefer, 2003).

School operating procedures are the last of the conditions that influence the teachers' sense of individual efficacy, job satisfaction, and organizational commitment. Under these procedures there are three sub-conditions. First of these is the quality of communication in the school. Second are the perceptions of teachers on the issue of school improvement planning and whether the priorities considered are fitting. Finally, evidence shows the positive impact of providing regular feedback on the focus and quality of school progress.

Leadership Practices That Directly Influence Teachers' Emotions

From recent research, we find that the emotionally consequential leadership practices reflect four sets of "core practices" for effective leadership (Leithwood & Jantzi, 2005; Leithwood & Riehl, 2005). These practices form a significant part of what most successful school leaders do in many different organizational and cultural contexts. Due to their transformational bias to leadership, these core practices involve:

- *Direction-setting*: The practices of school leaders that aim to build an inclusive sense of purpose in the school and appreciation of specific goals need to be encouraged if success is to be found and broader school purposes accomplished. Most successful school leaders set higher expectations for their own performance as well as those of their teaching staff and students.
- *Focusing on assisting teachers to improve professionalism*: The development of teachers' capacities includes most of the principal practices that influence teachers' internal states. These practices include: being genuinely collegial, considerate, supportive, attentive to teachers' ideas, and mindful of teachers' welfare. School leaders who provide individualized consideration and intellectual stimulation build the teachers' need to accomplish their own goals as well as those of the school. Success in building capacity is also achieved by buffering teachers from their distractions to instructional work as well as

modeling values and practices that are aligned with the teachers' core purpose.

- *Redesigning the organization*: This entails building a culture that is supportive and collaborative in teaching and learning, and creating and sustaining school structures that are consistent with such a culture. In this context, successful principals nurture productive relationships with parents and the entire community, and also develop connections with the wider environment so as to influence future policies and preempt situations that might affect the school.
- *Managing the instructional program*: This aspect of leadership basically requires instructional knowledge. It includes efforts by school leaders to ensure that their schools have highly competent staff, to observe the progress of students and the school improvement, to monitor teachers' instructional practices, and to provide supportive and helpful feedback to their staff.

The claim that the above core practices include much of what is needed to develop effective leaders assumes that these practices are formulated in contextually sensitive forms. Based on the extensive research carried out in non-school contexts, as well as that conducted in schools, it is evident that emotionally responsive practices are closely associated with social appraisal skills and abilities. These abilities enable one to appreciate the emotional states of others, find out what those states entail in complex social situations, respond in ways that are helpful, and manage one's own emotions.

Social and emotional intelligence are mostly linked to social appraisal skills. Mayer and Salovey (1990) state that, beyond emotional intelligence, we find emotional "meaning-making": the activity that leaders who are familiar with collaborative reflection engage in when interacting with their colleagues and teachers.

According to Beatty (2007a), transformational leaders are known for their emotional capabilities and are therefore prepared to include it in their professional life despite the fact that it may involve breaking traditions of professional culture and norms so as to maintain and repair relationships. This is because they realize that building trusting relationships is vital for a collaborative culture (Beatty & Brew, 2004).

In a recent international research study on successful school leadership, Day and Leithwood (2007), found that five out of nine studies revealed that successful principals were also good listeners. In one study, having a good sense of humor was stated to be important (Moos et al., 2007); this is a sign of good social appraisal skills in certain circumstances, such as defusing conflict and reducing tension. However, evidence on successful principal leadership, as reported by Day and Leithwood, does not reflect the social appraisal skills that are uncovered in wider leadership research. Nevertheless, it is tempting to infer from the indirect evidence—e.g., teachers' characterizations of successful leadership in Beatty's (2007a) research—that certain extensive social appraisal skills are inculcated within it.

One common element in both emotional intelligence and social appraisal skills is the discernment of others' emotional experience. This involves use of empathy to sense "what people are feeling, being able to take their perspective, and cultivating rapport and attunement with a broad diversity of people" (Goleman, 1998). However, there is a risk involved when a leader assumes that he or she knows what followers are feeling. According to earlier research by Denzin (1984), such a belief is often mistaken, since it is easy to misinterpret others' feelings. This is due to transference, as we often try to imagine how we would feel in their situation.

Assuming knowledge of others' feelings is potentially dangerous, especially where one is wrong. Engaging in respectful and reflective conversations is important for finding out if what we have "sensed" is indeed accurate. In light of evidence provided, it is clear that leaders who have emotional wisdom avoid assumptions as to what others are feeling. They instead prefer to commit themselves to emotional meaning-making with relevant parties. These leaders also recognize the importance of emotion in professional discourse, private reflection, and strategic analysis of situations. This kind of collaborative consideration of emotions is emerging as the key element for nurturing learning communities in the true sense of emotional leadership, even though it is a step ahead of present leadership practice (Beatty, 2007b).

Emotional leadership is said to be "future" leadership, because the research in schools exploring the particular connection between leaders' success and their social appraisal skills is still in its infancy. However, evidence from the non-school settings show that these skills do make a significant contribution to leadership success. Nevertheless, the magnitude of contribution varies in strength based on the job specification. An example of this is given by Wong and Law (2002), who state that emotional management skills are more strongly linked to performance in emotionally laborious jobs than those requiring less emotional labor. Emotional labor is linked with the emotions one feels or even generates in their line of duty. They state that teaching and school leadership undoubtedly qualify as a 10 on a 1 to 10 scale of being emotionally laborious.

Emotional Leadership Preparation

We have seen from teacher and leader studies and results, for example in Beatty (2002a, 2005), and the feeling of student connectedness with school goals (Beatty & Brew, 2005), that managing emotions should be on the topmost agenda in leadership preparation. In her research, Beatty states that school principals felt depleted when emotionally isolated and disconnected from others. This, she states, is an example of circumstances where emotions provide a kind of "knowledge" that continuously influences leaders.

When we look holistically at all the data available on cognitive, intellectual, and epistemological perspectives of leadership and their integration with other frameworks, we see the epistemological power of emotions. Simply put, emotions generate knowledge, and such emotionally acquired knowledge is strongly influenced by teachers' and leaders' understandings and misunderstandings of their emotions. Beatty states that there is hope of a shift in school culture from that of emotional silence to emotional engagement. She suggests that such a change has a probable impact on leader confidence, centeredness, wellbeing, and effectiveness, and might challenge leaders to "reculture" their schools.

The emotional epistemology framework shows progress on four levels. First, there is literal and figurative "emotional silence," in which emotions and their importance are denied. The next level allows self-evaluation and evaluation of others from what Beatty calls an "emotional absolutism" perspective, where emotions are classified as either being right or wrong and are rewarded or punished according to externally defined rules. However, internal emotional knowledge is denied. In the third level of "transitional emotional relativism," emotions begin to periodically take a position on the leadership agenda. However, this level is experienced when there is deeper emotional connectedness with oneself and others.

The fourth stance is that of "resilient emotional relativity," which shows a deepened and integrated use of emotional knowledge and meaning-making individually and with others integrated regularly in daily activities. In this phase, problem-solving and relationship-building are enacted as people learn to interpret emotion and remain non-anxious when they are before others (Beatty, 2002a, 2002b).

Students in the U.S. who participated in Beatty's emotional epistemology framework study reiterated that it had a powerful impact on the "reconceptualization" of their professional selves and in their leadership work (Beatty & Brew, 2004). In Australia, Beatty designed a new Master's in School Leadership degree based on the key elements of Sergiovanni's leadership framework, including human, cultural, technical, educational, and symbolic leadership. She accomplished this through positioning of emotional meaning-making and collaborative reflection as being fundamental aspects of school leaders' wellbeing, relational trust-building, collaborative cultures, and development of mutual connectedness both within and beyond the school environment. She restates the four major aspects of the concept of emotional epistemologies and reiterates that they are embedded and implicit in the support of transitioning across the various emotional perspectives.

According to Beatty's research, breaking the silence on emotion starts from the very first day, when students who have aspirations and are incumbent leaders, along with their mentors, attend orientation day on campus. For Beatty's Master's in School Leadership degree to succeed, the role of collaborative reflective practice needs to continue throughout—even during the two years of part-time study. From the outset, Beatty states, students learn to accept the pedagogy of discomfort by taking into account the power of "emotional wounding" in their professional experience. The transformational effects of addressing these emotional experiences through sharing directly or in an online reflection center by giving and receiving information between peers helps them in the integration of the students' personal, professional, and organizational selves (Beatty, 2000b).

As scholars, the students are bound to be judged in terms of personal and professional experience. Through the above process, they learn the practice of making sense of the tensions associated with increasing responsibilities in the school as they begin to institute changes in their own settings. Their acquired collaborative reflection skills serve as a source of strength and help protect them from the normative tendencies of fear, defensiveness, numbness, and detachment. Their collaboration with colleagues generally continues beyond graduation, thus providing ongoing, long-term support in bringing about change in their schools.

As early results from research studies on the efficacy of this approach proposed by Beatty emerge, there is a general indication that it is highly successful in the context of promoting leader preparedness in building collaborative school cultures and achieving sustainable change alongside maintaining leader well-being and resilience. Beatty holds that the results of both the U.S. and Australian utilization of emotional epistemologies framework in their leadership prepara-tion programs show that the generative power of emotional meaning-making, together with the leader's capacity to form trusting relationships, has the ability to bring about transformational change. Using the model of Beatty and Brew (2005), which looked at students' sense of connectedness with their school, the impact of increased trust in leaders by teachers and students could lead to a corre-sponding increase of student trust in their teachers, a stronger sense of belonging with peers, greater self-confidence, more academic optimism and engagement, and greater academic success.

Summary

There is compelling evidence, based mainly on primary/elementary schools, that shows that principal leadership has significant indirect and direct effects on student learning. The indirect effects largely depend on the extent to which leaders create, restructure, or refine the working conditions in their schools so as to nurture positive emotions towards teaching, develop teachers' instructional skills, and harness those skills in the students' best interests.

On the other hand, the direct effects are based on the nature and quality of the leaders' relationships with their teaching colleagues and the impact those rela-tionships have on the individual emotional predisposition to belonging and connectedness to school culture and the collective emotional climate in the school. To build such a climate, the leader needs to listen to, appreciate, and honor the feelings and ideas of his or her teachers, and create social spaces and structures in the formal agenda of the school for genuine dialogue concerning instructional improvement.

Building a sustainable climate is contingent on the leaders' ability and willing-ness to understand the complex internal states that cause or motivate teachers' actions, and to develop shared mental models of what the school can or ought to be. To achieve success, the leader must keep in mind both the emotions of him or herself, and those of the teachers (Leithwood & Beatty, 2008). It is also impor-tant for leaders to take emotions seriously, and consequently engage others in reflecting on the emotional toll of their own work, since, as we have seen, emotional "woundings" challenge, and can provide rich opportunities for redis-covery of oneself and new learning (Ackerman & Maslin-Ostrowski, 2004).

By opening up to their own feelings, leaders are able to connect with others' feelings. When they listen sincerely to the aspirations and ideas of colleagues and staff, their leadership efforts are more likely to shift from directing to enabling. This is a shift from the traditional leadership behaviors to a conceptualization of what leaders do when organizations are run through the lens of "complexity science" (Stacey, 1996).

Discussion Questions

1. Gardner and Stough state that the two most important aspects of effective leadership are the ability to monitor one's emotions and those of others. Do you agree? Why, or why not?
2. This chapter mentions a number of areas that are key to retaining teachers. If you were a teacher, what would encourage you to remain in your position? What would prompt you to consider leaving?
3. According to Wong and Law, emotional management skills are more strongly linked to performance in emotionally laborious jobs than those requiring less emotional labor. Name three aspects of school leadership that you would find "emotionally laborious." What could you do to lessen the negative impact of this labor?
4. In the vignette at the beginning of the chapter, Principal Cho must confront Mr. Raffles about his lack of emotional intelligence. What are three constructive things she could say that would allow him to connect more solidly with his students?
5. List two ways mentioned in this chapter in which a school leader can boost his or her emotional intelligence. Then think of two more things a school leader can do to improve in this area, and share them with the class.

Activities

1. Write statements such as "Why can't you understand?", "What a fascinating idea!", "Can you be quiet for one minute?", "You have a lovely smile" on index cards. Shuffle the cards and hand them out. Each person should silently act out how the card makes him or her feel, then read aloud the statement on the card. Discuss how language affects confidence, relationships, and trust.
2. In small groups, describe the teacher who had the greatest effect on you. How did that teacher make use of emotional intelligence?

Selected Readings

Chopra, D. (2011). *The soul of leadership: Unlocking your potential for greatness.* London: Rider.

George, J. M. (2008). *Emotions and leadership: The role of emotional intelligence.* CA: Sage

Moore, B. (2009). *Inspire, motivate, collaborate: Leading with emotional intelligence.* Westerville, OH: National Middle School Association.

West, D. L., & Reitzug, U. C. (2008). *"It's like not having a car for a road trip": Principal disempowerment and stress.* University Council for Educational Administration (UCEA) conference, Orlando, FL.

Zembylas, M. (2010). The emotional aspects of leadership for social justice: Implications for leadership preparation programs. *Journal of Educational Administration, 48*(5), 611–625.

Entrepreneurial Leadership

How Schools Can Learn from Business Leaders

Grover Cleveland Elementary was going through a difficult time. Its finances were in dire shape, and it seemed rudderless. The principal, Joe Alheusen, knew that it was up to him to get the school back on course, but he was having a hard time creating the required environment. Certain teachers came to his office from time to time with unconventional ideas that he would have to veto, but in the back of his mind he knew that he shouldn't be stifling their creative thinking.

One of the parents at Grover Cleveland, Oren Milner, was a wealthy financier and advisor for tech start-ups. One Friday evening, at a social get-together, Alheusen told Milner that he envied the freedom and energy of the start-up companies he dealt with, and said he wished he could bring those qualities to his school. Milner asked him a few questions, and realized that the school situation really wasn't that different from a company: creative employees had ideas that needed to be heard, it required sound leadership, and the finances had to be managed effectively. He suggested that he meet with a few of the school leaders.

After a month of Wednesday-afternoon meetings, Milner made three suggestions. He offered Alheusen the services of his accountant for a few weeks, to look at areas where the budget could be trimmed. He recommended implementing a new structure for staff meetings, in which all ideas would be heard, no matter how odd. The ideas would be discussed on their merits, and vetoed or promoted by the staff as a whole. And he advocated building stronger relationships between the "customers"—the parents—and the staff, to listen to complaints and receive ideas.

The U.S. education system is becoming increasingly modernized. Efforts in the business world to improve leadership have for a long time been ignored by school administrators, but there is currently a reawakening. Researchers are scrambling to propose models that would steer the education sector to new heights. Most of the efforts to improve leadership have sprung from the fact that now, more than ever, there is increasing pressure on school leaders from the government, communities, and various highly placed observers, all of whom are concerned about the state of education in America, especially in light of reports that have found American education wanting when compared with other developed countries.

One of the new ventures being considered as a leadership solution is entrepreneurial leadership. One aspect of entrepreneurs that stands out is their positive influence on innovation and economic growth, both of which are commodities of great global demand (Gold, Falck, & Heblich, 2010). In the modern age of tech start-ups and fast, easy global communication, schools can learn much from the agile new business models, as we saw in the opening vignette. School leaders can draw valuable lessons from entrepreneurs in the areas of being innovative, motivated, and goal-oriented. In this chapter, we will ascertain and examine skills and traits of entrepreneurs that could be useful for school leaders in achieving better outcomes.

Many studies have been dedicated to entrepreneurial leadership in the business sense, especially for small enterprises, but few have linked it to school leadership. Perhaps this is due to the fact that school leadership has traditionally been seen as separate, because its success is not measured in dollars. However, among many other commonalities, schools and businesses share an emphasis on results.

The entrepreneur's drive has been the main focus of many research studies. Schumpeter (1912) describes this drive as "the will to conquer," "the dream and the will to found a private kingdom," and "the joy of creating and of getting things done." While these developments accurately describe an entrepreneur's zeal to succeed, they do not explain where the so-called "Schumpeterian entre-preneurial endowments" are acquired from (Lazear, 2005). This will be the basis for our focus on entrepreneurial leadership.

Recently, researchers have recognized that entrepreneurs do not successfully build new ventures without effective leadership behavior traits (Bryant, 2004; Cogliser & Brigham, 2004). A good example of this is the requirement that business founders create a vision for their firm and inspire or influence others to see and understand their dreams. This is a good trait for attracting employees and acquiring the necessary resources for growing their ventures (Baum, Locke, & Kirkpatrick, 1998).

In addition, entrepreneurs have to set the initial goals in a way that rewards workers (Williamson, 2000). The need for entrepreneurs to show leadership stems from the fact that they are founders of their ventures and, as such, there are no established standard operating procedures or even organizational structures that they can fall back on while starting from scratch. This is the main difference between entrepreneurs and corporate managers, since the latter often have more well-defined goals, objectives, structures, and work procedures to guide them (Ensley, Pearce, & Hmieleski, 2006). This may be an advantage to entrepre-neurs, since the problem of substitutes and/or blockers of leadership that are usually associated with the larger and more established organizations are much reduced (Kerr & Jermier, 1978).

Though the importance of leadership in entrepreneurship has been established, there has been a research vacuum on the forms of leadership behavior that are required and prove most effective. Additionally, much of the entrepre-neurship literature on this kind of leadership has been one-sided, focusing mainly on empowering leadership behaviors (Covin & Slevin, 2002, 2004; Gupta, MacMillan, & Surie, 2004; Ireland, Hitt, & Sirmon, 2003; McGrath & MacMillan, 2000). However, Hmieleski and Ensley (2007) note the failure to acknowledge circumstances in which other behaviors, such as directive leadership, may be disadvantageous to any entrepreneur. Directive leadership in school leadership is instructional and, as we have seen in other chapters, instructional leadership remains at the core of any school leadership style.

The two researchers seek what they refer to as "one-best-way" models of entrepreneurial behavior, which often fail to take into account the full complexity of starting new ventures (Hmieleski & Ensley, 2007). This is why some researchers have suggested that, by failing to come up with more sophisticated cross-level models of entrepreneurial leadership, the field of entrepreneurship will fail to achieve the stature enjoyed by more established areas of management and leadership research, such as organizational behavior and strategic management (Davidsson & Wiklund, 2001; Low & MacMillan, 1988). The researchers suggest that, in advancing entrepreneurship research, it would be prudent to import some theoretical aspects from organizational behavior and strategic management, so as to develop cross-level models that can be applicable in new venture leadership.

Over time, there has been a question as to whether entrepreneurs are born or made. Before we continue into entrepreneurial leadership behavior, we need to find out if entrepreneurship is developed through nature or nurture. This is because it would be impractical to suggest a leadership style that requires certain "unlearnable" traits from school leaders that they might not naturally have. In their research, Gold, Falck, and Heblich (2010) argue that entrepreneurial endowments are acquired through a combination of innate genetics and education.

The researchers thus choose to focus on the role of socialization and pre-college schooling (i.e., adolescents' education in the broader sense, and also on the early formation of entrepreneurial endowments). However, there is no way to measure these early entrepreneurial endowments, since it is obvious that they are not directly observable. The next best alternative is to look at the entrepreneurial intentions of students, especially those in college. Through such a study, carried out in high schools, Falck et al. (2009) were able to prove that entrepreneurial intentions that arise in adolescence are a strong indicator of future actual entrepreneurship. It is this research that Gold et al. (2010) used to predict early endowments.

In their study on entrepreneurship, Gold et al. focused on college students, who they feel form the most significant subject pool, and one that represents an important source of innovative entrepreneurship. The researchers noted certain ascertainable factors for the growth of academic entrepreneurs, which are representative of the entrepreneurial endowments of students who are joining college for the first time. These entrepreneurial endowments form the basis for entrepreneurship education at all levels, and have been used with increasing popularity, especially in business schools (Katz, 2003).

Formation of Entrepreneurial Endowments

In ascertaining whether entrepreneurs are born or made and whether it is possible to learn and/or nurture entrepreneurial endowments, we first, as suggested by Gold et al. (2010), focus on the formation of these endowments. Research on what drives the creation of cognitive and non-cognitive skills has often been associated with a lifecycle perspective: i.e., every person has certain innate biological characteristics within them that shape his or her endowments. Researchers Nicolaou et al. (2008) and Nicolaou and Shane (2009) have analyzed this perspective in the context of entrepreneurship. They found that genetic factors can be used to explain individual differences in terms of the ability to identify entrepreneurial opportunities and the overall factors that tend to make one an entrepreneur.

The next aspects are those of socialization and schooling, which further contribute to the growth of entrepreneurial endowments with genetic factors as a foundation. Gold et al. (2010) state that, in socialization, parental role models play the first and most crucial part in developing entrepreneurial endowments. This is because children spend the years where they learn most in the company of their parents, which explains the strong impact of parenting on the preference for certain occupations. The researcher Marshall (1920) stated this plainly: "As the years pass on, the child of the working man learns a great deal from what he sees and hears going on around him." Later research by Aldrich et al. (1998), Dunn and Holtz-Eakin (2000), and Hout and Rosen (2000) confirmed that entrepreneurial parents more often than not leave a pronounced mark on their children, mainly due to their ability to provide contact between their relatively young children and their business workplace. In such cases, children receive continued exposure to the family business, and pick up, almost subconsciously, working knowledge of how to run a successful business enterprise (Lentz & Laband, 1990). Fairlie and Robb (2007) also attribute this acquired knowledge to the direct "entrepreneurial" effect that rubs off on the adolescents as they gain work experience while assisting with the family business.

There has also been an attribute linked to influence by children's peers in the process of socialization (Banduras, 1977), which could have a huge impact on the formation of entrepreneurial endowments (Falck et al., 2009). Gold et al. (2010) gives an example where the child's peers in the course of their socialization desire that they and their fellow peers become future entrepreneurs.

These children believe it is "cool" to be their own boss or run their own business, and not take orders from elsewhere. They are thus quite likely adventurous, fun to interact with, and act as the "leaders of the pack," engendering adoration and emulation by their peers (Akerlof & Kranton, 2002). Earlier research by Baumol (1968) had found out that one of the major influences on a child's entrepreneurial development are his or her peers, who may playfully reinforce entrepreneurial endowments, thus achieving what Schumpeter refers to as the "will to conquer" or "will to found a private kingdom." From the above findings, we see the influence of socialization and schooling on the development of cognitive and non-cognitive skills and any other abilities that generally fall under the rubric of entrepreneurial endowment.

The German Experiment

Gold et al. (2010) in their research analyzed the influence of pre-college education by looking at the differences in entrepreneurial skills in students in socialist East Germany (GDR) and West Germany before and after the 1990 reunification. This study demonstrated the differences in socialization and how they impacted entrepreneurial skills and leadership. Obviously, this example is the most suitable, since we know that entrepreneurship is primarily a capitalist resource, and therefore we would expect that there would be observable effects on students who studied under the different regimes.

Gold et al. used an empirical strategy to study this issue, and relied on a large sample of German university students. These students provided enough data for analyzing the effects of socialization and schooling on their individual entrepreneurial endowments. Specifically, the researchers looked at the influence of socialist education on the students' desire to become entrepreneurs. The findings suggest that both socialization and schooling contribute to the growth and development of entrepreneurial endowments, which eventually influence students' intentions to become entrepreneurs.

In order for us to get a better understanding of the relative importance of socialization and schooling, Gold et al. use the results of the study to consider the effect of pre-university education on student entrepreneurial intentions. The study used surveys of German university students, who experienced some part of their high school education under the socialist GDR regime and those students from West Germany who studied under an education system that taught the values of a market economy.

The researchers found significant differences in the entrepreneurial intentions of students from both academic regimes. They found that those East German students who completed their high school education before reunification in 1990 had lower entrepreneurial intentions than those completing it after reunification. However, the results were varied but robust for different specifications within student groups at West German universities, with the exclusion of "less alike" students, so as to rule out university selection and related biases.

These findings emphasize that entrepreneurial intentions are, to some extent, brought about endogenously within the process of socialization and schooling. They also demonstrate that policymakers can influence entrepreneurial endowments through the schooling system. However, the study is limited in the sense that it only proves that changes in the education system might affect entrepreneurial endowments, but does not provide us with any concrete evidence from which we can draw conclusions about the most effective model for increasing entrepreneurial endowments. This is an area that requires further empirical research.

We also learn from the results of the study on the subsample of German university students who finished their secondary education either in the GDR or in unified Germany, which suggests that teaching the values and benefits of a free market economy in schools affects the formation of entrepreneurial intentions. It is this finding that we are most concerned with, since it builds confidence that specialized entrepreneurship education could actually increase entrepreneurial endowments, i.e., develop the conditions necessary for the growth of this desire to be an entrepreneur.

For school leaders, the impact of this finding is twofold. First, they should create the most conducive atmosphere for students to acquire entrepreneurial intentions; and second, school leaders themselves can receive specialized education in the development of entrepreneurial traits that are vital for an entrepreneurial leadership style in the school setting. The only current setback is the limited research on how entrepreneurial courses at school can influence individual entrepreneurial intentions, but there is great scope for future research into this. In addition, Gold et al. state that the impact of entrepreneurship courses in colleges needs to be investigated more thoroughly.

What Does Entrepreneurship Entail?

Now that we have ascertained that entrepreneurs are not necessarily "born" but "made," we will take a closer look at entrepreneurship itself. In defining entrepreneurship, we depart from the earlier stated notion of an innovative, creative, and risk-taking Schumpeterian entrepreneur to include a multitude of meanings. Entrepreneurs, according to Wickham (2001), are ". . . creative, seek and discover niches for market innovations, bear risks, are growth oriented and driven by the maximization of profit or investor returns."

Another attribute is the "ability to lead the business and to be able to allocate business resources." This characteristic of entrepreneurship is the best correlative description of the term "entrepreneurship" in the light of "leadership," which includes many activities and entrepreneurial traits that are needed for successful entrepreneurial ventures. However, we are limited in this definition by the fact that the typical entrepreneurship process is actually terminated once the business becomes established. After that point, management becomes the driving factor. Consequently, when we refer to entrepreneurs in this sense, we are referring to "entrepreneurial leaders," who are in most cases the founder or owners of new business ventures.

There is also a bias toward leadership in small-sized enterprises. This is because entrepreneurial leaders in smaller businesses are directly involved in the day-to-day running of the business and are constantly bombarded by negative scale effects, unlike large business owners, who may delegate these tasks. Like Principal Alheusen in the opening story, most school leaders may relate more closely to the small-sized business entrepreneurs, who face daily challenges in performance of non-delegable tasks, since they face the same predicament in the day-to-day running of the school.

Entrepreneurs therefore have the arduous assignment of perceiving the different tasks required of them, which are dependent on different entrepreneurial abilities or require certain entrepreneurial qualities. A good example of this is that small and medium-sized enterprises must be market-oriented, to placing themselves in the best position to:

- adequately respond to customers' needs;
- open up new markets with existing products;
- efficiently organize flows of work;
- motivate employees;
- improve market development procedures and methods;
- modernize old distribution channels and discover new ones;
- secure old sources of finance and open new ones;
- discover and develop new products and new production processes;
- face insecurity by regulating risk.

The Global Village School Zone, recently implemented in Newark, New Jersey, is a fine example of a school system utilizing the above-mentioned tenets to create a new model. The Newark public school system is notorious for having one of the worst graduation rates in the country. Mayor Cory Booker has given his backing to the Global Village model, which essentially allows a number of public schools to act like charter schools. Committees formed of parents, principals, teachers, and other leaders make decisions, and are given the freedom to match curricula to students' needs. The schools are closely linked to advisors from various local universities, and have received opened new sources of funding, including grants from the Ford Foundation and the Victoria Foundation. Though there is certainly some risk involved, the schools are basing their programs on models that have proven successful elsewhere in the country, including the Harlem Children's Zone, where freedom from district-level oversight allows the schools to be more nimble and respond more accurately to students' needs (Hu, 2010).

Entrepreneurial Skills Required in Leadership

To adequately accomplish all of the tasks named in the previous section, the entrepreneur is required to be highly professional and competent in handling a business. The last two requirements—discovering and developing new products and production processes, and handling risk—require some level of professional qualifications and qualities that can be developed within the scope of entrepreneurial education and further education. One major area that calls for leadership from entrepreneurs is the task of developing human resources in order to gain a competitive advantage. The role and relevance of employees in service delivery cannot be overemphasized, and thus the entrepreneur has to show leadership in order to increase efficiency in the role of human resource management and also in ensuring employee satisfaction if they are to gain a competitive advantage over rival business ventures in the same industry (Heskett et al., 1990; Homburg & Stock, 2001; Lam et al., 2001; Normann, 1996; Sharpley & Forster, 2003). The role of the leader in human resource management includes the recruitment, development, and motivation of employees. We shall discuss these below, and examine the traits applicable to school leadership.

Recruitment and Development of Employees

Entrepreneurs are required to observe and interpret labor market changes to position their enterprises as players in the market. For smaller enterprises, certain problems are entailed in this requirement. First, entrepreneurs have to assess the qualification needs and consequently set clear standards for qualification, so as to maintain and develop a unique market position. Second, before these employees are hired, job design and the discretionary space of decision-making in the business have to be determined (Peters, 2005).

Communication, Motivation, and Control of Human Resources

Research has shown that the information and communication strategies within the business firm are strong determinants of service quality and the organizational culture. Entrepreneurial leaders therefore have to carefully conceptualize and implement practical channels and instruments of communication if they are to achieve meaningful results. Again, the small market enterprises (SME's) periodically face problems associated with nepotism and information/communication asymmetries (Peters & Buhalis, 2004; Peters et al., 2004) that their leaders have to deal with constantly.

Development and Empowerment of Employees

It has been proven in research that, in the long run, satisfied employees in business enterprises increase customer satisfaction (Heskett et al., 1997; Peters, 2005). This is why leadership tasks should include workplace design and implementation of some sort of reward and incentive scheme that is geared toward improving employees' service. The entrepreneurial leaders can choose to either design the service delivery process according to the customer/employees' needs between high and low complexity, or between high and low employee discretion.

Many employees in SME's have left their jobs for reasons such as bad manners in the company, not being appreciated, noncompliance with agreements, harassment by superiors, or a generally unconducive working atmosphere (Langer & Sviokla, 1988). Using empirical data, Peters (2005) shows that SME employees evaluate leader characteristics such as empathy or fairness and build a highly motivational culture in the enterprise. The more the entrepreneur assists employees in developing their careers, especially in preparation for international jobs (in the tourism sector), the more the employees value their jobs. Additionally, Peters observed that job satisfaction is strongly influenced by the job autonomy as well as satisfaction with the leadership style in the enterprise.

Analyzing the above results, we can assume that there are certain basic requirements that must be achieved for successful entrepreneurship. These include the installation of an appropriate wage system, team building, and a satisfactory internal communication system. Interestingly, the issue of wages can be interpreted as a satisfier but not necessarily a motivator. That is, appropriate wages may not always be expected, and thus an increase in employee earnings does not always lead to higher job satisfaction (Peters, 2005).

However, most, if not all of personal motivators are basically performance factors of high importance. Entrepreneurs in SME's should therefore take seriously long-term human resource instruments such as career planning, training, education, and job diversification. They should also communicate to their employees in a bid to show that they are concerned about these instruments.

In addition, the entrepreneur has a huge influence over the motivation of employees through the practice of fairness, freedom, and employee empowerment. Peters (2005) states that entrepreneurs can be divided into two clusters: those considered "employee friendly" and those considered "employee distant" in the eyes of employees. The former are judged to be more creative in designing the right motivational and communication structure in the enterprise. They offer empathy and fairness, which provide higher motivation and job satisfaction for employees than the "employee distant" leader. Nevertheless, the issuance of clear directives and command structures are not seen as negative aspects of leadership. Therefore, Peters calls for entrepreneurial leaders to find a balance between empathetic communication and the provision of clear directives that are more common in a hierarchical mode of leadership. Principal Alheusen, who we met in the opening vignette, would have to find a way to incorporate Oren Milner's suggestions about opening the communication avenues without eroding his authority and ability to give clear directives. The ability to find this balance, according to Peters, is the hallmark of the effective leader. Though he is referring to the business environment, we can assume the same is true for the school situation.

Peters recognizes that there is a challenge to entrepreneurs in allowing career development of employees so as to promote their occupational mobility because of the fear that they may lose the more highly qualified employees in the long run. However, good entrepreneurs allow their employees to grow and achieve their full potential, even though they risk losing them to better paying or bigger firms.

Peters adds that there is little evidence that an authoritarian leadership style and low educational attainment by entrepreneurs has a damaging effect on employee motivation, but we can nevertheless assume that higher fluctuation rates may be caused by inefficient human resource management and actions of leaders. As we have seen, there is no single effective leadership style: a more autocratic or more participative style may be called for, depending on the decision-making structures or the cultural settings involved (Herzberg, 1974; Kotter & Heskett, 1992; Lok & Crawford, 1999; Pennigton et al., 2003). In summary, Peters states that entrepreneurs should be aware of the fact that employees are motivated by a leader's high sense of fairness and empathy.

Empowering Leadership Behavior

This leadership behavior encompasses encouraging of self-reward systems, self-leadership, opportunity perception, participative goal setting, and autonomous behavior by followers, subordinates, and group members (Pearce et al., 2003). This behavior has been found to positively influence the perception of meaning, self-efficacy, team potency, and self-determination throughout the organization (Spreitzer, 1996).

Empowering leaders through positive emotional support and encouragement tends to increase the motivation and confidence of their subordinates and followers toward the accomplishment of their individual and organizational goals (Conger, 1989). We can therefore see how useful empowering leadership can be, particularly as a behavioral tactic for entrepreneurs, who must gain commitment from those they work with in order to compete against bigger, more established, and resource-rich enterprises (Ensley, Pearson, & Pearce, 2003).

In addition, empowering leadership behavior in entrepreneurs is likely to be very important in dynamic environments. According to Nicholls-Nixon (2005), entrepreneurs attempting to lead their ventures toward high growth while operating in dynamic conditions are more likely to benefit from adopting a more empowering leadership style. This view is in line with other complexity theories of leadership, which usually consider how leadership behaviors enable instead of guiding organizational effectiveness under uncertainty (Marion & Uhl-Bien, 2001).

From the above, we see empowering leadership as an effective method to distribute leadership throughout the management team. This enhances the formation of emergent strategy, which takes advantage of the individual talents of each team member that are most relevant to the current environment (Pearce, 2004).

However, there are some negative effects that come with empowering leadership, which have received relatively little attention in leadership literature. One of the disadvantages of empowering heterogeneous teams is that it can at times prove to be counterproductive (Gebert & Boerner, 1999). Gebert, Boerner, and Lanwehr (2003) found that empowering leadership can cause incompatibility among certain innovative initiatives.

In addition, empowered management teams can at times seek to acquire too much information before making decisions or attempting to follow too many opportunities without refining a single business concept that can be used to establish a solid basis in the market. These challenges are, however, more often experienced by firms with heterogeneous top management teams and that are more innovative than their homogenous counterparts (Bantel & Jackson, 1989; Elenkov, Judge, & Wright, 2005).

Though heterogeneous teams can be quite effective at considering multiple alternatives and making sense of challenging situations, they are, unlike other teams, much slower to reach consensus on decisions (Pfeffer, 1983). This stems from diverse perspectives within top management teams, which can produce conflict and slow the decision-making process (Amason, 1996).

We can therefore conclude that empowering the management teams is likely to provide greater opportunity for conflicts to emerge. These conflicts among team members are likely to be particularly detrimental to ventures operating in dynamic environments, where decision-making must be speedy in order to take advantage of the brief windows of opportunity that arise. Entrepreneurs should therefore be cautious about when and where to empower their management teams (Hmieleski & Ensley, 2007).

These two researchers hypothesize that, in high environmental dynamism, empowerment reduces the new enterprise's performance, causing the relationship between the top management team's heterogeneity and the new venture's performance to become increasingly negative as the empowerment increases. They add that, in more stable industry environments, this kind of empowerment leadership behavior will likely have a more positive effect on the performance of new ventures with heterogeneous top management teams than in the dynamic industry environments. This is because, in this context, the information available is less ambiguous and time is not of the essence. Thus, there is more time available for strategizing.

This stable environment allows the empowered top management teams to spend more time considering what alternative strategies are available, and exploring the potential for various innovative activities, since consensus and unified action are not urgent. As a result, there is generally less conflict within empowered heterogeneous teams operating in stable environments. In addition, we find that the high quality of information available within stable environments allows these heterogeneous teams to capitalize on their capacity to engage in reasonable strategic planning. This in turn enables empowered leaders to fully capitalize on the benefits of the top management team's heterogeneity and incorporate their diverse views into their venture's strategizing processes.

In the lower environmental dynamism, empowerment enhances the team's heterogeneity on the new venture's performance, enabling the relationship between the two to become increasingly positive as empowering leadership increases.

In the vignette at the beginning of the chapter, Oren Milner, the entrepreneur, immediately recognized that the teachers at Grover Cleveland Elementary were not empowered. Though they had creative ideas, there was not an appropriate forum for receiving those ideas, and thus creativity was being stifled. Effective school leadership should pay attention to the lessons learned from entrepreneurs, and particularly those from fast-moving start-ups, which tend to be highly creative. They should strive to create environments in which positive ideas are encouraged and in which there is ample opportunity for those ideas to be implemented.

Directive Leadership Behavior

Directive behavior is the process through which entrepreneurs instruct and command followers to carry out their designated tasks, assign responsibility in the form of specific non-negotiable goals, and use what Pearce et al. (2003) call "contingent reprimands" to bring about cooperation from followers, subordinates, and group members. Much of the leadership literature has focused on the negative rather than the positive effects of directive leadership (Cruz, Henningsen, & Smith, 1999; Larson, Foster-Fishman, & Franz, 1998; Moorhead & Montanari, 1986).

However, there are several notable benefits that can be attributed to directive leadership behavior, especially in new ventures operating in dynamic industry environments and having heterogeneous top management teams. Hmieleski and Ensley find that directive leadership can facilitate the foundation of a collective vision by heterogeneous top management teams founded by entrepreneurs (Mumford, Feldman, Hein, & Nagao, 2001; Shalley & Gilson, 2004). Ensley and Pearce (2001) argue that this collective vision of the new venture's top management teams is one of the most important determinants for the sustainability and growth of new ventures.

Hmieleski and Ensley attribute these positive effects partly to the fact that unified teams are more likely to make fast decisions. Several studies have identified a positive link between the speed of strategic decision-making and solid performance in dynamic industry environments (Baum & Wally, 2003). Eisenhardt (1989) demonstrated that it is not just the speed of decision-making that counts, but specifically the speed at which comprehensive decisions are made. Even though, as we found in empowerment, heterogeneous teams within dynamic environments may not have adequate time in order to fully examine various decision options, their diversity alone provides greater comprehensiveness in strategic decision-making. Additionally, even where directive leaders do not invite team members to participate actively in strategic decision-making, they may still require the diverse knowledge of heterogeneous top management team members to provide them with the necessary information to make important decisions.

Hmieleski and Ensley thus suggest that, for exceptional entrepreneurial leadership, there must be a combination of directive leadership, together with traits such as empowerment, recruitment, motivation, and communication. The result of such a combination would be the harmonization of the organization's objectives with those of the entrepreneur's subordinates and other employees.

However, there are several instances in which leadership can inhibit the management teams from considering diverse perspectives (Larson et al., 1998; Moorhead & Montanari, 1986). In a stable environment, there is less urgency to quickly reach a consensus on strategic decisions. Directive leadership may therefore be unnecessary in bringing together the diverse views of heterogeneous teams within dynamic environments.

At this stage, leaders should be more flexible and allow diverse views to incubate and sprout without forcing a plan on the team. In fact, strategic decisions should be made by the group and not by the entrepreneur (Kahai, Sosik, & Avolio, 1997). Consequently, directive leadership may cause unnecessary conflict in the heterogeneous new venture top management teams operating in stable industry environments. However, the problem may not be common in homogenous top management teams, whose views are most probably unified with their leaders (Larson et al., 1998).

Principal Alheusen, who we met in the opening story, knew that one of his failings was the inability to field and sieve through the multitude of creative (and sometimes crazy) ideas thrown up by his staff. A school setting with a traditional top-down, heavy-handed approach to management does not generally have the structures in place to listen to such ideas. Oren Milner, the entrepreneur, might note that traditional tech companies such as IBM suffered because of a similar stifling environment. The newer, more nimble companies, such as Facebook and Google, are aware that creative ideas are the beating heart of their organizations. Google famously gives employees one day a week to work on projects of personal interest, and Mr. Milner might note that the Google founders Larry Page and Sergey Brin say that the biggest threat facing their company is the failure to innovate. He might suggest formats for staff meetings other than the traditional one in which the principal stands in front and lectures. He might suggest a circular seating arrangement or small groups, with a mechanism for receiving and writing down ideas. The study by Hmieleski and Ensley (2007) examines the interaction between entrepreneur leadership behavior, new venture top management team heterogeneity, environmental dynamism, and the performance of new ventures. Their study is just one of the many works on leadership that have recently reasserted their focus on the contextual concerns of entrepreneurial leadership (Griffin & Mathieu, 1997; Osborn, Hunt, & Jauch, 2002). Another discovery in their research was the fact that the top management team's heterogeneity and environmental dynamism is linked to the influence exerted by empowering and directive leadership, either positively or negatively in relation to performance. The advantage of this study over others in this context is the link between the interaction of team heterogeneity and environmental dynamism with leadership behavior. This gives us a complete model on entrepreneurial leadership that we can relate to school leadership.

However, this study has some setbacks. First, it assumes that the entrepreneur relies more heavily on the top management of the venture than he or she does on the employees. This is because it does not factor in the impact of entrepreneurial leadership on employees. Also, the study does not directly measure the underlying processes and mechanisms through which the observed interactions between its variables occur. However, this is a common shortcoming in much of the entrepreneurial leadership literature, which fails to consider the underlying mechanisms by which entrepreneurial leadership behaviors influence group processes (Yukl, 2002). Nevertheless, this research by Hmieleski and Ensley (2007) will enable us to draw parallels between business entrepreneurship and school leadership.

Parallels Between Entrepreneurial Traits and School Leadership

In order to understand the commonality between entrepreneurship and school leadership, we must first create some parameters. We begin with our earlier analysis on the SME's and how they are faced with day-to-day leadership challenges. This aspect relates to principal leadership, who have to deal with similar problems, such as unmotivated teaching staff, poor student outcomes, low budgets, and cases of indiscipline.

Our next comparison is in the latter study by Hmieleski and Ensley (2007), which factors the concepts of a top management team, industry environment, and directive leadership into entrepreneurship. While the concept of the top management teams may not be fully congruent to the school setting, since most principals make most of the strategic decisions on their own, it is relevant for the popular distributed model of leadership, in which the school leader allows various actors to participate in decision-making process. A dynamic environment in the school setting is one where these policies keep changing and the school leader constantly has to beat set deadlines. A stable environment would be one where the school leader has been entrusted with almost complete control of the school. In some aspects, dynamic environments could be considered applicable to public schools, while stable environments would most probably relate to private schools. Finally, directive leadership relates to instructional leadership in the school setting.

We then compare the traits for the entrepreneur in the SME that Peters (2005) outlines, and consider how such entrepreneurial endowments may influence school leadership.

Recruitment and Development of Employees

Though most school leaders may not have a part to play in the recruitment of teaching staff, they are largely responsible for their development. Career development in teachers is dependent on the school culture and environment (Robinson, 2008; Spillane et al., 2004). School leaders, like entrepreneurs, are required to shape their school systems in a way that allows the teachers' professionalism and instructional capacity to grow.

Additionally, school leaders are supposed to shape teaching staff to acquire other skills through assigning duties and responsibilities that are non-academic in nature: e.g., bus duty, sports supervision, and coaching instruction. Similarly, school leaders should do their best to retain the most productive teachers without stifling their growth. This is the same predicament that befalls entrepreneurs in SME's. In summary, an entrepreneurial school leader strives to ensure that his or her school retains the most competitive and productive teaching staff, which is a sure recipe for achieving better student results.

Communication, Motivation and Control of Teaching Staff

Peters (2005) states that good entrepreneurs conceptualize and implement practicable channels and instruments of communication to achieve meaningful results. School leaders could use this trait directly in dealing with teaching staff as well as students. Communication has always been identified as an important part of leadership. Since successful entrepreneurs are good communicators, school leaders need to keep their communication channels open and develop good listening and negotiation skills.

As well as ensuring communication channels are open, school leaders need to keep teaching staff motivated. As seen earlier, satisfied employees produce better results (Heskett et al., 1997). Therefore, it is up to the school leader to come up with innovative motivation techniques that keep staff satisfied. While school leaders may not have the same powers as entrepreneurs in paying teachers' wages, they have to come up with non-monetary motivation techniques, such as creating a conducive workplace with reduced stress and burnout levels, and a friendly school culture (Leithwood & Beatty, 2008).

Since most teachers quit work because of reasons similar to those of other employees, including lack of appreciation from leaders, non-compliance with agreements, harassment by superiors, or generally unconducive working environments (Langer & Sviokla, 1988), entrepreneurial school leaders should avoid making the mistakes that lead to the above situations. As Peters (2005) states, employees associate leader characteristics of empathy and fairness with a highly motivational culture in the enterprise. Therefore, school leaders should endeavor to develop these traits. Additionally, Peters observes that job satisfaction is strongly influenced by the sense of job autonomy as well as satisfaction with the leadership style employed.

The basic requirements that must be achieved for successful entrepreneurship, Peters (2005) summarizes, include appropriate wage systems, team building, and a satisfactory internal communication system. However, since we have already seen that wages are not necessarily a motivator (appropriate wages may not always be expected, and thus an increase in employees' earnings does not always lead to higher job satisfaction), team-building and internal communication systems are most applicable to the school setting.

Using Peters' (2005) separation of entrepreneurs into "employee friendly" and "employee distant," we assess the applicability of these two entrepreneurial characters in relation to the perception of the school leader by the teaching staff. As we saw, "employee friendly" leaders are more creative in designing the right motivational and communication structure in their organizations, and possess traits such as empathy and fairness, which provide higher motivation and job satisfaction for employees than the "employee distant" leader. These two perceptions of leadership have an impact on the motivation of teachers, since they would almost certainly prefer the friendly leader over the distant one.

The above preference, however, does not affect entrepreneurial leadership, since, unlike other leadership types such as emotional leadership, it is more concerned with ends than means (Leithwood & Beatty, 2008). Additionally,

Peters states that the issuance of clear directives and command structures by the "distant" leader does not necessarily have a negative effect on leadership outcomes. In fact, he advocates that entrepreneurial leaders find a balance between empathetic communication and the provision of clear directives that are common in hierarchical modes of leadership.

Peters (2005) adds that there is little evidence that an authoritarian leadership style and low educational attainment by entrepreneurs has a damaging effect on employee motivation, but we can nevertheless assume that higher fluctuation rates may be caused by inefficient human resource management and actions of leaders. This can be translated in school leadership to mean that the entrepreneurial school leader should not shy away from adopting an instructional type of leadership that involves issuance of commands and assigning responsibility where it is an absolute necessity. This is due to the absence of a proven single effective model of leadership, thus calling for prudence on the part of the school leader. However, Peters states that a more autocratic or participative style is often more suitable, depending on the decision-making structures or the cultural settings involved. Peters recommends that entrepreneurs focus primarily on employee motivation through fairness and empathy, and therefore that school leaders should strive to work on these two traits.

Empowering Leadership Behavior

Empowering leadership behavior, as earlier described, encompasses encouragement of self-reward systems, self-leadership, opportunity perception, participative goal-setting, and autonomous behavior by followers, subordinates, and group members (Pearce et al., 2003). In the school setting, autonomy should be granted to teachers insofar as classroom instruction is involved, and they should also be involved in decision-making processes.

Empowering school leaders also increases the motivation and confidence of their followers toward the accomplishment of school objectives through positive encouragement and support (Conger, 1989). Since empowering leadership is a useful behavioral tactic for entrepreneurs, who must gain commitment from those they work with in order to compete against bigger, more established, and resource-rich businesses, it is equally important for school leaders, who, similarly, must succeed in achieving better outcomes.

In addition, empowering leadership behavior in entrepreneurs is particularly important in dynamic environments. Similarly, dynamism in schools, in the sense of changing policies and school leaders' tasks, calls for reliance on teaching staff, and their cooperation goes hand in hand with the leader's empowerment techniques. Hmieleski and Ensley (2007) saw empowering leadership as an effective method to distribute leadership throughout the management teams in order to take advantage of the individual talents of each team member. In the school setting, the school leader should distribute leadership among senior staff-members, who can assist in certain school administrative functions such as ensuring discipline in students, running sports activities, and participating in tasks that can be said to be delegable.

In addressing the negative aspects that come with empowerment, such as counter-productiveness in decision-making, school leaders should simply draw a line between the issues that need consensus and those where they should inter-vene and make quick decisions. Hmieleski and Ensley (2007) refer to the differ-ences that arise from heterogeneity in management. As schools are certainly heterogeneous, due to the variety of careers and interests that converge in the school setting, school leaders should be careful not to allow the problems that are stated to come from heterogeneity to slow down decision-making processes (Bantel & Jackson, 1989; Elenkov, Judge, & Wright, 2005). We also learn from the research that empowering the heterogeneous top management teams is likely to provide greater opportunity for conflicts, which are especially detrimental to the performance of ventures operating in dynamic environments, where decision-making should be quick (Hmieleski & Ensley, 2007). It is therefore advisable that entrepreneurial school leaders in dynamic environments where there is external pressure should avoid complex decision-making processes.

However, in stable environments, such as private schools, where the school leader enjoys some level of autonomy, they can allow the empowered staff to spend more time considering what alternative strategies are available and exploring the potential for various innovative activities, since consensus and unified action are not urgent. We also find that the high quality of information available within stable environments allows heterogeneous teams to capitalize on their capacity to engage in reasonable strategic planning. This enables entrepre-neurial leaders to fully capitalize on the benefits of diverse views in strategizing processes.

Directive Leadership Behavior

Directive leadership behavior in the context of the school setting is instructional in nature. School leaders should instruct teachers on matters regarding the curriculum, formulation of rules, and state policies on educational matters. Like entrepreneurs, school leaders must instruct teaching staff to carry out their desig-nated tasks, assign responsibility in the form of specific non-negotiable goals, and employ the use of contingent reprimands to bring about cooperation from students and teachers alike. Hmieleski and Ensley (2007) found that directive leadership facilitates creation of a collective vision in heterogeneous top manage-ment teams. Similarly, school leaders can create a common vision in their school through the setting of rules and by enforcing them through instruction. The benefits of this type of leadership are often attributed to faster decision-making and clarity of goals.

Hmieleski and Ensley (2007) suggest that exceptional entrepreneurial leader-ship entails a combination of directive leadership and the other mentioned traits, such as empowerment, recruitment, motivation, and communication. This should also be the approach adopted by school leaders who wish to pursue this entrepreneurial perspective in their running of the school. However, there should be more emphasis on the non-directive aspects, especially in stable envi-ronments, since they yield more results in terms of motivating teachers.

In these environments, school leaders should be more flexible and allow diverse views to grow without forcing a plan of action on the team. If possible, most of the important strategic decisions should be made in consultation with the school's stakeholders. Thus, Principal Alheusen in the opening story would be wise to use staff meetings and parent-teacher forums not only for airing minor complaints, but also for floating and discussing major decisions. In conclusion, we find that entrepreneurial leadership, as suggested by Peters (2005) and Hmieleski and Ensley (2007), involves the inculcation of various entrepreneurial traits in the day-to-day administration of the school. Additionally, we find that a model of entrepreneurial leadership that is inclusive, participative, motivating, and directive seems to be the most suitable in any entrepreneurial venture and, by extension, the school setting.

Summary

A great deal of criticism has been leveled at the various contextual models of leadership (Ashour, 1973; Schriesheim & Kerr, 1977; Vecchio, 1983). Most of the failures associated with previous contextual examinations of leadership have been two-fold. First, these previous studies failed to test and measure the various suggested models of contextual or situational leadership adequately (House & Aditya, 1997). These shortcomings, which are mostly methodological, are at the source of the scholarly attacks on the past situational leadership studies (House & Aditya, 1997). However, in the models of entrepreneurial leadership that we have relied on for this chapter, we have ensured that we do not overlook this concern.

Second, the studies of the past have oversimplified the contextual framework within which leadership takes place. A good example of such criticism is that by Schriesheim and Kerr (1977) and Vecchio (2003) on the contextual models of leadership that only specify single moderators and account for lesser levels of variation in performance. In the studies by Peters and by Hmieleski and Ensley, we examine a substantial portion of the variance in performance when contextual factors that are both internal and external to the samples are considered together.

Recently, there has been a resurgence of the studies into these contextual models of leadership (Osborn et al., 2002). While this can be attributed to the sudden demand for leadership in American schools, researchers like Hmieleski and Ensley (2007) suggest that deeper research is needed in this area before these models can be applied directly to organizations. They challenge other researchers to develop contextual leadership models further, using multiple internal and external variables.

When it comes to entrepreneurial leadership, we find that research on the application of this model in the school setting is rare if not completely nonexistent. However, since the model has been used successfully in the business sector, we can relate the factors that enhance its success to the school setting by drawing parallels as we have done in this chapter. It is quite probable that most school leaders may be entrepreneurs in their private undertakings and therefore would embrace this leadership style, since it would involve the use of talents they may already possess.

Discussion Questions

1. According to Akerlof and Kranton, children with entrepreneurial spirit are adventurous, fun to interact with, and act as the "leaders of the pack." How can this spirit be transmitted to children in the classroom setting? List three practical activities.

2. The reasons employees leave companies—not being appreciated, noncompliance with agreements, harassment by superiors, etc.—are very similar to the reasons teachers leave schools. According to business analysts, what can an entrepreneur do to lower the attrition rate? List three things.
3. List four traits of a successful entrepreneurial leader. Then show how each of these could be useful in school leadership.
4. Effective leadership requires effective money management. What can a school learn from a business about managing money?
5. In the vignette at the beginning of this chapter, entrepreneur Oren Milner gives the school three suggestions. Can you add two more, based on material in this chapter?

Activities

1. Think of a successful company (e.g., Google, Apple, Facebook). Make a drawing or chart showing the relationships among the following within the company: leadership structure, employees, product, customers. Now think about a school setting. Make a similar drawing or chart. What are the equivalents for product and customers? Use the charts as a starting point to discuss how the school system might be streamlined or improved.
2. In small groups, discuss the pros and cons of comparing a school to a business. What are some of the key differences between the two? Share with the larger group.

Selected Readings

Ball, S. J. (2007). *Education Plc: Understanding private sector participation in public sector education.* Routledge: London.

Christopher, G., & Gregg, V. (2008). Talent development: Looking outside the education sector. In F. Hess (Ed.), *The future of educational entrepreneurship* (pp. 23–44). Cambridge, MA: Harvard Education Press.

Hentschke, G. C. (2009). Entrepreneurial leadership. In Davies, B. (ed.), *The essentials of school leadership.* London: Sage.

Kempster, S. & Cope, J. (2010). Learning to lead in the entrepreneurial context. *International Journal of Entrepreneurial Behavior and Research, 16*(1), 6–35.

Woods, P. A., Woods, G. J., & Gunter, H. (2009). Academies schools: Sponsors, specialisms and varieties of entrepreneurial leadership. *Journal of Education Policy, 23*(3), 100–103.

Xaba, M. & Macala, M. (2010). Entrepreneurial orientation and practice: three case examples of historically disadvantaged primary schools. *South African Journal of Education, 30*(1), 75–89.

Chapter 7

Strategic Leadership
Those Who Fail to Plan, Plan to Fail

At Elm Circle High School, a sixty-five-year-old principal who had emphasized traditional methods of teaching and leadership retired. For seven years, the school went into a nosedive under the leadership of three principals, each of whom lasted a couple years. Finally, the school board hired Connie Johns, a young and energetic principal who had some new ideas.

After talking with the staff, Principal Johns realized that the three interim principals had been what she termed "firefighters": they spent all their time solving day-to-day problems, and the general structures, which had been put in place thirty years before, were unchanged. No wonder the school was having trouble.

Principal Johns delegated most of the day-to-day administrative tasks to various subordinates, and spent the first six months of the year in dialogue with teachers and members of the community, coming up with a five-year plan to redefine and reenergize the school. Some of the ideas included networking with other schools via the Internet, creating a more bottom-up listening structure, and holding monthly meetings open to the community, in order to ensure the plan was on track.

The effects of Principal Johns' restructuring were not apparent during the first or even the second year of her tenure, and some members of the school board were skeptical. However, halfway through the third year, higher test scores and lower teacher attrition showed that the school was finally taking a turn for the better.

We have previously seen that educational leadership in this age is complex and demanding, due to various factors. Cheng (2010), in his Three Wave Model of Strategic Leadership, states that the challenges include reestablishing novel national visions, crafting new educational aims for schools, restructuring education systems at different levels, privatization, and diversifying school education, all at the macro-level.

At the meso-level, involvement of parents and the community in management of schools is a new challenge. At the site level, it requires ensuring high-quality education, ethical standards, and accountability in educational institutions; decentralization; school-based management; enhancing teacher quality; and teachers' professional development. The challenges at the operational level include using information and communication technology (ICT) in both learning and teaching, applying new technologies in school management, and making a paradigm shift in the assessment of learning and teaching. Cheng refers to the above as the nine trends of educational changes.

The above-mentioned contextual changes in school leadership have created serious challenges to the traditional thinking and practices of educational leadership, and have consequently led to the emergence of a new brand of strategic thinking and leadership in education (Cheng, 2002a, 2002b). School leaders are now expected to be more strategic in their running of schools and to become more proactive in facing up to these contextual challenges using various strategies. Cheng (2010) states that the concept of strategic leadership is still vague, and that the domain of study in this kind of leadership is "relatively diffused" and often uncharted. He states that leadership is strategic if it includes the following:

- It is proactive in light of contextual changes.
- It involves a SWOT analysis of internal and external contexts and positioning of the institution in a changing environment to inform repositioning in response to these changes.
- It involves planning and management of key action programs (strategies) to achieve effectiveness, survival, and development of the institution so as to meet the contextual challenges.
- It causes the institution to implement these action programs and evaluate their impact so as to inform future planning.

This chapter aims to explore how the above-named contextual challenges are related to the emergence and change of the concept of strategic leadership in education and to analyze the various proposed models of strategic leadership aimed at guiding educators, school leaders, policymakers, and researchers in understanding and analyzing the complex nature and practice of strategic leadership in a dynamic environment, and particularly one that includes numerous educational reforms.

As stated earlier, the challenges from contextual changes facing American schools, as well as other schools worldwide, have tremendously changed the practice and context of education and its leadership. The novel visions of education crafted by state governments and district school boards, increased competition between schools, closer interface with the community, greater stakeholders' expectations, external participation and collaboration, multi-level developments, and technological and cultural changes demand that school leaders become more strategic and sensitive to these changes.

Cheng (2010) states that these leaders are now expected to perform strategic leadership within broad horizons, with foresight and innovative perspectives, strong social networks, and proactive action programs. Cheng's three-wave models of strategic leadership represent different paradigms that are employed in the conceptualization of the context and practice of strategic leadership in education when it comes to facing the increasing complexities brought about by educational reforms. Through these three models, we can understand and analyze the paradigmatic diversities of strategic leadership.

Based on these different models in education, strategic leadership is conceptualized as internal, interface, and future strategic leadership. Strategic leadership in education helps school leaders face up to contextual challenges and develop appropriate strategies for their schools to be effective in achieving good outcomes, surviving in a competitive market environment, and remaining sustainable in pursuit of a brighter future for their students, teachers, and community. In the three models proposed by Cheng (2010), strategic leadership in education is defined through different assumptions of the education environment, such as education reforms, positioning of the institution, nature of learning, concept of effectiveness, nature of school competition, and the demand for sustainability. In light of this, we find that the key features of strategy, leadership roles, and strategic concerns of educational leadership are totally different across the three models.

First-Wave Model: Internal Strategic Leadership

Cheng states that, since the 1980s, there has been an effective school movement in the U.S. (Townsend, Avalos, Caldwell et al., 2007). The educational environment is usually assumed to be relatively stable and predictable, with little competition, while the role of education is perceived as aimed to provide the necessary manpower to serve an industrial society (Blackledge & Hunt, 1985). Education provision and content are also assumed to be under centralized planning, and the management of the school seen to be under external control of central bureaucracies with very little autonomy. Education is perceived to be knowledge delivery and learning: a process by which students receive knowledge, skills, and cultural values from their teachers and curriculum.

The first-wave model of educational reform aims to improve the internal processes of learning, teaching, and leadership while enhancing the internal effectiveness of schools in the accomplishment of pre-planned educational aims and targets. Changes in internal processes are those that involve school management, quality of teachers, curriculum design, teaching methods, evaluation criteria, resourcing, and the learning/teaching environment (Gopinathan & Ho, 2000; Kim, 2000; Tang & Wu, 2000; Abdullah, 2001; Cheng, 2001; Rajput, 2001; MacBeath, 2007).

Within this model, the school is positioned as a provider of planned knowledge, skills, and cultural values from teachers and curriculum to students in a comparably stable society. School effectiveness is a kind of "internal effectiveness," defined by the achievement of planned goals and tasks of delivery of knowledge, skills, and values in learning, teaching, and schooling. Under central manpower planning, competition among schools is comparatively bounded and mainly controlled by the central bureaucracy and its given regulations and standards.

Correspondingly, school sustainability may not be a major concern of school leaders in such a stable education environment. The school strategy developed by leaders is a kind of internal improvement strategy, mainly based on a kind of technical rationality in SWOT analysis and planning, with a focus on the technical improvement of internal operations in teaching, learning, and management to enhance the achievement of planned school goals. The key initiatives of the school strategy are often oriented toward the short term and narrowed in obligation to bureaucratic regulations (Eacott, 2008a).

In the first-wave model, the role of strategic leadership is mainly a form of internal leadership, with strategies focused on assuring internal school effectiveness through improving school performance in general and enhancing contents, methods, and processes of teaching and learning in particular. Internal strategic leadership is used in reference to concepts such as structural leadership, human leadership, instructional leadership, curriculum leadership, and micro-political leadership (Cheng, 2003, 2005a). We know the strategic concerns in leadership through the answers to the following questions:

1. How can the internal processes of education such as learning, teaching, and school management be organized to impart the planned knowledge, skills, and values?
2. How can the imparting of knowledge and skills from teachers to students be ensured while practically improving schooling, teaching, and learning?
3. How can the teachers' instructional capacity be practically and technically improved and developed within a limited time period and allocated necessary resources to meet expectations?
4. How can students achieve progress and higher standards in the planned curriculum and in public examinations?
5. How can the so-called internal process be changed to maximize the use of allocated resources?

However, the first-wave model has certain limitations, such as the fact that it may be too inward, looking into planning and action without taking into account the complexities, diversities, influences, and expectations of the external environment. Its positioning is also narrowly focused on the technical and operational aspects of education and the school. It gives more attention to the instruction and guidance of the central bureaucracies, rather than the changing environment and stakeholders' expectations. Due to the technical, short-term, and internal nature of the first-wave model of leadership in education, it is often not seen as being very strategic.

Since the late 1980s, there have been several attempts at reforming the first wave, though these efforts at reform have been limited and inadequate to satisfy the increased needs of contemporary education. There was increased doubt as to the efficiency of these improvement initiatives, and the internal leadership as a whole, in meeting the various diverse needs and expectations of parents, students, and other stakeholders in the school. There was an increased need for the education service to be accountable to the public and also to ensure that education practices and their outcomes were relevant to the changing demands of the community. Therefore, most of these challenges were concerned with the interface between schools and the community. This meant that strategic leadership should not only focus on internal process of school improvement but also on the interface between schools, stakeholders' satisfaction, and accountability to the community.

Second-Wave Model: Interface Strategic Leadership

As a result of the above challenges to internal strategic leadership, mainly concerning educational accountability to the community and quality of education that satisfies stakeholders' expectations, a second wave of educational reforms emerged in the 1990s. These reform efforts were aimed at ensuring the internal and external stakeholders of the quality and accountability of schools (Coulson, 1999; Evans, 1999; Headington, 2000; Mahony & Hextall, 2000; Goertz & Duffy, 2001; Heller, 2001).

In the U.S., there was a growing trend toward quality education and increased competitiveness in schools, all emphasizing quality assurance, school monitoring and review, parents and community involvement in school governance, school charters, parental choice, student coupons, and performance-based funding (Cheng & Townsend, 2000; Mukhopadhyay, 2001; Mok, Gurr, Izawa et al. 2003; Mohandas, Meng, & Keeves, 2003; Pang, Isawa, Kim et al., 2003).

In this wave, education is seen as providing a service to many stakeholders in a commercial and consumer-oriented society, and thus learning is the process by which students receive a service. The school is thus a deliverer of educational services whose quality should satisfy the expectations and needs of key stakeholders in the school setting. The wave therefore emphasizes interface effectiveness between the school and the community, defined by stakeholders' satisfaction, market competition, and accountability to the community.

Cheng finds that the education environment caused by these second-wave reforms is highly unstable and dynamic due to uncertainties and competition. Additionally, the provisions for and contents of education are mainly driven by changing market needs and the diversity in stakeholder expectations. To meet the challenges and needs inherent in this wave, strategic leadership in this model calls for an accountability framework with the participation of key stakeholders such as parents, teachers, alumni, and community leaders.

Schools in this domain have some bounded autonomy with certain aspects of centralized monitoring and external review. In the U.S., competition among schools for resources and survival is serious, particularly where there is a student population decline. The short-term survival of schools is obviously of more concern than their long-term sustainability in development (Cheng & Walker, 2008; Cheng, 2009).

The school strategy that leaders develop is a kind of interface satisfaction strategy that is based on the market rationality, SWOT analysis, and strategic planning, focusing on competition, survival, resources, stakeholders' satisfaction, and cost-return calculation. These strategic initiatives often aim for short-term or middle-term success.

However, successfully managing the interface between schools and the community in a competitive and dynamic environment is consistently challenging for school leaders. The concepts of second-wave strategic leadership are different from those in the first wave, even in environmental, public relations, and brand leadership (Aaker & Joachimsthaler, 2000; Cheng, 2003, 2005a). The strategic concerns of leadership can be established through the following questions:

- How should the school ensure that it provides services that are competitive in the education market?
- How can teaching and student outcomes meet the stakeholders' expectations and needs?
- How can a school ensure that education services offered are structured in such a way that they are accountable to the public and stakeholders through packaging, monitoring, and reporting?
- How can the school influence its stakeholders to ensure support for its survival and development through its interface and branding, marketing, partnership, and public relations activities?

- How can the school take advantage of its external resources and build a stronger network for support?

The limitations of the second-wave model of strategic leadership are that it might be too market-driven in its SWOT analysis, strategic planning, and action programs, thus deviating from the core values and purpose of education. Its initiatives might also be too focused on school competition, market survival, and PR, rather than education activities. It may sometimes react only to the stake-holders' short-term needs, without considering the long-term and sustainable development of students, staff, and the entire school community.

Third-Wave Model: Future Strategic Leadership

At the beginning of the new millennium, the effects of rapid globalization, phenomenal influences of information technology (IT), and the urgent demands for economic and social development stimulated deeper international reflection on educational reform. This is in line with the assumption that the world is moving toward lifelong learning and a multiple-development society, within a quickly changing environment that is impacted by globalization and technological advances. In attempting to keep up with these changing times and ensure that the younger generation meets future challenges, researchers, policy-makers, and school stakeholders recognize the need for a paradigm shift in both learning and teaching. Such a shift would bring about reforms in the aims, content, practice, and admin-istration of education, to ensure that student learning remains relevant for the future (Burbules & Torres, 2000; Cheng, 2000a, 2000b; Stromquist & Monkman, 2000; Daun, 2002; Cheng, 2003; Ramirez & Chan-Tiberghein, 2003).

There is thus an emerging global third wave of educational reform, which heavily emphasizes future effectiveness, and which refers to the relevance of education to meet future needs of individuals and the society. The 21st century is thus characterized by the need to meet the changing purposes and functions of education, and to adopt new ways of thinking that take into account multiple intelligences and the novel concepts of globalization, individualization, and localization (Baker & Begg, 2003; Maclean, 2003; Cheng, 2005a).

The major difference between this third wave and the first and second waves is that the nature of learning is aimed at developing multiple intelligences of learners. These are relevant to future multiple and sustainable developments in the technological, social, political, economic, learning, and cultural contexts in both local and global arenas (Cheng, 2005b). This third wave is driven by the notion of world-class education, and these are the standards used to define the effectiveness and improvement of education.

In this wave, schools might have sufficient autonomy to achieve their own visions for the future with an aspect of local and international benchmarking in school management and educational practice. The school aims to position itself as a world-class institution that facilitates multiple and sustainable developments of both students and society in the context of globalization and change. Just as in the second wave, competition among schools and other educational institutions is rife, but it may be more related to long-term development locally, regionally, and even globally, rather than short-term achievement at the local level.

Strategic leadership in this wave is primarily concerned with the sustainability not only of the school but also of the teaching staff, students, and the wider community. The strategy relied on here is a type of "future development strategy" that is based on the future relevance and rationality in the SWOT analysis and strategic planning, with an emphasis on the sustainable development of students, staff and the school, globalization, localization, and individualization in education systems and unlimited opportunities for lifelong learning. These strategic initiatives are designed for long-term multiple developments at various levels.

In Emeryville, California, a fiscal crisis, together with declining student scores, forced officials to "think out of the box." The leaders realized that the situation in the schools was deeply intertwined with the situation in the community. As in so many urban areas in the U.S., schools in Emeryville were seen as separate from the rest of the community. John Flores, a city manager, spearheaded efforts to create the Center of Community Life. This would bring together members of the business, civic, and education spheres to place the school at the heart of the community, creating a place where "lifelong education" could occur. Among the initiatives are mixed-income housing, recreational facilities open to all, and community health services. A member of the school board involved in the project, Josh Simon, noted that it "involves an interaction between programs and design . . . and a great deal of ongoing conversation."

In a similar way, Principal Johns in the opening vignette eschewed the role of "firefighter." She spent her first year creating structures that might not achieve immediate results (and might even irk board members), but that paid off in the long run by achieving lower teacher attrition and higher student test scores.

In the third wave, strategic leadership can be described as future leadership with an inclination toward the pursuit of a new vision and aims for education, change in learning, teaching, and the curriculum; lifelong learning; an international outlook; sustainable development; global networking; and the integration of IT in education (Cheng, 2001; Pefianco, Curtis & Keeves, 2003; Peterson, 2003). Learning opportunities for students are maximized through the concept of "triplication in education," which is an integrative process of globalization, localization, and individualization of education. It also, as seen in the example of Emeryville, aims to involve all members of the community.

Cheng (2005a) states that inviting a new paradigm of school leadership to the third wave of educational reforms is a key challenge. However, new concepts of school leadership seem to be emerging in this wave, such as triplication, multi-level learning, sustainable development, and multiple-thinking leadership (Cheng, 2010). In summary, the common strategic concerns that school leaders have in this wave may be illustrated through the following questions:

- How can the school change its learning, teaching, and management toward globalization, localization, and individualization, both practically and culturally?
- How can the school increase students' learning opportunities through creation of an IT environment, networking, and changes in teaching and learning?
- How can schools bring about development and sustainability of students' self-learning as a lifelong process?

- How can students' ability to triplicate their own learning be properly developed?
- How can the CMI's of students be continuously developed?
- How can the different kinds of intellectual resources be used globally and locally to support the concepts of world-class teaching and learning?

The third-wave model of strategic leadership, like the earlier two types, also has limitations in its conceptualization and practice. First, it is too forward-looking in terms of its SWOT analysis, strategic planning, and action programs, which may be impractical or unrealistic and thus result in serious setbacks and failure in implementation. Secondly, the implementation of this leadership is heavily dependent not only on a paradigm shift in leadership, but also on the cultural and technological support required for system change.

Again, this strategic leadership model may ignore existing market needs and stakeholders' expectations, resulting in strong resistance to its action plans and thus presenting difficulty in implementation. Cheng (2010) concludes by stating that this model of strategic leadership in the school may be considered as not technically efficient or market strategic, especially during its inception.

Elements of Strategic Leadership

To determine the traits in schools that make them effective in the short term and sustainable and successful in the long term, we rely on a model of strategic leadership formulated by Davies, Davies, and Ellison (2005). The model states that there are two elements that make up strategic leadership: strategic processes and strategic approaches.

Strategic processes are very important in making a strategy a reality and a force for change in schools. Several maxims related to leadership and management are relevant here. One is: How we undertake an activity is as important as what we do to build long-term success. Therefore, care and attention should be given to the process of building strategic capability through the maxim "process is policy." This suggests that policy is not merely formed and then implemented, but that there is an interaction of processes that create the complete policy. The "how" part of strategic processes is divisible into four elements that build strategic direction for the school. These elements are conceptualization, involving people, articulation, and implementation.

The element of conceptualization mainly focuses on the processes of reflection, strategic thinking, analysis, and creation of new ways of understanding through the formulation of mental models of the novel reality. The "involving people" part of the strategic process involves facilitating increased participation, leading to greater levels of motivation and strategic capability. The element of articulation brings out the oral, written, and structural means of communication and development of a strategic purpose. The last element of implementing policy involves translating strategy into action, alignment, and takes into account the elements of strategic timing and abandonment.

Strategic approaches refer to the means by which strategy developed through strategic processes is deployed. The Davies et al. (2005) model focuses on four approaches. First, it considers the pro-active approach to strategic planning, which is the predominant traditional approach to strategy, and one that assumes that the school understands the goals through which it wishes to achieve measurement of outcomes, and how to plot the journey toward achieving those outcomes. The methodology in this approach is similar to that of the school-development and school-improvement movements. However, it contrasts with the reactive approach of emergent strategy, which is a means of utilizing current experience to inform future strategy. This is a common practice in circumstances where schools learn by doing.

If the school is indeed a reflective and learning organization, a pattern of success and failure is formed. The school formulates strategy by repeating activities that engender success and avoiding a repetition of those that cause failures. Consequently, a pattern of actions emerge that, when put together in a collaborative manner, produce a more coherent strategic framework. Therefore, emergent strategy is a reflective and reactive process that draws on experience to predict and improve future patterns of behavior.

The researchers in their model also considered decentralized strategy as a model of strategic development. This is where senior school leaders determine values and set the direction of the school, but delegate implementation of policy to other staff. Decentralized strategy is dependent on values and a degree of trust among the various actors in the school setting. The last approach is strategic intent, the method by which capability and capacity building achieve significant strategic change. This approach sets clear objectives (intents) that the organization is committed to meeting, but recognizes that it is vital to build capability and capacity first, so as to fully understand how and when they can be achieved.

Understanding Strategy and Strategic Leadership

Strategy involves decision-making aimed at shaping the direction of the organization. In a school, strategizing is a medium- to long-term activity, i.e., three to five years and beyond. Strategy also includes taking into account broader core issues and themes for development in the school, instead of day-to-day imperatives. Davies et al. (2005) state that in understanding what strategy entails, it may be useful to consider it as being related to strategic thinking and a strategic perspective, rather than the traditional conception of strategy as mechanistic plans. Note as well that this concept may have to be elucidated to all stakeholders in the organization. Principal Johns, in the opening vignette, implemented strategies that she knew would take at least two years to achieve results. Members of the school board were skeptical, however, and perhaps Principal Johns could have spent more time explaining her position and strategy to all involved.

In their model, the researchers perceive strategy and strategic planning as distinct concepts, and put forward the idea that strategy involves development of strategic processes that can ensure the effective development and deployment of strategy through appropriate strategic approaches. These two elements, as earlier mentioned, are driven by effective strategic leadership in schools. Strategic planning is held to be one among a number of development approaches. While strategy can be thought of as a framework to set future direction and action, it can also be used as a template or backcloth to judge current activities.

Davies et al. (2005) define a strategically focused school as one that is educationally effective in the short term, but also has a clear framework and set of processes to translate the core purpose and vision into excellent educational provision that is sustainable in the medium to long term. Such a school has leadership that enables short-term goals to be met, while at the same time building capability and capacity for the long term.

Strategic leadership can therefore be said to link the strategic function with the leadership function, as suggested in its definition. School leaders play the role of defining the organization's moral purpose, which is summarized as "why we do what we do." The values and beliefs that inform this moral purpose are linked to the organization's vision of "where we want to be and the sort of organization we want to be in the future."

Through strategic leadership, this broad activity is linked to shorter-term operational planning, responses to immediate events, and the long-term strategic direction. In simple terms, strategic leadership defines the vision and moral purpose of the school and translates them into desired action. It is necessary to set the direction and build the capacity for the organization to achieve change. This translation of vision and purpose requires a proactive transformational mindset that strives for better outcomes, rather than maintenance of the status quo, which is an approach of transactional leadership. In the vignette at the beginning of the chapter, for example, Principal Johns needed to create a fresh mindset, which operated as a springboard to propel the school out of its set patterns. Similarly, the Center for Community Learning in Emeryville is a proactive, long-term strategy focused on improving not only student test scores, but community wellbeing as a whole.

These ideas on strategic leadership suggest that it is strongly linked to the organization's vision. Earlier, researchers Beare, Caldwell, and Millikan (1989) were of the opinion that "outstanding school leaders have a vision for their schools—a mental picture of a preferred future—which they share with all those in the school community." They further state that:

- Outstanding leaders must have a vision for their organizations.
- The vision should be communicated in a way that secures commitment from other members of the organization.
- Communication of the vision requires communication of its meaning.
- Focus should be given to the institutionalizing of the vision if leadership is to be successful.

In many other books on educational leadership, there is considerable emphasis on vision. However, strategic leadership consists not only of the vision element in leadership ability, but also encompasses other wide-ranging factors. The question thus remains how we can develop a coherent model that informs us about what strategic leadership truly entails.

Strategic Leadership: Findings from the Research

In their analysis of data from interviews with leaders possessing high-level strategic skills, Davies, Davies, and Ellison (2005) split their research findings into two categories—what strategic leaders do and what characteristics they possess. Their analysis established that strategic leaders involve themselves in five main activities in each of two categories.

1. They Set the Direction of the School

This activity relates to the traditional definition of strategy as a pattern of decisions that set the direction of the organization. Freedman (2003) states that strategy is the actual framework of choices that is relied upon to determine the nature and direction of an organization. Earlier, we had seen that this comprised a strategic plan of three to five years and beyond, concerning itself with the broader thrust of the school's activities. It is moderately different from extending a short-term view by a year or so. Rather, it develops a medium-term perspective. Strategic leadership involves several planning approaches aimed at building capacity so as to understand the feasibility of different future possibilities.

The development of strategic direction involves a process in which we don't just look forward from the present, but we also establish a picture of what we want the school to look like in the future and set guidelines and frameworks on how to move forward to that position. As we have seen above, from the conversations with strategic leaders, there must a clear understanding of the direction the school is headed in. From conversations with these leaders, Davies et al. (2005) summarize what strategic leaders do as follows:

- They set the direction of the school.
- They challenge and question—they are dissatisfied with the present.
- They translate strategy into action.
- They prioritize their own strategic thinking and learning by building new mental models to frame their understanding and that of others.
- They align the people and the organization with the strategy.
- They display strategic wisdom based on a clear value system.
- They determine effective strategic intervention points.
- They have powerful personal and professional networks.
- They develop strategic capabilities within the school.
- They have high-quality personal and interpersonal skills.

2. They Translate Strategy into Action

While most schools establish plans, few translate them into action. The research by Davies et al. (2005) found that strategic leaders are good "completer-finishers." According to Mintzberg (1995), they were capable of not only "seeing ahead" but also "seeing it through." This characteristic of strategic leaders is born of their ability to focus on a limited number of issues and move forward on those issues.

In the business world, there is debate about the extent to which traditional strategic plans get implemented. Most studies suggest that only 10–30% of all plans are achieved, with the rest remaining on shelves. Davies and Davies (2005) question whether school plans merely provide frameworks for external audit or whether they get implemented. One of the leaders interviewed in the Davies study stated that, "It's not enough just to think and reflect, people actually want to see results."

It is key that a leader be seen as a person who not only builds a sense of purpose and direction in the school, but also as one who translates them into reality. The importance of this perception is reinforced in the statement by one of the leaders in the study, who said, "If you can implement two or three things effectively and the staff can see the benefit they are more likely to work with you when it comes to a major change because they can see something will come of it."

Davies and Davies (2005) state that there is a danger where strategy is seen as a desirable activity, and in consequence so much time is spent designing strategic frameworks and plans. Thus the question that emerges is: "How do we translate these frameworks into the capacity to move toward better outcomes in the school?" To answer this, a strategic leader uses his or her strategic ability to translate strategic vision into action. Fullan (2004) describes strategic leaders with this ability as "doers with big minds." In conclusion, school leaders need to articulate the strategic view, but they are also needed to implement the strategy as efficiently as they designed it.

3. They Align the People, the Organization, and the Strategy

It is vital that school leaders build in-depth capacity within the school to deliver the strategy. Davies (2003) suggested a four-stage approach that, first, articulates the strategy, be it in oral, written, or structural ways; second, builds a common understanding through shared experiences; third, creates a shared mental image of the future through dialogue; and fourth, defines the desired outcomes. The processes described help to build a powerful understanding within the teaching staff to enable them to contribute fully to implementation of the strategy. Novak(2002) states that the difference in strategic change comes from "doing to" staff and very often results in "doing them in." He argues for the need of "doing with" as a way of building long-term commitment to strategy implementation.

In conclusion, we can see that strategic leaders pay a great deal of attention to establishing a sustainable strategy that is inclusive of all those who work in the school. While traditional approaches may suggest aligning the staff to the strategy, it may be much better to think of empowered organizations that align the people, organization, and strategy.

4. They Determine Effective Strategic Intervention Points

An important aspect of strategic leadership is that knowing when to make a change which is as significant as the change itself (Davies & Davies, 2005). This critical issue of timing arises from rational analysis, but can also stem from leadership intuition (Parikh, 1994). The distinction between "Chronos" time and "Kairos" time, according to Bartunek and Necochea (2000), is very important for strategic timing. While the former refers to the normal ticking of a clock and the passage of time, the latter refers to those intense moments in time when critical actions and decisions are made. These are the points at which good strategic leaders make successful interventions.

Interviewed leaders in the Davies, Davies, and Ellison (2005) research recognized the importance of strategic timing. They stated from experience that if they waited until all staff were "on board," the opportunity to change may have passed, and where they moved too quickly, without enough support, the change was more likely to flounder. Therefore, discerning when both external circumstances and internal conditions can be effectively managed to bring about successful change is significant in effective leadership.

The issue of strategic timing goes hand in hand with the concept of strategic abandonment. Davies and Davies (2005) define it as the ability to abandon some commenced activities to create the capacity for undertaking new ones. The issue that comes up is that of differentiating between abandonment of things that are not working well and abandoning those that were satisfactory in pursuit.

In conclusion, a key ability of strategic leaders is not only knowing when to make a change, but also in knowing how to free up organizational space so as to have the capacity to move into a new strategic direction.

5. They Develop Strategic Capabilities in the School

This concept of developing strategic capabilities was earlier articulated by Prahalad and Hamel (1990) as "core competencies," and by Stalk et al. (1992) as "strategic capabilities." Both relate to the fundamental attributes within the school setting. A good example of long-term competency is the fundamental understanding of learning and the varying needs of students. This can be effectively compared to the shallow understanding of the latest specific skills that arise from an imposed curriculum from the government. Strategic leaders agree that more focus should be on the development of long-term abilities. Davies and Davies (2005) use the analogy of a tree, in which the trunk and branches are above the surface, while below are the roots that hold everything together.

If leaders develop strategic capabilities or competencies, then they would achieve more depth and range in the form of a reflective-learning culture in teaching staff, a no-blame problem-solving approach, and a deeper understanding of learning. Consequently, when the school faces new challenges, it would draw from the latter abilities without having to rely on current skills. In summary, we find that, while strategic leaders have the capacity to manage and shape the "now" of school life, they also have the ability to allocate time and resources to build strategic capabilities in order to ensure that the school remains sustainable and develops over the long term.

Characteristics of Strategic Leaders

Davies, Davies, and Ellison (2005) in their research found certain personal characteristics of school leaders who employed strategic leadership in the running of their schools. The study found five main characteristics that strategic leaders display.

I. They Challenge and Question: They Are Dissatisfied with the Present

One key characteristic of strategic leaders is their ability to envision the different ways their organization might perform in future. They always have a desire to challenge the *status quo* and improve for the future. This means that strategic leaders have to deal constantly with their dissatisfaction with present arrangements, while facing the challenge that they are not able to change things as quickly as they might want.

Leaders, as change agents in their organizations, constantly ask questions such as:

- What are the things taught that have been clearly successful or unsuccessful in the past?
- What accounted for the success or failure?
- What do we need to do differently in the future?
- Which relationships between the school and students, parents, or the wider community have been successful or unsuccessful, and why?
- What can be done to change things for the better?
- How can we assess what we do to challenge the current understanding and operations?
- As a school, are we cruising and strolling or are we challenging and creating?

Collins (2001) classified leadership into five levels. The highest is level five, which has leaders who are modest in character, but ambitious when it comes to their organizations, and they always challenge average performance. Collins states that the defining characteristic of level-five leaders is their demonstration of an unwavering resolve to do whatever is necessary to achieve the best long-term results without concern about its difficulty.

2. They Prioritize Their Own Strategic Thinking and Learning, and Build New Mental Models

Davies et al. (2005) state that this characteristic is one of the most significant in strategic leadership. In order for a leader to envision the future and develop new approaches, he or she requires knowledge and experience. In the study by Davies, strategic leaders were conscious of their learning needs, and they prioritized and set aside time to meet them. They also constantly sought to broaden their repertoire of skills. New challenges require new skills, hence the need for continuous professional development to achieve those skills. Strategic leaders frame their new understandings in mental models, which they utilize to communicate with other staff. From this, it is clear that leaders need to be active learners to enhance and develop their existing skills. Davies et al. agree with the suggestion that school principals change their titles to "lead learners," in order to emphasize the importance of leaders being learners themselves, and also setting a good example for others in the school.

One challenge that school leaders face is that they lead very busy lives. Thus, prioritizing time for their own learning to the exclusion of other tasks may be difficult. Earlier research by Schön (1987) makes a distinction between reflection-on-action and reflection-in-action. Honing the skills needed to develop reflection-in-action, Schön claims, can build the leader's capacity to determine his or her learning needs and build frameworks aimed at meeting them.

These mental models suggested in the form of pictures or frameworks capture reality, which is complex and dynamic. Through their creation, leaders can make sense of reality for themselves and their staff, and develop a clearer interpretation of the world. By engaging in this process of reflection, all school stakeholders share a common definition and understanding of their roles, and this builds a common purpose.

3. They Display Strategic Wisdom Based on a Clear Value System

Through the earlier definition of strategic leadership, we can see it as a link between values, vision, and operational matters. By using a clear value system based on ethics, leaders create the bedrock for all their activities. This is because wisdom to make the "best" decisions is based not just on a good understanding of possible changes, but also on what is in the best interests of students. The interviewees in the Davies study stated that they used a series of value statements to guide their interaction with colleagues and to set the framework for their strategic decisions.

Wisdom in this context is defined as the ability to take the right action at the right time. In his presentation during the International Thinking Skills Conference in 2002, Robert Sternberg stated that leaders need wisdom because they:

- Need creative ability to come up with ideas.
- Need analytical ability to decide whether the ideas are good.
- Need practical ability to make their ideas functional and convince their followers that their ideas are valuable.
- Need it to balance the impact of the ideas on themselves, others, and their institutions in the short and long run.

In describing the nature of wisdom in depth, Stenberg stated that wisdom is:

- Successful intelligence.
- Balancing of interests.
- Balancing of time-frames.
- Mindful infusion of values.
- Aligning of responses to the environment.
- Application of knowledge for the common good.

4. They Have Powerful Personal and Professional Networks

As seen earlier, knowledge plays a critical role when making strategic decisions. This knowledge is gathered from networks of fellow professionals and from local, regional, national, and international organizations, so as to gain fundamentally in both understanding and benchmarking current knowledge.

The research by Davies et al. (2005) found that effective strategic leaders put a great deal of time and effort into the maintenance and extension of their networks. The importance of networking is illustrated by Fullan (2004): ". . . if you want to change systems, you need to increase the amount of purposeful interaction between and among individuals and indeed within and across systems."

Leaders therefore need to develop extensive networks that can provide them with insight needed to fulfill the complex functions of their posts. In common practice, most organizations provide introductions to networks, but what is important is the will and enthusiasm of the leader to utilize these formal networks to add to their own personal professional networks.

5. They Have High-Quality Personal and Interpersonal Skills

In their study of strategic leadership in schools, Davies and Davies (2005) stated that the maxim on leadership and management, "getting things done through people," was evident across those interviewed. The leaders sampled described how they built greater personal understanding on how to boost their confidence and resilience, and also in understanding others in their staff. Most noted that honest relationships and finding time to listen to others were the cornerstones of their strategic efforts. One leader said, "I am constantly trying to listen and support people so as to really understand where they are coming from. They need to trust and believe me and feel I am working in their best interests."

In the context of the previous discussions on wisdom, personal qualities of leaders have been stated as vital for leadership. Davies and Davies state that, additionally, leaders should be passionate, hold on to their values, inspire and stimulate others, and be socially intelligent. While all of the above qualities affect the way leaders learn and their capacity to change, Boal and Hooijberg (2001) state that most leadership research shows that leaders have to develop important interpersonal skills, such as empathy, motivation, and communication. According to Bennett (2000), if a leader is to practice moral leadership and re-engineer pedagogy successfully, he or she requires a firm set of personal values.

While many leaders are likely to develop their own lists of values they consider necessary, integrity, social justice, loyalty, humanity, respect, and a clear distinction between right and wrong as mandatory in those lists. Strategic relationships that have been already built are likely to flounder unless a value system is upheld and exercised regularly and consistently.

Although Bennett does not include it in his comprehensive list, social intelligence is paramount for strategic leadership, since the decision-making, solution-implementation, and organizational improvement processes are rarely free of emotion. Social intelligence involves possessing a thorough understanding of the social context, and, as Gardner (1985) stated, it is the ability to notice and make clear distinctions among other individuals in important aspects such as their moods, motivations, temperaments, and intentions. In summary, the key element of social intelligence is the ability to discern emotion in oneself and in others.

The leader's ability to connect with followers' involvement and resolve conflicts is vital to the development of strategic relationships and discovery of creative solutions. Bennett (2000) also points out strength and courage as personal values that are important. He concludes that visionary projects that are delivered with passion are likely to fail unless the leader has the capacity to counter adversaries and remain confident until the end.

As we saw with Connie Johns in the opening vignette, it takes a strong and confident leader to enact real, lasting change. Transformative, systemic change is a slow process, and one that requires an immense amount of dialogue, keeping the connections among all stakeholders strong and active. Principal Johns, by spending the first six months of her tenure in dialogue, was able to get everyone on board, and implement changes. However, in the case of Elm High, creating lasting change also required tenacity in the face of objections from members of the board.

Lessons from the Statewide Systemic Initiatives Program

The Statewide Systemic Initiatives Program was started in 1990 by the National Science Foundation (NSF). The projects supported by the Directorate for Science and Engineering Education in the U.S. intended to increase the impact of, accelerate, and widen the effectiveness of improvements in the subjects of science, mathematics, and engineering in K–12 and post-secondary levels (Heck & Weiss, 2005).

These projects, funded as statewide systemic initiatives (SSIs), aimed at aligning various parts of the education system in several states to produce comprehensive, coordinated, and sustained change. These initiatives harmonized curriculum goals, content of instructional materials, instructional practice and assessment, teacher recruitment and preparation, and the professional development of teachers and school administrators under the umbrella of systemic reform.

SSIs targeted for change the various "ways of doing business" in the school, such as its organizational structure, articulation within the system, decision-making, allocation of resources, and accountability. They were also designed to involve various stakeholders in their reform efforts, which included scientists and mathematicians, local school system decision makers, leaders of parent and community-based organizations, and business and community representatives.

Examining these SSIs, we are able to draw valuable conclusions as to the nature of strategic leadership in educational reform. From 1991 to 1998, the NSF funded 26 initiatives, in amounts of up to $2 million per year for five years. While four of these SSIs terminated early, eight continued to receive funding for a second five-year phase. Through the study by Heck and Weiss (2005), we are able to analyze the "thinking" behind these SSIs, including how and why they were designed, implemented, and assessed with the SSI leaders, and their documents as the primary data sources for the study.

Heck and Weiss designed their study specifically to explore the concept of "strategic leadership," and they state that their framework for examining the concept was informed by various literature materials on strategic leadership for sustainable development in an array of fields. They state that most of the literature offered perspectives that were helpful in choosing the aspects to investigate and the methods of interpreting data on SSIs (e.g., Farrell & Hart, 1998; Goldsmith, 1996; Hickson, Butler, Cray, Mallory, & Wilson, 1989; Koteen, 1989).

Heck and Weiss state that they focused on three criteria of strategic leadership:

- Leaders' understanding of the SSI's capacity to succeed, and how it could be used to effect change within the school system.
- Leaders' conceptualization of the context in which the SSI functioned.
- The convergence point between directions pursued by SSI leaders and the conditions they were attempting to change.

The researchers' interpretations relied on theoretical conceptions of strategic thinking toward sustainable change, which include the extent to which SSI leaders provided direction, prioritized utilization of resources, anticipated and dealt with uncertainty, and how they maintained a basis for quality control and progress assessment (Goldsmith, 1996; Koteen, 1989; Shrivastava, 1985).

Lessons Learned

In summary, Heck and Weiss drew the following conclusions on the role of strategic leadership in school reform.

- Strategic leaders have a vision of the reformed system and how to achieve it.
- Strategic leaders create a broad understanding and support for the reform vision at the highest levels.
- Strategic leaders bring commitment of school and district leadership to the reform vision and its implementation.
- Strategic leaders rely on the use of interventions to translate the reform vision into practice.
- Strategic leaders recognize that, for reform to be achieved, one has to start small, refine activities as needed, and provide evidence that interventions lead to desired outcomes.
- Strategic leaders develop system capability and capacity to scale up reform with quality.
- Strategic leaders enhance and facilitate development of formal policies that provide guidance and incentives for reform.
- Strategic leaders avoid controversy.
- Strategic leaders develop capabilities for the next generation of reform leaders.

Summary

Many researchers have considered strategic leadership as the role of a single leader. Through our analysis of the various models, we have seen the activities that are required of these leaders and the characteristics they possess. Through these models, it is hoped that the reader gets a clearer understanding of what strategic leadership in the school scenario entails and its pros and cons, as derived from the three-wave models of Cheng (2010). All in all, the development of what Cheng (2010) refers to as "total strategic leaders" in the educational world should be comprehensively addressed by education reformers and scholars. A good starting point would be a better understanding of the waves of educational reforms in light of strategic leadership in education and subsequently drawing policy implications that can guide efforts to rationalize education reform and develop the capacities of strategic leaders in schools to cope with the various challenges in the education sector.

Discussion Questions

1. Fullan describes effective leaders as "doers with big minds." What is the relationship between vision and implementation? How much time should be spent on each? What is necessary to successfully implement a vision?

2. In the vignette at the beginning of the chapter, Principal Johns implements severa strategic reforms. Can you think of two more ideas Elm Circle High could implement to reenergize the school?
3. What are the roles of the principal, the teachers, the parents, and the community in implementing strategic reform? Provide one example for each.
4. Cheng's third-wave model of reform strategies focuses on the "multiple intelligences" of learners. What are multiple intelligences? Give examples of three people with very different learning styles. How might they benefit from the third-wave model?
5. Choose three of the questions posed to present the common strategic concerns that school leaders have in implementing the third-wave model of strategic leadership, and provide answers based on material in this chapter.

Activities

1. Present a skit in which two learners with very different "intelligences" (e.g., a gifted athlete and a gifted mathematician) are confronted with a problem (e.g., how to rescue a kitten from a tree). How do each of them solve the problem using their gifts? How could they have worked together to solve the problem? Why is it important to teach to all "intelligences"?
2. Choose one problem at your school (present or past). Create one-week (short-term), one-year (middle-term), and five-year (long-term) plans to address the problem. Discuss the advantages of each.

Selected Readings

Burns, J. M. G. (2010). *Leadership*. New York: Harper Perennial.
Davies, B. (2006). *Leading the strategically focused school*. London: Sage.
Davies, B., & Davies, B. J. (2005). Strategic leadership. In B. Davies (Ed.), *The essentials of school leadership* (pp. 10–30). Thousand Oaks, CA: Corwin Press.
Eacott, S. (2008). Strategy in educational leadership: In Search of Unity. *Journal of Educational Administration, 46*(3), 353–375.
Fullan, M. (2003). *Change forces with a vengeance*. London: Routledge Falmer.
Honig, M. I., & Coburn, C. (2008). Evidence-based decision making in school district central offices: Toward a policy and research agenda. *Educational Policy, 22*(4) 578–607.
Jones, G. (2007). *Organizational theory, design, and change*. (5th ed.) Upper Saddle River, N.J.: Pearson.
Razik, T. A., & Swanson, A. D. (2009). *Fundamental concepts of educational leadership*. Boston, Mass: Allyn and Bacon.

\able Leadership
..... Is Won by Those Who Endure

During the great recession of the late 2000s, many families from poor socioeconomic back-grounds fled inner city areas and moved to thriving, middle-class cities nearby. Principal Joseph Gutierrez's school was located in a district that straddled a middle-class area popu-lated mainly by European Americans and a much poorer area, where the housing was relatively inexpensive. During the flight from the inner cities, many socioeconomically disadvantaged families, most of them African American and Hispanic, moved into the poor area, and the number of minority students at his school nearly doubled.

Faced with a sudden drop in test scores, frictions between the middle-class and lower-class students, and an increased dropout rate, Principal Gutierrez realized he had to completely overhaul his school program. Quick-fix solutions like begging the community for mentors to help disadvantaged students study during testing periods were not going to do much in the long run. After extended discussions with staff members and the school board, he instigated monthly meetings for parents. He got local restaurants and taxi services to commit to providing free food and rides to and from the meetings, and teachers volunteered to provide activities for the children. The parents held directed discussions on issues such as nutrition, bedtimes, and homework, with an emphasis on creating structures that would assist each other. Out of the discussions grew a network that extended across the socioeconomic lines. Over time, students' test scores stabilized, and the communities grew closer together.

Building a sustainable system that goes beyond myopic interests and short-term policies is an arduous task for any school leader. In the U.S., our education system has been criticized for being too shallow in curriculum and unsustainable in the long run. In fact, a 2007 report by UNICEF concerning children's wellbeing in 22 countries ranked the U.K. and the U.S. at the bottom of the industrialized nations in the survey. Hargreaves (2007) laments that these two countries, in their single-minded pursuit of economic competitiveness and development at all costs, are destroying the planet, while "eating their young."

To add to this, most of the seemingly fashionable educational reform strategies have threatened to treat teachers and other human resources as expendable waste, in the same way multinational companies and politicians have hindered the sustainability of our natural resources. Most of the damage to educational sustainability in the U.S. comes from imposed short-term targets, endless and meaningless testing, and the pursuit of quick political ends at the cost of true learning for all students.

In *Teaching in the Knowledge Society*, Hargreaves (2003) argues that teaching and learning in schools need to be reconfigured to prepare youth to participate in transforming the country into an innovative knowledge economy and also gain opportunities for employment at the highest levels of these economies, providing high-quality skills and earning high wages. He adds that many countries aspire to be knowledge societies. Knowledge societies, in this age of electronic, satellite, and digital technologies, address how information and ideas are formed, used, circulated, and absorbed at great speed in "knowledge-based communities," which he defines as networks of individuals working hard to produce and circulate new information/knowledge.

In knowledge societies, prosperity, wealth, and economic development are dependent on the people's capacity to "out-invent" and outwit competitors, understand the desires and demands of the consumer markets, and change their jobs or acquire new skills as required through the economic fluctuations and downturns. A distinct feature of these knowledge societies is that the above-listed capacities do not just belong to individuals, but also to organizations, which then share, create, and apply the new knowledge continuously and consistently in cultures of mutual learning and endless innovation.

Hargreaves states that, for sustainability, knowledge society organizations develop the individuals' capacities, by providing them with better opportunities for lifelong training and retraining, by breaking the barriers to learning and communication, by getting individuals to work in diverse and flexible teams, by using problems and mistakes as learning opportunities rather than occasions for blame, by including everyone in the organizational vision and mission, and by developing "social capital" through networking and relationship-building, which provides people with support and opportunities for further learning.

According to Hargreaves, the knowledge society is a learning society, and its economic success and culture of continuous innovation is dependent on the capacity of its constituents to keep learning throughout their working lives. This is why schools that purport to prepare students for the knowledge economy have to break with the concepts of the past.

Hargreaves suggests that the present model of one teacher per class, with its emphasis on basic literacy and numeracy, needs to be replaced with a wider, more cognitively challenging and innovative curriculum. He adds that there is a need for teachers to work together rather than teaching alone in classrooms; for professional learning to be continuous and not episodic; for teachers' judgments to be guided by objective as well as subjective evidence, by experience as well as intuition; and, finally, for the teaching profession to be more predisposed to taking risks and accepting change instead of just sticking to proven procedures and comfortable routines.

In summary, Hargreaves states that the demands of knowledge economy schooling require that schools put aside the outdated industrial and agrarian educational models, and also abandon their reinvention in narrowly focused, highly intensified, and over-tested standardized reforms that bring about restrictions in the curriculum, undermine professional morale, inhibit creative learning, and reduce the supply lines of leadership recruitment.

In *Sustainable Leadership*, Hargreaves and Fink (2006) discuss the development of the concept of sustainability in the environmental movement, its definition in the Brundtland Commission Report of 1987, and the UN Decade of Education for Sustainable Development (2005–2015). They argue against what they refer to as "quick-fix Anglo-Saxon" educational reform strategies, which impose short-term achievement targets, set a "hurried" curriculum to be taught to young age groups, promote the culture of "teaching to the test," and encourage quick-fix turnaround strategies for use by teachers in poorly performing schools.

The Current Sociopolitical Context

This sociopolitical context refers to contemporary ideologies, regulations, policies, conditions, laws, practices, traditions, and events that define America's education. Nieto (2007) states that these ideologies, practices, laws, and policies are responsible for the current structural inequality in the education sector. She argues that societal ideologies, assumptions, and expectations, which are often taken for granted, and which relate to people's identities, race, ethnicity, gender, sexual orientation, social class, language, and various other differences—together with other material and concrete conditions in the society—work toward creating barriers to educational progress.

Nieto is of the opinion that, consciously or unconsciously, these social assumptions and ideologies define what the society collectively believes about certain people. These perceptions may often determine who gets access to education, housing, health care, and employment, among other material needs. This sociopolitical context is also used to determine whose language is considered "standard" and which lifestyle is "normal."

In the U.S., many young students have been marginalized by their schooling experiences. However, this situation is not unique to the U.S., and many societies around the world are facing the same situation due to globalization and other factors such as immigration and war, which are making urban areas increasingly cosmopolitan. We therefore find that, independent of location, the sociopolitical context affects every society due to the connection between democracy and public schools. Nieto notes that it is mostly through public schools that children get the opportunity for a better life than the one their families have.

According to Nieto, public schools have the capacity to fuel democracy. In the common discourse, however, because of privatization and other market-driven schemes, this important connection between public schooling and democracy seems to have been lost. The sociopolitical context, at the school level, influences policies and practices, such as the curriculum, pedagogy, parent outreach, discipline, and hiring of staff, among others. In matters of curriculum, the sociopolitical context guides the knowledge that is required to teach through the perspective that is advocated for. The sociopolitical context in this case determines who benefits and who loses in the curriculum.

At an individual level, teachers, school leaders, and other educators are largely influenced by the ideologies and beliefs in society and, consciously or unconsciously, act on them whether they believe them or not. Racism and other biases manifest themselves through school policies and also through teachers' and school administrators' practices and decisions. For example, decisions about which students are gifted and which require special education are often affected by teachers' biases (Harry & Klingner, 2006; Oakes, 2005). Teachers' relationships with their students are also affected by the sociopolitical context, since their perspectives and expectations are occasionally influenced by prevailing societal attitudes about people from particular backgrounds (Valenzuela, 1999; Flores-Gonzalez, 2002).

The context includes changing demographics in the population since as we had earlier seen shifts in population are redefining national identities. In the U.S., particularly, 30% of the nation's residents are African Americans, Asian/Pacific Islanders, Latinos, and American Indians (U.S. Census Bureau, 2000a). However, what is more dramatic than the current population statistics are the future projections by the Census Bureau, which estimate that, by 2050, people of color will be over 50% of the total population of the U.S. and, for the first time, European Americans will be the "minority" (U.S. Census Bureau 2000b). Currently, there are over 450 languages spoken in the U.S., and nearly a fifth of the total U.S. population speaks a language other than English at home, which makes the country a truly multilingual nation, in practice if not in philosophy (U.S. Census Bureau, 2004).

On the other hand, statistics show that the profile of teachers has changed very little compared with the population profile. Though statistics may differ slightly, almost all sources show that 85–90% of U.S. teachers are European American, monolingual English speakers, who mostly have had little experience with students of color and those whose native language is not English (National Collaborative on Diversity in the Teaching Force 2004; National Center for Education Statistics 2005).

Nieto finds, concomitant with the growth in diversity, a growing "achievement gap" between European American students and students of color. Statistics gathered in 2006 by *Quality Counts 10*, the tenth annual report on the results of standardized education in the U.S., show that, though student achievement has generally improved, the achievement gap between African American and Hispanic students compared to European American students is still very large. The gap is the equivalent of two grade levels or more, which is close to what it was in 1992 (Olsen, 2006). However, Nieto states that the attention to the achievement gap focuses on students, rather than the institutionalized policies, practices, and structured inequality in education that affect their learning.

In many countries, there has been a growing culture of standardization and bureaucratization that forms part of the sociopolitical context. In the U.S., standardization has been mainly influenced by federal legislation with rigid accountability structures, most recently the No Child Left Behind Act. This is despite glaring evidence that testing rather than increasing student learning is leading to higher dropout rates and less engagement with schooling (Nichols & Berliner, 2007).

Additionally, these hyperactive accountability structures are joined by the issue of segregation according to race, ethnicity, and social class, which is now worse than at any time since the 1954 decision in *Brown vs. Board of Education*. Nieto (2007) states that, at present, the most segregated of all students are the low-income Latinos, though poor children of all backgrounds, and particularly poor children of color, are the most marginalized through this segregation (Orfield & Lee, 2005).

Nieto suggests that the most significant aspect of the sociopolitical context is probably the long-standing and growing structural and social inequality, which invariably results in poverty, inadequate housing, poor access to health care, and unemployment. She states that, though teachers can make a significant difference in terms of life-chances and opportunities for their students, it is apparent that they alone cannot take on the entire responsibility for student achievement due to the existence of inequality and structural barriers created by racism and other biases, such as lack of resources in poor schools, poor infrastructure, and unfair and bureaucratic policies.

In the U.S., educators such as Jean Anyon and economists such as Richard Rothstein, among many others, are of the opinion that it is mainly the macro-economic policies—i.e., policies that regulate such issues as the minimum wage, availability of jobs, tax rates, medical care, and affordable housing—that are primarily responsible for causing school failure. In addition, they argue that educational policies cannot by themselves transcend these policies. Anyon (2005) writes:

> As a nation, we have been counting on education to solve the problems of unemployment, joblessness, and poverty for many years. But education did not cause these problems, and education cannot solve them. An economic system that chases profits and casts people aside (especially people of color) is culpable.
>
> (p. 3)

Rothstein (2004), who was at the Economic Policy Institute in Washington, D.C., states that if education reform is pursued without any additional investments in health care, housing, early childhood education, after-school and summer programs, or any other social and economic support, then the achievement gap can never be closed. He warns of the consequences of sustaining a society increasingly being characterized by very few "haves" and many "have-nots." He states that:

> If as a society we choose to preserve big social class differences, we must necessarily also accept substantial gaps between the achievement of lower-class and middleclass children. Closing those gaps requires not only better schools, although those are certainly needed, but also reform in the social and economic institutions that prepare children to learn in different ways. It will not be cheap.
>
> (p. 149)

Defining Sustainable Leadership

The study by Hargreaves and Fink (2006) draws on research into 30 years of educational leadership in eight U.S. high schools and available literature on environmental and corporate sustainability. From their study, we find the definition of sustainable leadership:

> Sustainable educational leadership and improvement preserves and develops deep learning for all that spreads and lasts, in ways that do no harm to and indeed create positive benefit for others around us, now and in the future.

The two researchers give an example of a school district that employs a heroic principal to turn around an underperforming school, then sees all his work unravel within several months of his subsequent promotion. Another example of unsustainable leadership is where a charismatic leader decides to accept to become the principal of a nearby school and consequently takes all his teacher-leader disciples with him, thus undoing his work. Similarly, a principal of a "magnet" school increases her institution's reputation by attracting the top students around the school area, consequently taking away the best talent from the nearby neighborhood schools, and causing the overall performance of the area to plummet. Teachers in high schools observe four principals pass through their school in a span of five years and decide that they can easily wait out all other principals and then change their agendas in future after they have left. Another example is where a school district attempts to water down a highly unionized school by assigning to it a succession of increasingly authoritarian principals, only for the union's resistance to change to become even more deep-seated.

The researchers state that the above examples of unsustainable leadership and improvement efforts are actually not hypothetical, and were found in a study on educational change funded by the Spencer Foundation over a period of 30 years in eight U.S. and Canadian high schools, as observed by over 200 teachers and school administrators who worked there in the 1970s, 1980s, and 1990s (Hargreaves & Goodson, 2004). The study has been used by researchers to show that one of the key elements that influence change or continuity in the long term is leadership, its sustainability, and succession. Hargreaves and Fink (2006) state that most of the processes and practices of school leadership in their study show or create temporary and localized "flurries" of change, with little lasting or widespread improvement in the long run.

However, there were several exceptions to this norm. Hargreaves and Fink found that, from the first day of appointment, some school leaders thought hard about the issue of succession, especially regarding how to identify and groom their successors. An example is given of one founding leader of an innovative school who was careful not to "poach" the best teachers from neighboring institutions, thus avoiding the injustice or jealousy that comes from doing so. In other schools, some courageous leaders responded to standardized testing by improving learning for all—in the belief that eventually better scores would follow—rather than becoming obsessed with results, thereby stifling the learning process. These two leaders did more than manage change or implement reform: they pursued and modeled sustainable leadership.

The Seven Principles of Sustainable Leadership

The main responsibility that all education leaders have is creating a learning system that engages students intellectually, emotionally, and socially. Sustainable leadership therefore goes beyond the temporary gains in achievement scores to create long-lasting, meaningful improvements in learning processes (Glickman, 2002; Stoll, Fink, & Earl, 2002). Hargreaves and Fink (2006) give two examples.

The first is Talisman Park High School's principal, who reacted to a new mandate to issue a tenth-grade literacy test that students were required to pass in order to graduate by attempting to shield his experienced staff from the time-consuming test-related activities that are entailed in such policies. The principal decided that the most expedient way to achieve good results was for them to concentrate on boosting the achievement of those students who were more likely to fall below the passing grade. Though the main strategy was to raise the school's scores, the other students who needed help with literacy were generally ignored.

A second principal was in charge of the neighboring, more ethnically diverse Wayvern High School. This principal reacted to the same mandated test by concentrating on the improvement of literacy for all students in the long run. Teachers in this school worked together to evaluate and improve their literacy practices and, with the help of parents and other school stakeholders, focused for one month on improving the literacy learning of all students. While the first-year results were not dramatic, by the second year, the school improved and scored above the district means. By the third year, the school was the district's number-two performer and was well ahead of the privileged Talisman Park High School, whose principal had opted for a quick fix.

Keeping the above example in mind, let us look at the particular principles that define sustainable leadership.

1. Sustainable Leadership Lasts

One of the major characteristics of sustainable leadership is that it involves planning and preparing for succession—not just as an afterthought, but from the first day of the school leader's appointment. In the Hargreaves and Fink (2006) study, there were some rare glimpses of thoughtful and effective succession management and sustainable leadership. A certain school sampled built on its ebullient and optimistic principal's success in forming a democratically developed plan for school improvement by grooming his assistant principal to replace him when he retired.

However, the study showed that leadership succession is rarely successful. This is mainly because charismatic leaders are often followed by less-dynamic successors, who find it difficult to maintain the momentum of school improvement. Additionally, the study shows that leaders who turn around underperforming schools are usually transferred or promoted prematurely even before their improvements have had a chance to stick.

In the 30 or so years that Stewart Heights High School was under observation, we saw what is known as "revolving-door principalship" (MacMillan, 2000; Hargreaves et al., 2003), which is mostly found in today's reform-driven climate. In the early 1990s, Stewart Heights was drifting in terms of performance. It had an aging staff nostalgic about its former days as a "village school," who had never accepted the challenges that come with increasing urbanization and cultural diversity. The school's principal actually confessed that he did not have a particular objective for the school, but just wanted to buffer his teachers from the so-called "outside forces," so they could concentrate on classroom instruction. When the principal finally retired, the district appointed the dynamic, experienced, and abrasive Bill Matthews as his replacement.

Matthews was of the opinion that, no matter what, students came first. He communicated his expectations clearly, and was relentless in his determination to serve his students and the community. By the end of the third year, with Matthews at the helm, and after the school had made several curriculum changes, planned for school improvement, restructured the process of student guidance, and created a more welcoming environment, there was a dramatic increase in student and parent satisfaction. Then, abruptly, Matthews was promoted to a district leadership role and, with shortages in leadership surfacing across the district, his assistants were also transferred.

In the ensuing chaos, the district appointed first-time principal Jim West to the school. While West might have preferred to feel his way carefully, he and his ill-prepared assistants had to focus on implementing a newly mandated reform agenda. Within a few months, everything that Matthews had accomplished in school improvement had been undone. The traditional power blocs, such as the group of department heads who had dominated opinion before Matthews' arrival, reasserted their former authority, since West needed their support to ensure that there was compliance with the mandated reforms. West displayed indecisiveness, which led some of the teachers to regard him and his assistants as ineffectual. As Hargreaves and Fink reiterated, "nice people can't cope." In just three years, West was transferred. The school had had four principals in six years, and the staff became cynical.

As seen above, sustainable leadership requires that leaders pay serious attention to the issue of leadership succession. This can be achieved through grooming successors for them to continue with reforms, keeping successful leaders in schools much longer, especially if they are making great strides in promoting learning, resisting the urge to search for "irreplaceable charismatic heroes" to become the saviors of schools, requiring that all district and school improvement plans include succession plans, and slowing down the rate of principal turnover to avoid teachers becoming cynical about having to "wait out" all their leaders (Hargreaves & Fink, 2006).

2. Sustainable Leadership Spreads

A suitable way for leaders to leave a lasting legacy in their schools is to ensure that they share and help develop their vision with other school actors. Leadership succession in this sense therefore means more than grooming one's successor. It actually means distributing leadership throughout the school through its professional community so that others can carry the torch of school improvement after the current principal is gone (Spillane, Halverson, & Drummond, 2001).

One example is the founding principal of Durant, an alternative U.S. high school, who believed that the original vision of bringing about independent learning in real-life settings in the school would only survive if teachers, parents, and students shared in that vision. He emphasized dialogue and shared decision-making among school stakeholders, and the staff came to believe that they were all part of the administration. Even after the principal had retired, all the teachers and members of the school community continued their resistance of the standardizing district and state policies, holding on dearly to their founding vision by seeking waivers for their distinctive education program.

In contrast, Durant's neighbor, Sheldon High School, was at the time experiencing the full impact of "white flight" to the suburbs and magnet school competitors in the early 1980s. As a result, like Principal Gutierrez's school in the vignette at the beginning of the chapter, Sheldon experienced a major shift in its racial balance and intake of students with special needs. Most of the majority European American teaching staff felt frustrated in the face of these changes, and also shut out of crucial school decisions.

As a way of venting their frustrations and leadership impulses, the teachers turned to their union, which grew more assertive. The district in turn responded by appointing several autocratic leaders, who were selected in the hope that they could stand up to the union. The resulting standoff caused the school to become completely unable to respond effectively to its student population. The teachers argued that there was a lack of disciplinary support from the principal's office, and consequently refused to change their own traditional practices.

These two case studies serve to show that sustainable leadership cannot just be the responsibility of one person. The school is a highly complex institution, and no one leader can control everything without assistance (Fullan, 2001). In summary, sustainable leadership is and must be a shared responsibility. If we look back at the opening vignette, we see that Principal Gutierrez enlisted the parents in his efforts to get his school back on course. Monthly meetings in which parents discussed issues as basic as adequate nutrition and bedtimes went straight to the root of the problems, and put some of the onus of creating a healthy school on the community, rather than on the school leadership.

3. Sustainable Leadership Is Socially Just

Another aspect of sustainable leadership is that it aims to benefit all students and schools, and not just a few at the expense of the rest. Sustainable leadership is conscious of the fact that the so-called magnet, lighthouse, and charter schools and their leaders can have an impact on surrounding schools. It is also sensitive privileged communities "poaching" from the local leadership pool. Sustainable leadership therefore recognizes and takes full responsibility for the fact that schools in one way or another affect each other in interlinked webs of mutual influence (Baker & Foote, in press). In this aspect, and in cognizance of the above facts, sustainability is tied to social justice.

Hargreaves and Fink (2006) give an example of Blue Mountain High School, which went to great lengths to ensure that they did not raid all the best teachers, students, and leaders from nearby schools. The schools' leaders, in consultation with the school district and the other high school principals, operated on a quota system, which ensured that they would not draw disproportionately from any one school or age group of teachers in the district. Through this behavior of showing care to other schools, the principal exercised social justice and also avoided inviting envy and resentment from neighboring schools.

In sharp contrast, the one magnet school in the study, Barrett High School, grew at the expense of neighboring schools. The school was founded in the late 1980s to stem the tide of "white flight" out of the city by pursuing higher standards and selective intake of "appropriate" students and teachers from the other schools in the district. While *U.S. News* described the school as among the top 150 high schools in the U.S., some of its high-achieving students were actually drawn from a neighboring school. Eventually, the school was plagued by low attendance, high rates of violence, and a creativity-sapping curriculum that robbed teachers of their social mission and professional discretion. In the words of the two researchers, "by concentrating excellence in some specialized pockets, the district created a system of high standards for authentic learning and flexible teaching for the privileged magnet schools and their teachers but introduced 'soulless' standardization in the other schools."

We can therefore conclude that sustainable leadership is not just about maintaining improvement in one's own school, but school leaders who truly care about sustainability should accept responsibility for the schools and students and be aware that their actions have an effect on the wider environment.

In numerous instances, as we saw in the opening vignette, problems in schools are caused directly or indirectly by the socioeconomic situation of some or all of the students. Poverty is almost always accompanied by poor nutrition, poor sleep habits, inability of parents to help with homework, and lack of structured time at home. Principal Gutierrez's actions to create a better school environment will have far-reaching consequences if parents are able to change their home environments as a result of the discussions he instigated.

4. Sustainable Leadership Is Resourceful

The systems of sustainable leadership provide certain intrinsic rewards while at the same time offering extrinsic incentives that attract, motivate, and retain the best and brightest in the leadership pool. These systems provide time and opportunity for school leaders to network, support, and learn from one another, while at the same time coaching and mentoring their successors. Sustainable leadership is therefore described as "thrifty without being cheap." It carefully utilizes its resources to develop the talents of its educators instead of lavishing rewards on selected proven leaders. The systems of sustainable leadership take care of leaders while encouraging them to take care of themselves.

However, in the study, demands for reform, resource depletion, and the resultant rush to retire in all schools sampled led to rapid turnover of principals and serious reductions in assistant principals and middle-level leaders such as department heads. Additionally, school districts significantly reduced support from consultants and assistant superintendents, among other officials, leaving principals overwhelmed and alone. The culture of supervision and support for school leaders has mostly been replaced by "depersonalized demands" of test-based accountability.

As a consequence, teachers and administrators feel burned out by excessive demands and reduced resources, and may lack the physical energy or emotional capacity to build professional learning communities (Byrne, 1994). As we noted in an earlier chapter, school leaders' emotional health is a scarce but crucial resource. Therefore education reformers and policymakers may find that they push for short-term gains by mortgaging the entire future of school leadership.

Hargreaves and Fink give the example of Principal Charmaine Watson, who helped build a collaborative learning community at Talisman Park High School, but was suddenly transferred after only three years. She grieved that there was still work to be done. While she took the same inspirational drive and commitment to her next school, she found that in the new context of reduced resources and unrealistic implementation timelines, the system could no longer support collaboration and she was reduced to modeling optimism (Blackmore, 1996). Finally, the emotional strain took its toll and, after several stressful months, she retired early.

Under these reforms, principals in the study escaped to district administration and early retirement, or, in some cases, were even hospitalized under the pressure. In certain situations, they narrowed their role from leadership to management in order to cope. Eventually, leadership is only sustainable when it sustains the leaders themselves.

5. Sustainable Leadership Promotes Diversity

Leaders who promote sustainability cultivate and recreate environments that stimulate continuous improvement on a broad level. They enable people to adapt and prosper in increasingly complex environments by learning from each other's diverse practices (Capra, 1997). Most innovative schools create and promote this diversity. In the study, we find three such schools that have unfortunately regressed under the standardization reform agenda.

An instance of this situation led Durant Alternative School to standardize its teaching and student assessments away from school-developed history courses that previously engaged students of diverse backgrounds. Rather than build on shared school improvement, principals in these innovative schools found themselves having to force through implementation of mandated policies. These once-loved leaders may have attempted to encourage debate on these questionable change agendas, but many teachers still felt that they had sold their schools and souls to the districts and states.

Hargreaves and Fink (2006) state that standardization is the "enemy" of sustainability. Sustainable leadership cultivates and acknowledges many kinds of excellence in teaching, learning, and leading, while providing networks for sharing of these diverse kinds of excellence in cross-fertilizing the processes of school improvement (Louis & Kruse, 1995; McLaughlin & Talbert, 2001). In conclusion, sustainable leadership does not in any way impose standardized templates on entire communities.

6. Sustainable Leadership Is Activist

Standardization has increased the problems that traditional schools had. In the Hargreaves and Fink (2006) study, it turned the sampled schools into less-motivated versions of their former selves. Moreover, formerly innovative schools have lost their edge. However, Durant High School has proven most resilient not because of its strength or innovativeness as a learning community, but due to its leaders' activism (Oakes, Quartz, & Lipton, 2000). The school engages assertively with its wider environment in a pattern of mutual influence.

Over the years, Durant High School's brave new principal has actively utilized his personal and professional networks to forge strategic alliances with the immediate community in a dedicated campaign to ensure that the school's mission is preserved. The principal has written articles for both local and state newspapers, appeared on various radio and TV programs, and joined students and parents who symbolically protested in straitjackets outside the district offices. He has also organized several conferences discussing the adverse effects of high-stakes testing and has worked with his allies throughout the state to push for some sort of group variance from state tests. As a result of his efforts, his school got a temporary exclusion from state policy. Through these occurrences, we see that, in an unhelpful environment, sustainable leadership must include some sort of activism.

7. Systems Must Support Sustainable Leadership

From the examples given above, which were extracted from the study, most inspiring school leaders did more than manage change—they actively pursued and modeled a form of sustainable leadership. The long and short of developing sustainability is the commitment to and protection of deep learning in schools by attempting to ensure that school improvements last over time, especially after the charismatic leaders have left, by distributing leadership and responsibility, by taking into account the impact of their leadership on schools and communities in their neighborhood, by persisting with their vision and avoiding stress and burnout, by promoting and bringing about diverse approaches to school reform instead of standardized prescriptions for teaching and learning, and by activism.

While most school leaders want to achieve goals that matter and inspire others to assist them to accomplish those goals so as to leave a lasting legacy, they are often not responsible for their school's failure, since most of the blame rests with the systems in which they lead. This is why the study suggests that sustainable leadership cannot be left to individuals, irrespective of talent or dedication. Therefore, for us to institute change that matters, spreads, and lasts, we must ensure that the systems in which leaders work must make sustainability a priority.

Past, Present, and Future of Sustainable Leadership

Sustainable leadership builds on the past in a bid to create a better future for schools. This is against most educational change theories, which do not find a place for the past, since the "arrow of change" is thought to move only in a forward direction. Past problems are generally either ignored or overcome in a rush to get to the future (Hargreaves & Goodson, 2004; Goodson, 2001).

Hargreaves (2007) finds that, for those leaders attracted or addicted to change, the past is seen as a repository of regressive and irrational resistance for those whom they consider as favoring the *status quo* or emotionally incapable of letting go of old habits and beliefs. These leaders consider the past to be a dark era of weak or poor leadership practices that leave negative legacies, models of schooling, or "uninformed" professional judgment in classroom instruction that gets in the way of modernization (Fullan, 2003).

Hargreaves (2007) is of the opinion that reform based only on the present or future becomes the antithesis of sustainability. Sustainable development has the characteristic of respecting, protecting, preserving, and renewing all the valuable elements of the past and learning from those elements to build a better future. One way of getting in touch with the past is to see teacher resistance and nostalgia among members of the profession not as obstacles to change, but as sources of wisdom (Goodson, Moore, & Hargreaves, 2006). Change theory must strive to build proposals that are built upon past legacies instead of trying to ignore or obliterate them. While contemplating changes, sustainable leadership calls on leaders to look to the past for precedents that might be reinvented, refined, or used as evidence of policies that have succeeded or failed before.

However, the above proposal does not mean that leaders live in the past, but value and learn from it. Abrahamson (2004) calls for an end to what he terms "creative destruction," where leaders see the need to obliterate the past in order to create a future that usually leads to endless back-and-forth movements, increased employee burnout, and the unnecessary waste of expertise and memory that had been accumulated over time. He proposes a creative recombination of the best parts of the past in a craftsman-like manner that is resourceful and renewing.

Through sustainable leadership, leaders should find new structures, technology, and people by finding, redeploying, reusing, and recombining mismatched parts that have been lying around in the school's organizational "basement" (Abrahamson, 2004). Sustainable leadership and improvement is concerned with both the future and the past. It refuses to treat people's knowledge, careers, and experience as disposable waste rather than as valuable and renewable resources. In conclusion, sustainable leadership does not blindly endorse the past, but respects and learns from it.

Four Forms of Forgetting That Affect Sustainable Leadership

The main challenge to educational reform is not to retreat to the past but to build an intelligent relationship that acknowledges its existence, understands its meaning, and learns from it. However, in certain instances, an organization may choose to forget elements of the past. De Holan and Phillips (2004) found that there are four kinds of "organizational forgetting." They categorized these kinds of forgetting based on whether they were intentional or unintentional or whether they applied to long established or recently acquired knowledge. De Holan and Phillips summarized the options for organizational forgetting and their outcomes as follows:

> Some companies forget what they need to know, incurring huge costs in replacing the lost knowledge. Other organizations fail to forget the things that they should and they remain trapped by the past, relying on uncompetitive technologies, dysfunctional corporate cultures, or untenable assumptions about their markets. Successful companies are able to move quickly and adapt to rapidly changing environments by being skilled not only at learning, but also at forgetting.
>
> (De Holan & Philips, 2004b)

I. Dissipation

Dissipation occurs when new knowledge is brought into the organization, but there is no goodwill or ability to make it stick in people's memory to enable the organization to become or remain effective. Dissipation is easily prevented by passing on the new knowledge and sharing it with others. Most charismatic leaders find this a difficult task.

In two of the four innovative schools sampled in the Spencer Foundation, charismatic leadership was employed in their founding periods. However, these charismatic leaders failed to deal well with the psychological turmoil that accompanies succession. This characteristic can be seen in most leaders who refuse to face succession or the ultimate mortality that these succession events anticipate.

Hargreaves (2007) gives two examples of dissipation. The first occurred where the founding principal in one of Canada's most innovative high schools in the 1970s left "shoes that were too big to be filled." She was a calm and guiding leader who helped rebuild the once fractious and fragmented school, only to have all her efforts undone when she was transferred to another school before she could groom a successor. In the second example, the son of a policeman, who brought about an energetic and interactive staffroom culture, was succeeded by a former guidance counselor whose laid-back approach neither blended with nor built on the work of his predecessor. In both cases, new knowledge was never passed on to successors and consequently dissipation occurred.

De Holan and Phillips suggest that it is not only through mentoring or succession that new knowledge is passed; it can also be transmitted when leaders strive to explicitly connect it to people's existing knowledge. In one of the schools in the study, there was an ability to adapt innovations such as computer technology by relating them to the school's long-standing experience and technically creative past.

2. Degradation

This kind of forgetting occurs when well-established knowledge is lost accidentally (De Holan & Philips, 2004). Knowledge degradation among professionals commonly occurs when there is a high turnover of critical personnel who are unable or unwilling to create collective knowledge that would enable a successful collective action without the professionals' presence or immediate supervision. Frequent leadership succession in periods of less than five years across most of the study schools caused erasure of organizational memory, or the incapacity of incoming leaders to understand and draw reasonable inferences from it.

High turnover in teaching staff also brings about similar difficulties, mostly in innovative schools, where distinctive goals, practices, and structures keep being reviewed or renewed every time new teachers come and existing ones leave. The sudden downsizing or elimination of "waste" in middle-level management can also cause degradation, since management losses and budget cuts in the school districts, as evident in the Spencer study, reduce the capacity of middle-level managers to support the principals in their running of schools.

3. Suspension

While most of the organizational forgetting is usually accidental, some of it is quite deliberate and is part of a willful strategy to bring about change and improvement. This is reflective of the earlier statement by De Holan and Phillips (2004b) that organizations need to be skilled not only at learning, but also at forgetting. Collins and Porras (1994) found that one of the factors that leads to long-standing success in business is the capacity of companies to engage in diverse experimentation, know when to keep successful innovations, and know when to "forget" the rest. This is what Peter Drucker calls "organized abandonment" (Drucker, 2001).

According to Drucker, the purpose of this abandonment is to free up resources that are no longer producing results. A good change leader puts everything on trial on a regular basis to check on its viability. Organized abandonment is therefore important in getting rid of practices that reduce effectiveness or impede the introduction of superior ones. However, Drucker argues that abandonment cannot be successful if it is just a vague intention. This is because it is hard to let go of things spontaneously. To effectively practice organized abandonment, there is a need to have regular meetings where tough and focused decisions are made on what to leave behind and free up space for innovation ahead.

There is need for organized abandonment in the educational policy in the U.S. This can be achieved by cutting back on the curriculum, giving exemptions to schools that succeed in using other designs, reducing the load of external accountability, minimizing the impact of external testing on students and their teachers, transferring many of the administrative tasks that burden teachers to other personnel, and improving infrastructure in schools that serve poor communities to make them better suited for student learning (Teachernet, 2005).

While it is easy and desirable to abandon tasks and practices that one never wanted in the first place, research has found that it is harder to let go of those practices that they found comfortable. The Spencer study gives the example of certain Canadian schools, where several mandated policies, such as the demand for meetings in the work-to-rule action and the policy of "destreaming" or "detracking," were removed. Most teachers were delighted, as they felt that the policies had been forcing them into difficult and unfamiliar practices. However, none of the schools and teachers found it easy to abandon practices that they liked and found comfortable. Hargreaves (2007) suggests that, to achieve this, a much more organized, systematic, and focused process is required to make organizational abandonment feasible, deliberate, and desirable.

4. Purging

It is a good trait to forget, or at least unlearn, some of our poor practices, bad habits, and outdated ways of doing things that do not meet the needs of changing cultures and times, through systematic organizational purging. However, unlearning practices we feel are effective and exchanging them for new ones where our initial competence is low can be uncomfortable. The temptation to cling to the past is normal and understandable.

Eventually, all change brings about loss. When what is lost is comfort and competence, that loss will understandably be mourned, and probably resisted (Marris, 1974). However, Hargreaves finds that some purging of organizational memory is unproductive, especially where the old and experienced are deliberately disvalued. According to him, when purging involves teaching literacy, assessment processes and attitudes, communication procedures with parents, or approaches to school administration, there are two core issues that must be considered. First, we have to ask whether the areas for unlearning have been diagnosed correctly, and whether this unlearning is educationally desirable or just politically expedient. Second, we need to find out whether the process of knowledge conversion is managed in a supportive or a traumatic manner.

There is a need for schools to forget the right things in the right manner. Where the above two core issues are not addressed, school leaders will likely find themselves facing the formidable obstacle of teacher nostalgia, where teachers retreat to the past due to their present feelings of embitterment and exclusion.

Hargreaves gives an example of a group of teachers in one of the Canadian schools, which was the embodiment of bitterness and nostalgia. The members of this "kaffeeklatsch" of older teachers (many of them department heads) regularly met before school in a staffroom corner, where they recalled how the students in the school had changed from being mostly European American students, who had fewer problems and a lot of money. These students apparently came from comfortable homes, were ready and able to learn, and identified with the school's family culture. In sharp contrast, the teachers felt that current students, being more diverse and less affluent, had far too many problems to deal with than earlier generations.

These new students came from single-parent homes, which had problems finding food, clothes, and basic amenities. More students in the school required ESL support, and did not consider the school the social hub of their lives. Other teachers lamented that there were increasing discipline problems, poor work habits, and low concentration levels. Others felt that students' attitudes toward authority had been negatively affected by the lack of parental guidance. An English teacher who had 33 years of teaching experience could not imagine today's students learning the classics such as Shakespeare. A coaching colleague was unhappy that, for the first time in the school's history, they didn't have a senior football team, since there weren't enough students from a background interested in football.

This nostalgia was mostly prompted by teachers' concerns that government reforms were moving too fast (Goodson, Moore, & Hargreaves, 2006). There was also a feeling among teachers that they were being used as scapegoats for the failures in the public system. Other reported opinions were that parents were anxious that their children would not measure up and therefore didn't want to be involved, that education reforms were underfunded, teachers lacked control over students, reforms didn't help students, the entire reform process was too "mechanical," and that there were too many unanswered questions in education reform.

Hargreaves states that all nostalgia is a recollection of the past that becomes infected by an embittered experience of an unpleasant present. The nostalgia that teachers have for professional autonomy and lost missions is characterized by a backdrop of contemporary reform calls against narrowed school vision, standardization of education, and lost autonomy. There is also nostalgia for European American students, who wanted to learn in what Hargreaves refers to as a "more professionally intimate" environment, which sharply contrasts with the contemporary classroom characterized by growing racial diversity, increasing numbers of poor students, and a wide range of students with special educational needs.

Hargreaves is of the opinion that the reason large-scale educational reform often fails is because it dismisses nostalgia or derogation of teachers' professional pasts. While dismissal of nostalgia may appeal to public opinion and prejudice, it alienates the profession and dismisses the missions it holds dear. Anti-nostalgia is ethically contentious and strategically problematic since it amplifies the widespread resistance to change, and worsens entrenched and embittered nostalgia among older teachers who feel that change blocks their efficiency. As a reaction, the experienced teachers seek refuge from the present by romancing the past.

The emphasis of reform should be for the experienced teachers to improve their practices. Purging and other acts of forced forgetting have the impact of throwing educators back into the false memory of defensive nostalgia, which leads to the wasting of the teachers' wisdom as professional elders and makes them demoralized and disgruntled.

Renewing the Past

As we have previously seen, overconfident reformers are always prone to dismiss the past, forgetting that the targets of reform are always inclined to romanticize it. While present-day change addicts are trapped in what Hargreaves (2007) calls a "narcotic bubble" that insulates them from romanticism of the past, the challenge that confronts most leaders is creating a more successful and sustainable future. Leaders therefore need to acknowledge the past, and preserve it and learn from it where possible. However, while we should engage with the past, we should not retreat to it. In addition, it is prudent to remember the past but avoid distorting it through nostalgia or anti-nostalgia.

The past remains a subject for intelligent and not blind endorsement. It should be understood and connected to change in the future through "coherent life narratives." It should serve as a motivator and not a museum. In the words of the great English romantic poet William Wordsworth, "let us learn from the past, to profit the present, and from the present to live better in the future." Sustainable leadership therefore needs both a rear-view mirror and a windshield. Without the mirror, it is possible that things will keep overtaking us. While the past can be a point of pride and something to be honored, it can be a painful one marked by conflict, grievances, and mistreatment, which in this case means that it has to be healed to avoid repeating mistakes. This affliction of repetitive change has been the downfall of many leaders and their policies.

Through sustainable leadership, societies can pass knowledge from one generation to another by effectively managing succession and by distributing this responsibility widely. Hargreaves states that the past is part of our future. Prosperity for all seems to be a proper goal, but we must ensure that it is not achieved at too great a cost. Instead, sustainability and survival must be our main priorities. Standardization policies and target-driven competitiveness can do nothing to bring about sustainability in the long run. This knowledge and information society should be structured in such a way that it can coexist with a strong and supportive welfare state. In Hargreaves' (2007) words, "the lion can lie down with the lamb." Should prosperity and security also co-exist side by side? Hargreaves gives a fitting summary:

The last two decades have been dominated by "Anglo-Saxon" strategies of soulless standardization, measurement-driven improvement and forceful intervention that have incurred only widespread poverty and inequity as well as other social waste. It is time for other more sustainable sensibilities to take their place and the climate is certainly ready for it.

Summary

Leaders develop sustainability through their approach, commitment to, and protection of deep learning in their schools. It is also determined by how they sustain themselves and those around them to promote and support deep learning, how they are able to sustain themselves in this endeavor in a way that ensures they persist with their vision and avoid burnout, how they ensure that the improvements they bring last over time, especially after their departure, how considerate they are of the impact their leadership has on schools around them, how they encourage and perpetuate diversity rather than standardized teaching and learning in their schools, and, finally, how they engage with their environments through activism.

It is a common trait that most school leaders want to do things that matter, inspire others to join them in their vision, and leave a lasting legacy. As earlier stated, in most cases, it is not leaders who let their schools down, but the systems through which they lead. Sustainable leadership therefore calls for a collective effort from all leaders and stakeholders in the school. Additionally, if change is to matter, spread, or last, sustainable leadership must be a fundamental priority of the education systems in which school leaders work.

Discussion Questions

1.   The threat to educational sustainability in the U.S., according to Hargreaves, comes from short-term targets, endless and meaningless testing, and the pursuit of quick political ends. If you were to design a sustainable educational system in the U.S., what structures would you put in place to counter each of these threats?
2.   Segregation in schools according to race, ethnicity, and social class is worse than at any time since 1954. In the vignette at the beginning of this chapter, Principal Gutierrez instituted monthly meetings to try to bridge the dividing lines in his school. What are two more ideas he could implement to do this?
3.   The chapter notes that there is a need for schools "to forget the right things in the right manner." Give three examples of things a school should "forget." In what manner should they forget them?
4.   Eighty-five to ninety percent of teachers in the U.S. are European American, and monolingual in English. However, by 2050, people of color will outnumber European Americans in the U.S. What are three sustainable initiatives that could be instituted now to prevent friction in the future?
5.   Compare and contrast the case studies involving the Durant and Sheldon high schools. What could the principal at Sheldon High School have done differently to prevent the European American teachers from insulating themselves from the changes? Give two concrete examples.

Activities

1. In small groups, decide on the issues affecting the school system in your area. Place the issues into short-term, medium-term, and long-term categories. Then create structures that address the long-term issues, focusing on sustainability, and present these to the larger group.
2. Draw a map of your city or area, indicating schools and other educational institutions, and delineating racial, social class, and economic divisions. What initiatives are in place to bridge the gaps? Where should future initiatives be placed in order to best meet the needs of all members of the community?

Selected Readings

Bolman, L.G. & Deal, T.E. (2008). *Reframing organizations: Artistry, choice, and leadership* (4th ed.) San Francisco, CA: Jossey-Bass.

Delagardelle, M. L. (2008). The Lighthouse Inquiry: Examining the role of school board leadership in the improvement of student achievement. In T. L. Alsbury (Ed.), *The future of school board governance*, (pp. 191–223). Lanham, MD: Rowman & Littlefield.

Hargreaves, A. (2009). Leadership succession and sustainable improvement. *School Administrator, 66*(11), 10–15

Hargreaves, A. (2009). Sustainable leadership. In B. Davies (Ed.), *The essentials of school leadership*. London: Sage.

Chapter 9

Invitational Leadership
Developing a School Culture of Trust, Respect, and Hope

Angela Murray, an art teacher at Blue Ridge Elementary, came to Principal Frank Anderson one day with a problem. While using a shared computer in the staff room, she had discovered an email exchange between two other teachers that made snarky comments about her off-putting mannerisms and even the way she dressed. Ms. Murray was hurt. However, even though she'd discovered the emails by accident, she didn't feel comfortable confronting the teachers because of privacy issues.

Principal Anderson sympathized with Ms. Murray's problem, but he also realized that she was not wholly blameless. The art teacher's social skills were somewhat lacking, and her creative outfits were causing merriment among students and teachers alike. She was a relatively new teacher, and a few small changes, he thought, might make her job easier.

Principal Anderson had a dilemma. Should he just deal with Ms. Murray, and ignore the email exchange, which was certainly private? Or should he bring in the other teachers and lecture them on respect? Which direction would create the best future for the school?

Invitational Leadership as Comprehensive Design

Invitational leadership is a new comprehensive model that promises to guide today's education leaders through complex times. Designed by Purkey and Siegel (2003), it is based on the invitational theory of practice. Purkey (1992) had earlier stated that invitational theory is "a collection of assumptions that seek to explain phenomena and provide a means of intentionally summoning people to realize their relatively boundless potential in all areas of worthwhile human endeavor." He added that the purpose of invitational leadership:

> is to address the entire global nature of human existence and opportunity, and to make life a more exciting, satisfying and enriching experience. Unlike in any other system reported in professional literature, it provides an extensive framework for a variety of policies, places, programs, and processes that fit with its basic components.
>
> (p. 5)

Invitational leadership as a model has a comprehensive design that includes many vital elements needed for success in today's educational platforms. Contemporary school principals are now, more than ever, required to go far beyond their daily tasks of making budgets, preparing schedules, and dealing with student behavior and angry parents. According to Bolman and Deal (2002), the most crucial responsibility for the school leader is not to answer every question fully or make every decision correctly, but to serve a more powerful and durable role when they act as models and catalysts for values such as caring, justice, excellence, and faith. These values, often described as "servant values," are an inherent element of the invitational leadership model.

Review of the available literature today firmly supports the need for changes in leadership so as to adequately meet the needs of current educational institutions (Bolman & Deal, 2002; Day, Harris, & Hadfield, 2001; Kouzes & Posner, 2003; Rosener, 1990). Halpern (2004) opined that rapid changes often require new leadership styles: leaders with the necessary knowledge to achieve goals and those who can keep a school afloat amid the uncertainty of continuous change. The need for a change in leadership is further related to the need for an ethic of caring, which is strongly supported in current literature (Bolman & Deal, 1997; Bolman & Deal, 2002; Grogan, 2003; Halpin, 2003; Patton, 1997; Tallon, 1997).

Grogan (2003) stated that leadership is predicated on caring about those the leader serves. Invitational leadership as a model exemplifies caring as an integral part of its primary principles and fundamental beliefs. Halpin (2003) described social capital, which is the crucible of trust, as the ability of people to work together for common purposes. Invitational leadership builds on the growth of social capital by caring for and supporting other peoples' efforts and initiatives.

Invitational leadership is comprehensive in nature, since it consists of many positive and essentially sound educational elements, which, if adopted and well laid out, can serve as the leadership model that will impact positively on the diverse and changing needs of today's educational institutions.

Invitational Education Theory

Popularly referred to as IET, invitational education theory is simply invitational leadership in action in the school setting. Barth (1991) noted that improving the interactions among teachers and between teachers and school principals plays a significant role in the process of school improvement. According to researchers Purkey and Novak (1996), IET can offer a systematic approach to the educational process and provide strategies that make schools more inviting.

IET also provides educators with principles of practicing behavior that can integrate—creatively and ethically—research, theory, and practice. The objective of IET is to build schools with a climate that invite everyone in the school to experience success together. Strahan and Purkey (1992) state that the school climate should in one way or another reflect a sense of excitement and satisfaction for both students and staff.

In their model on IET, Purkey and Novak (1984) suggest that educators should take on their tasks from a consistent stance of trust, respect, optimism, and intentionality. Literature on the role of school climate and its impacts is widespread, with most findings supporting the notion that, as a variable, it has an effect in improving student achievement and also on relationships within the school (Anderson, 1982; Brookover et al., 1977; Lezotte, Hathaway, & Miller, 1980; Stronge & Jones, 1991).

The effectiveness of leadership lies in personal resources of people. Lately, leadership styles have become a chief concern among school leaders as a means to produce patterns of interactions that are meaningful and make participants feel attached to organizational events.

Comprehensive Description of Invitational Leadership

As today's school leaders seek to acquire the skills and knowledge that are necessary for effectiveness in current educational institutions, they should realize that there are no simple answers or shortcuts to achieving leadership excellence. Bolman and Deal (2002) state:

> When you look at examples of effective leadership, it becomes clear that it's not related to any one style, personality, gender or ethnicity. Many pathways point to effective leadership. But some qualities are consistent across effective leaders.
>
> (p. 1)

The important task however, is to find the right combination of qualities and characteristics that will consistently provide the leader with skills and knowledge required to succeed on a regular basis. Purkey and Siegel (2003) made an attempt to blend several leadership qualities, values, and principles when they built the invitational leadership theory. They described the model as shifting from emphasizing control and dominance to focusing on connectedness, cooperation, and communication.

The model aims at "inviting" all interested stakeholders to succeed (Day, Harris, & Hadfield, 2001; Purkey, 1992; Purkey & Novak, 1996; Purkey & Siegel, 2003; Stillion & Siegel, 2005). Day, Harris, and Hadfield (2001) define "invitations" as messages communicated to people, which inform them that they are valued, able, responsible, and worthwhile. The messages are sometimes transmitted by interpersonal action, but are mostly disseminated through the institution's policies, programs, practices, and physical environments.

In the vignette at the beginning of this chapter, Principal Anderson is faced with a situation in which trust has been breached, and there is a lack of open communication among the parties. The invitational model would suggest that he find a way to bring Ms. Murray and the gossiping teachers together in a nonthreatening environment, to enable all sides of the conversation to be heard.

As the vignette illustrates, invitational leadership has a highly personal and ethical character, which is included within its modular constructs. Stillion and Siegel (2005) found that invitational leaders strive to create an environment where stakeholders are able to achieve their goals and potential while simultaneously participating in the shared vision and mission of the entire group. These authors further showed that invitational leadership intentionally creates positive physical workplaces and establishes policies that reflect the optimism of the leader, both of which lead to trust and respect among the school actors. These core values and principles are similar to those of ethical leadership and Greenleaf's servant leadership theory (Stillion & Siegel, 2005).

Invitational leadership is based upon four basic assumptions, which exemplify the characteristics of invitational leaders. These assumptions are optimism, respect, trust, and intentionality. Day et al. (2001) described them as follows:

Optimism – The belief that people have untapped potential for growth and development.
Respect – The recognition that every person is an individual of worth.
Trust – The possession of confidence in the abilities, integrity, and responsibilities of ourselves and others (Purkey & Siegel, 2003).
Intention – A decision to purposely act in a certain way so as to achieve and carry out a set goal, (Day et. al, 2001). Stillion and Siegel (2005) define it as having knowledge of what we intend to bring about as well as how we intend it to happen, thus giving clarity and direction to our work.

Let's look at the above assumptions as they relate to the vignette. If Principal Anderson was cynical, he might dismiss Ms. Murray as a hopeless case, and laugh along with the other teachers. However, the invitational model shifts the focus from negative to positive. Using the above assumptions, Principal Anderson would understand that Ms. Murray was still a work in progress, and he would believe in her potential. He would realize that her creativity and quirkiness were, if tapped appropriately, assets rather than liabilities, and would attempt to transmit that notion to the other teachers. He would work with Ms. Murray, helping her hone goals that would make her a better teacher.

According to social reformer John Gardner (1990), the prime function of a leader is to keep hope alive. Stillion and Siegel (2005) state that an optimistic leader is one who can reframe problematic situations as opportunities and view the impossible as merely difficult.

Judging from today's challenges and high accountability standards, optimism could be a dynamic element to ensure success for educational organizations. Stillion and Siegel (2005) were of the opinion that optimistic leaders embrace both the challenges and change, while expecting that the outcome will be positive. Therefore, today's school leaders and other stakeholders need to experience the positive outcomes that optimism may bring.

Respect is one of the most innate needs of human nature (Purkey, 1992). Purkey stated that people are valuable, able, and responsible, and thus should be treated with respect. Respect in other stakeholders shows a basic belief in the worth and value of fellow teachers, students, parents, and school leaders. Respect among organizational members leads to an inviting and inclusive workplace where diversity is seen as the norm and every individual has capacity to flourish (Stillion & Siegel, 2005).

Trust is closely related to respect. Purkey and Siegel (2003) define it as having confidence in the abilities, integrity, and responsibilities of both ourselves and others. Trust is an important value, which contributes directly to the success of an organization. On the other hand, lack of trust is a barrier to cohesive teamwork and efforts. Lencioni (2002) found that trust is at the heart of any functioning cohesive team. In its absence, teamwork is all but impossible. Therefore, building trust is quite a critical element that any successful leader should have.

Intentionality is another vital element in the invitational leadership model. Stillion and Siegel, (2005) suggested that knowledge of what we intend to bring about and how we intend it to happen gives us clarity and direction in our work. Therefore, the development and maintenance of specific and clear intentions facilitates organizational growth and success. As Purkey (1992) stated, intentionality can serve as a tremendous asset for educators and others in their professions, since it acts as a constant reminder of what is truly important in their service. Invitational leaders are therefore required to be purposefully intentional in their work and their endeavors together with all stakeholders.

In addition, Purkey and Siegel (2003) suggested a framework through which schools can become more "invitational" by concentrating on five areas that contribute to either success or failure: policies, programs, places, processes, and people. They articulated that each of the above elements contributes to the creation of a positive school climate and, in the long run, a healthy and successful school.

The personality of a place is noticeable to observers at the first glance. It is immediately apparent when an environment is empty, sterile, and lifeless or when, in contrast, it is warm, exciting, and filled with the personalities of the inhabitants. Purkey (1992) states that places are the easiest to change, since they are the most visible part of any environment. Places also offer a direct opportunity for immediate improvement, since they are quite visible, easy to promote in a positive manner, and are more readily managed aspects of the organization's image.

Policies are also a component of success or failure in invitational leadership. School leaders must determine if their policies restrict, confine, and squeeze out all sense of individuality or whether they create productive opportunities for the institution (Fowler, 2004). School policies that are both successful and create a positive school culture seek to encourage a win/win result. Stephen Covey (1989) described a win/win as a mindset that continuously seeks to benefit people mutually in all their interactions. Schools that develop such policies create a cooperative rather than competitive arena.

Development of appealing programs is another element in Purkey and Siegel's (2003) framework for creating a positive and successful organization. More often than not, school leaders are guilty of giving very few options. Hansen (1998) states that students often feel "disinvited" in school, due to the fact that they are often overlooked. In such circumstances, no one cares enough to encourage them to participate in sports or other school activities, they receive test papers with a grade without any additional comments, and their absence is rarely, if ever, noticed by their teachers. Hansen explains that such students suffer from a caring disability, since educators did not care to invite them to participate in school life.

Witcher (1993) found that schools with a positive school culture appear to make greater efforts to provide a variety of creative and attractive programs. Rigorous and comprehensive academic courses taught by outstanding teachers serve to increase the effectiveness of the instructional program while raising the standards for academic achievement (Edmonds, 1979; McCombs & Whisler, 1997).

Another important component of the invitational leadership model is processes. In most schools, the participation process is confined to "here's the deal, take it or leave it" (Cleveland, 2002). Cleveland opined that some school leaders feel the need to be presumed to be in charge. However, those leaders who make the effort to nurture a successful school culture seem to be more aware of the need to include as many stakeholders in as many of the decision-making processes as possible. Schools that have a positive school climate encourage decision-making through participation, cooperation, and collaboration. In this manner, students feel encouraged to take responsibility, be involved, and speak with their own voices.

The final component of Purkey and Siegel's (2003) framework is the people aspect. The most crucial element for building a successful school is the people who comprise the school and its facets. She adds that people are the one resource most guaranteed to make a difference in the creation of a positive school culture. Hansen also noted that investment in people often results in effective change. Therefore, we find that involvement of people in many activities that require cooperation is an excellent way to assist individuals to become part of an effective team. Involvement is also a good starting point in developing a more positive working and learning environment. Hansen noted that it is very important to provide people with the recognition that they have already earned.

Another aspect of meeting people's needs in the organization is the formation of relationships (Bruffee, 1999; Katzenbach & Smith, 2003; Lencioni, 2002; Tallon, 1997). These positive relationships are an integral part of creating a successful school. Earlier research stated that:

> Every child deserves to learn in a school that is inviting, academically challenging, and safe. The overall ambiance of the school and the quality of instruction are better enhanced as the school develops a concordant relationship among the students, parents, teachers, and administrators.
>
> (Kelly et al., 2008, p. 62)

The framework described above is often referred to as the "five P's" of invitational leadership. Purkey and Siegel (2003) suggest that these five P's are the means by which leaders "invite" others professionally. They find that these P's are highly significant for their separate and combined influence on invitational leadership in the organizational setting. The two authors affirm the importance of the five P's in their statement that their combination offers an almost limitless number of opportunities for the invitational leader, since they address the total culture or ecosystem of any organization. These P's also significantly help in making invitational leadership a unique and holistic leadership model (Stillion & Siegel, 2005). It is the connection between the four basic assumptions and the five P's that makes the invitational leadership model comprehensive.

Whittaker Middle School in Portland, Oregon, provides an excellent example of invitational leadership in practice (Brewster, 2003). The school had been chosen as one of 14 schools that needed "emergency action." Its test scores were low, and during one school year, half the staff left, and the school went through three principals.

Principals Tom Pickett and Lynn Beudefeldt were chosen to restructure the school and lead it out of the morass (Brewster, 2003). Pickett brought Student Management Specialist Cottrell White on board to help with the restructuring effort. White's focus was trust among stakeholders. He noted, "I have always been interested in the role of trust in the process of student learning and achievement. I have had many discussions [with the principal] about how it feels to be a staff member and what it means to be trusted (Brewster, 2003)." The Trust Evaluation Committee he helped establish allowed each staff member to present ideas without fear of reprisal. It also chose two co-facilitators to work with the staff to promote trust. As a result of White's efforts, the school was able to qualify for a Comprehensive School Reform grant, which was contingent upon staff support and agreement to work together toward agreed goals. The result was increased test scores and higher morale and cohesiveness among the staff.

Invitational Leadership Compared with Other Leadership Models

Invitational leadership shares with participative/distributed leadership a belief in promoting active participation of all interested stakeholders and also on the fundamentals of moral/ethical leadership. However, closer scrutiny reveals that invitational leadership is more inclusive and holistic, since it addresses the "total environment" in which leaders function. While invitational leadership believes in allowing active participation of all organizational members, it also seeks to achieve a balance of authority and influence throughout the same organization (Day, Harris, & Hadfield, 2001; Purkey, 1992; Purkey & Novak, 1996; Purkey & Siegel, 2003; Stillion & Siegel, 2005).

If we look back at the opening story through the lens of invitational leadership, we can see that Principal Anderson has an opportunity to influence many facets of the school environment by dealing with the situation holistically. By talking to and working with Ms. Murray, he will be influencing her teaching and her impact on the students. By meeting with the emailing teachers, he has the opportunity to create a healthier staff environment. And merely by agreeing to tackle a situation another leader might view as petty, he shows that he is interested in the wellbeing of the entire school.

The leadership styles of transformational and servant leadership have been among the best received and most highly acclaimed over the last few decades (Davis, 2003; Leithwood & Duke, 1999; Leithwood, Jantzi, & Steinbach, 2000a, 2000b; Spears & Lawrence, 2004; Yukl, 2006). In both models, there are similar principles that call upon leaders to lead in an exemplary manner. As with invitational leadership, these models attempt to help leaders to support their followers in empowering ways (Davis, 2003; Farling, Stone, & Winston, 1999; Hoyle, 2002; Sergiovanni, 2000; Spears & Lawrence, 2004).

Invitational leaders, according to Stillion and Siegel (2005), accept the basic tenet of servant leadership that those who would lead must be ready and willing to serve, but they go beyond this premise in their attempt to describe the values and roles that they must serve in their organizations.

Invitational leadership, in truth, holds many of the same beliefs and tenets that describe both transformational and servant leadership. One such similarity is that of forming and sharing a vision. Purkey and Siegel (2003) suggested that invitational leaders seek to invite their associates to share in a vision of greatness and offer them a vivid but compelling picture of human endeavor. The three leadership types also share the elements of trust and respect. Purkey and Siegel (2003) in their invitational leadership model state that trust is critical to invitational leadership since it acknowledges the interdependence of human beings. Further, the two authors delineated the importance of respect in their model in their statement that:

nothing is more important to invitational leadership than the respect for people – the belief that we and our associates are able, valuable, and responsible, and should be treated accordingly.

(p. 7)

Another shared component between invitational leadership and the two models is that of morals and ethics. Invitational leadership is described by Purkey and Siegel as being at heart a moral activity, intentionally expressing respect and trust in the leaders themselves and in others, both personally and professionally. In a similar manner, it seeks to empower followers by asking others in the organization to meet their goals as a condition for their own success. In other words, encouraging others in their quest for self-fulfillment is a characteristic embedded in the invitational leadership model. The authors conclude that invitational leadership is a mutual commitment between colleagues, instead of a series of orders issued from the top down.

While we see many shared components between the invitational leadership model and participative, transformational, and servant leadership models, there are also a few intrinsic and decisive differences. First of these are the twin elements of optimism and intentionality. The five P's that contribute to success or failure are also unique to the invitational model. As earlier seen, optimism and intentionality are viewed as important characteristics for effective leaders. The focused effort on values and principles that apply to policies, programs, places, processes, and people are also important for effectiveness in leadership. We then find that these important and unique qualities serve to make the invitational leadership model quite an excellent choice especially in these times of critical need and increased accountability for school leaders (Day et al., 2001; Purkey, 1992; Purkey & Novak, 1996; Purkey & Siegel, 2003; Stillion & Siegel, 2005).

The Case for the Invitational Leadership Model

Earlier, we touched lightly on the problems that have presented themselves in the U.S. education sector, particularly in the eyes of school leaders. We have also seen evidence from several literature reviews that have substantiated the tremendous need for direction in school leadership and that have involved numerous characteristics of what researchers consider "effective" leadership (Caldwell & Hayward, 1998; Davis, 2003; Fullan & Miles, 1992; Furman, 2004, Hallinger & Heck, 1999; Muijs & Harris, 2003; Schein, 2000). There is also a rising need for leadership that will transcend all previous models and theories (Bolman & Deal, 2002; Day et al., 2001; Kouzes & Posner, 2003; Rosener, 1990).

This need for leadership that transcends previous models is common in various literatures. Many of the concerns raised include increased standards for accountability issues, the need for effective leadership that will suffice during these progressively difficult times, the need for growth in organizational health, perception of the leader as a change agent, and the creation and development of a positive school culture.

Many researchers are now calling for a more participatory approach to leadership in these difficult times in education. Several challenges (e.g., cost containment, public accountability, globalization, integration of technology, and measurement of student outcomes) require more participatory forms of leadership than those exhibited in the past. In addition, Day et al. (2001) found that the evidence available is sufficient to suggest that the existing theories of leadership don't sufficiently reflect or explain the current practice of effective leaders.

There is unanimity among the above-mentioned authors that most of the literature available supports a person-centered philosophy that mostly emphasizes the improvement of teaching and learning by having high expectation of others. These authors affirm that current leadership theories of leadership are inadequate to meet the needs of current day leaders. We therefore find that, as public scrutiny and accountability standards increase, a change in leadership theory appears to be warranted.

In addition to the above challenges, there is growing demand for today's schools to become institutions of academic excellence and also for schools that serve all interested stakeholders (Bolman & Deal, 2002; Grogan, 2003; Halpin, 2003). Bolman and Deal (2002) articulated the increased need for caring school systems that serve the best interests of the institution and its various stakeholders. They acknowledged that this discovery implies a more profound and challenging responsibility for leaders to understand the growing concerns of those they serve.

The above challenges and concerns are uniquely answered by the invitational leadership model. Various researchers have found that invitational leaders impact their organizations in so many positive ways (Day, Harris, & Hadfield, 2001; Purkey, 1992; Purkey & Novak, 1996; Purkey & Siegel, 2003; Stillion & Siegel, 2005). This is in line with the earlier finding by Ogawa and Bossert (1995) that leadership must not only affect individual actions; it must also influence the system in which those actions occur.

Invitational leadership can step in to satisfy the need for a leadership model that systematically and holistically addresses both the internal and external elements of an organization. Invitational leaders focus on creating organizations that are people-centered and success-oriented, while at the same time dealing with all the other necessary aspects of the organization (Purkey, 1992; Purkey & Novak, 1996; Purkey & Siegel, 2003; Stillion & Siegel, 2005). According to Day et al. (2001):

Invitational leaders engage in people-centered leadership, constantly creating, reviewing, maintaining and renewing the learning and achievement cultures of students, staff and close communities of parents.

(p. 26)

The authors additionally established that invitational leaders modeled school culture through the thousands of daily interactions by which common standards, relationships, visions, expectations, and definitions of effectiveness were created, framed, supported, and analyzed. Invitational leadership also provides required guidelines and direction to support the organizational growth and success of the school.

Ideally, Principal Anderson in the opening story would use the situation presented by Ms. Murray and the gossiping teachers as an opportunity to model openness and adherence to previously established guidelines. He might encourage Ms. Murray to vocalize the complaints she is hearing, then ask her to come up with ways to neutralize the complaints. In addition, he might devise a structure that would enable Ms. Murray and the gossiping teachers to hear each other and find closure. Petty though the situation might seem, in the invitational model, with its emphasis on personal interaction and ethical guidelines, dealing with these situations consistently and openly is key.

In summary, we find from the above literature review that the invitational theory of practice (also known as ITOP) may be the best answer to Kouzes and Posner's, Ginsberg and Plank's, and many other researchers' pleas for a more comprehensive leadership model designed to meet the needs of today's educational climate. Various researchers have voiced their support for invitational leadership as a viable model in today's educational setting.

Stanley, Juhnke, and Purkey (2004) noted that ITOP presents a way of creating and maintaining school systems that are safe and at the same time conducive to academic success. They further found that schools that have applied ITOP in their administration policy have reported positive changes. These changes have been mainly improvements in areas such as student performance levels, the morale of teachers, faculty attendance rates, and the general safety of the school.

Halpin (2003) also reported that invitational leadership contributes positively to the school because it cares for and supports the efforts of others. Further corroboration of the supremacy of invitational leadership as a model for positive influence in today's educational schools comes from researchers Stoll and Fink (2003), who argued that the result of an invitational kind of leadership is a "moving school," which comprises colleagues who are committed to learning together and who share the belief that learning should be valued for its own sake and for the wellbeing and development of others. The literature supports the belief that the invitational leadership model will indeed serve as a positive source to assist in the preparation of tomorrow's school leaders.

Establishing the Significance of Invitational Leadership

In this section, we draw mainly from the study by Egley (2003), which sampled 149 school districts within the state of Mississippi, each of which had a performance index rating assigned to their district. The study excluded agricultural schools and school districts on probation. School districts in the study were ranked according to performance ratings: Level 1 and 2 had 36 school districts, Level 3 had 80 school districts, and Level 4 and 5, 33 school districts. Seventy-seven out of the 149 districts agreed to be involved in the study, and a total of 283 survey responses were received.

Egley used the leadership survey developed by Asbill, which was a 45–item instrument designed to measure teachers' perceptions of their administrators personally and professionally, inviting behaviors in relation to IET. The survey operated on the assumption that teachers' perceptions of the principal were effective agents of school improvement. The survey was also designed to yield an invitational quotient reflecting the professionally and personally inviting behaviors and practices of principals as perceived by the teachers in the school.

School principals from the participating districts were provided with a packet of information to survey each teacher. It contained information and instructions that detailed the necessary steps needed to gather the desired data on teachers.

The principal was also instructed to ensure that all teachers complete the survey and return it to the researcher in a self-addressed and stamped envelope. The study required teachers to rate their administrators' behaviors based on 44 items by selecting responses they felt best described their perceptions. Item 45 was in the form of an open-ended question that allowed teachers to express any additional comments relating to their principal's leadership style, practices, and behaviors. Items 1-37 reflected the elements of invitational leadership: i.e., trust, respect, optimism, and intentionality. These components defined the personally and professionally inviting behaviors of principals.

Items 38–40 indicated the relationship between the administrators' invitational quotient and effectiveness. Item 41 was designed to show the relationship between the administrators' invitational quotient and the principal as an agent of school improvement. Items 42–44 were designed to rate the teachers' satisfaction with the principal and their job satisfaction.

The data gathered were used to test five hypotheses related to IET and its relationship to other factors. The study showed that a relationship exists for each of the five hypotheses, but the most practical significance was that there is a relationship between the behaviors and practices of principals and teachers' perceptions of them. From the results of the study, several inferences were made. One was that the relationship between teacher and principals is supreme in the school setting.

The study found out that teachers' job satisfaction was positively correlated with the professionally and personally inviting practices and behaviors of principals. This corroborated earlier research on the strong influence of leadership within the organizational setting (Barth, 1991; Louis & Murphy, 1994; Sergiovanni, 1992). Additionally, a positive relationship was found to exist between the principals' invitational quotient and the perception of the principal's effectiveness as an agent for school improvement. The study conclusively found that principals who were perceived as being more effective showed more traits of professionally and personally inviting behaviors.

Through this study, we see that the tenets of IET are a worthwhile theory that can be positively applied in the preparation of leadership programs for future administrators. Earlier research by Daft (1999) found that people and task orientation behaviors are important leadership variables that require attention. He also noted that leadership that has concern for people tends to be related to higher employee satisfaction and fewer personnel problems in many situations.

The findings of the Egley (2003) study contended that IET has merit in transforming the educational setting. These findings add impetus to the understanding of IET as viable leadership. Other researchers have also found that organizational quality can be significantly improved by focusing more on the interactions of individuals within that setting (Ogawa & Bossert, 1995).

Several recommendations were made based on the Egley study. The first was that replication of the study should be conducted in other districts and states in the U.S., since the initial study was limited to the state of Mississippi. Another was that similar research be undertaken to examine IET in elementary and middle schools. Finally, the researcher recommended that a study be conducted to determine the correlation between the tenets of IET and the Interstate School Leaders Licensure Consortium standards. The above study was limited in the sense that it only concerned itself with people, which is just one of the five areas in which IET plays a role in the school setting.

Effectiveness of Invitational Leadership

To examine the effectiveness of invitational leadership, we look into the research studies which show a comprehensive review on the topic. Most of the literature is focused on effective leadership characteristics and how they relate to invitational leadership (Purkey, 1995; Purkey & Siegel, 2003; Bolman & Deal, 1997; Katzenbach & Smith, 2003; Yukl, 2006).

Finding 1

One of the first research questions looked into was whether there is a significant difference between the usages of the values of invitational leadership in effective schools as compared to less effective ones. When analyzed, we find that a significant difference does exist. In fact, the difference was so significant that one can in full confidence conclude that school leaders who are effective are constantly practicing leadership behaviors that produce positive results. There was a consistent pattern in the manner by which the teachers scored the leaders in effective schools.

This was mainly because, as the teachers and principals answered the interview questions candidly and honestly, it became more apparent that the teachers and principals in the effective schools were cognizant of the effective leadership skills that led to the organization's success.

We find that effective leadership is intentional. The school leader should be proactive, compassionate, and willing to serve others. The consistency in the use of invitational leadership principles was found to assist greatly in the creation of a successful and healthy school.

Finding 2

The second research question involved discerning the invitational leadership characteristics effective school leaders exhibit that lead to organizational success. The interviews showed that teachers and principals had strong opinions concerning the four values of trust, respect, optimism, and intentionality that constitute invitational leadership. All four characteristics were seen by interviewees as important contributing factors when building a successful organization.

In the analysis of both teachers' and principals' perceptions, the following results were found:

1. *Trust* – Most of the individuals interviewed for the study agreed that trust was a crucial component of effective leadership. One of the principals who responded in the interview stated that, "I feel that trust is the most important aspect of leadership, for trust nurtures all the other assumptions that make up effective leadership." A teacher interviewee confidently stated, "If a leader doesn't have the trust of their staff, they will not be an effective

leader." This statement summarizes what appears to be general consensus among teachers and principals.

2. *Respect* – The value of respect in the area of leadership is basic to organizational effectiveness. It denotes the simple belief that people have worth and value and should therefore be treated as such. As Stillion and Siegel (2005) articulate, "There is recognition of the fact that all individuals are valuable and therefore must be respected so as to create an inviting and inclusive workplace where diversity is seen as the norm and every individual has an opportunity to flourish." Respect was frequently mentioned in both written responses of principals and teachers, with most identifying it as a critical element of overall leadership effectiveness. One interviewee stated, "I don't feel my principal respects me, so I feel ill at ease every time I am in her presence." Another participant felt differently: "My principal is always positive and treats each person with respect. Feeling respected for what I do means the world to me." Another interviewee affirmed:

> "I feel respect is very important. If a teacher and/or student are respected, they can optimally perform up to their potential and understand the intentions set forth by administrative policies. If respect is evident, the work place will be more positive and a trust will then be established."

Most of the interviewees were of the opinion that when a school principal shows respect for his or her staff, a positive atmosphere is created that brings about excellence and satisfaction within the school. It is thus obvious that the invitational leadership value of respect is definitely pivotal to a successful acquisition of effective leadership.

3. *Optimism* – As we saw earlier, the optimistic leader is an individual who is capable of reframing problematic situations as opportunities and considering the impossible to be merely difficult. Again, many participants in the survey were positive that their leader's ability to be both encouraging and enthusiastic was vital for effective leadership. A respondent said "My principal is very enthusiastic and positive, and that contagious spirit spreads." One principal from an effective school accepted that:

> "I believe attitude is contagious. I try to remain positive at all times and communicate future visions for our school in positive terms. I confront behaviors that are negative and try to help the staff member turn those behaviors to positive ones."

Another of the sampled principals acknowledged, "You can't be afraid to deal with negative behaviors in your building. Working to turn the negatives to positives helps to create a sense of optimism for the future. I always try to live by the following: 'Praise in public, constructively criticize in private.' " One teacher said of her principal that, "His ability to take things in stride and remain positive spills over to his staff; this creates a sense of optimism in our building. It is quite simply a fun place to work." It is thus undeniable that the invitational leadership assumption of optimism contributes tremendously to increase members' desire to work while assuring excellence and success.

4. *Intentionality* – Hockaday, Purkey, and Davis (2001) define intentionality as the ability of individuals to intertwine their inner consciousness and perceptions with their actions. It is simply having an end in sight. The ability to be purposeful and focused is a very significant aspect of invitational leadership. However, during the interview process, the interviewees were not quite certain of this aspect of their leader's behaviors. Nevertheless, after further probing, it was discovered that leaders of effective schools appeared more distinctly purposeful in their vision and mission than the leaders of less effective schools. Thus the leaders of effective schools were more likely to believe strongly in the aspect of intentionality than the less effective school leaders. A principal from a school considered to be effective stated:

> "Everything you do must be with clear intent. If you don't know where you're going you're never going to get there. As a leader it is critical that everything we do is with purpose."

One teacher had this to say about her principal:

> "She strives to be clear with her intentions at all times. Occasionally her intentions don't always mesh with the will of the majority, but she follows through with the path she sets. I believe this has helped bring us to a better place as a school."

When another was asked about intentionality, the teacher from a school considered less effective had the following words concerning her principal:

> "I guess he tries to have a plan and work that plan, though often he seems very disorganized and making things up as he goes. It seems there is little purpose to what or why things are done."

As with the other characteristics, intentionality is a key element that school leaders should adhere to in their desire to bring about effectiveness, long-lasting change, and excellence in their schools.

Since the main intent was to look into the role that leadership characteristics play in creating organizations that are effective, it was important to establish the perceptions of current educators on the total effectiveness of their leader. It is interesting to note that both principals and teachers from schools considered to be effective were much more likely to respond with an "agree" or "strongly agree" on all four questions concerning effectiveness than their less effective counterparts.

Apparently, teachers are generally clear on whether their leader is effective or not. According to the results of the interviews and written statements, teachers' opinions clearly revealed what effective leadership is all about. In the long run, effective leadership skills that are practiced consistently lead to effective and generally better outcomes than the haphazard ordering of leadership skills that one ascribes to. Since the best possible outcome of effective leadership is to help transform the perceptions of followers in positive ways, the comments of one teacher aptly sum up the goal of effectiveness when she stated, "My principal is encouraging and enthusiastic – she makes me look forward to coming to school despite student challenges." This is clearly invitational leadership at its best.

Finding 4

The last research question of the study sought to determine the aspects of invitational leadership teachers and principals considered most influential in contributing to an effective school or organization. The aspect that teachers and principals overwhelmingly agreed on was the crucial role of people within the organization.

While the interviewees and reports touched on the other factors of places, policies, programs, and processes, it was interesting to note that each respondent offered the same answer to the question asking whether people are the most influential element in an organization. This was true regardless of the background of the teachers and principals or whether they were from effective or less effective schools. As one teacher wrote:

"All people of an organization have to be what is most important. Sadly, not all leaders are well versed in this critically important skill. When you work under a leader that lacks in people skills, all you can think about is how you can get out of this negative situation."

In the same manner, a principal commented that:

"I believe the number one reason why people lose their job is because of their lack of people skills; whether they are the teacher, principal, or superintendent you must treat people in a positive manner."

Almost all participants had stories of leaders who had either placed high priority on people within the school or had mistreated them. The question led to an unexpected theme, repeatedly made manifest in the written comments and interviewee responses, which was that of favoritism for certain members of an organization. Interestingly, the problem was more prevalent among less effective school leaders. However, there were a few leaders from effective schools who demonstrated this trait as well. One interviewee said:

"Some teachers are allowed to not follow the rules and others are held accountable to the letter of the law. Some teachers are the principal's 'buddies.' "

Another stated that, "My principal sometimes comes across as having 'favorites' and others don't get a chance to shine." Yet another shared:

"I have pretty much given up trying to excel at my job. Since I'm not one of the 'in teachers,' it really doesn't matter what I do, my principal won't pay any attention to what I achieve. The worst part is, because I'm not one of her 'favorites' my students ultimately suffer in the long run."

In the final collation of survey information, it was apparent that there were specific patterns of responses that prevailed for certain principals. It was also clear that a few principals had teachers who were among their favorites, while some were just not favored. In summary, as leaders consider the influential aspect of people, it is of great significance that they remain aware of how they treat each and every member of their institution. This is definitely a matter of respect and consideration, which, as we saw, is necessary for effective leadership.

Summary

Novak (2009) argues that educators should be focused on creatively allowing all people to realize more of their emotional, moral, social, intellectual, and creative potential. While this is true of a school's curriculum and pedagogy, it is also true of leadership interactions. Novak views invitational leadership as part of the school leadership's ethical responsibility to mould a positive culture where staff members show respect, care, optimism, and intentionality to each other and to students and parents.

He advocates for leaders to give more emphasis in relationship building, especially on doing-with rather than doing-to, participation in leadership, and not dictating the decision-making process. Through the development of goodwill and trust, taking a real interest in the people with whom one works helps them achieve goals and objectives that are meaningful to them while respecting confidences.

One major problem that leaders have is that they tend to communicate more with their peers: people who are most like themselves. These kinds of groupings may unintentionally exclude other people. Good leaders should embrace diversity and form teams of people who have different strengths and weaknesses and who share different opinions on matters.

Another very important aspect of invitational leadership theory not mentioned in most studies is that it can be applied to the self. More often than not, leaders let themselves become run down by their total commitment to a particular task without finding time to nurture their own personal growth.

In conclusion, we should consider our own behaviors and also consider the intentions of others. School leaders need to be continuously reflecting and analyzing their actions and words to find out if they are guilty of unintentionally "uninviting" others to excel together in the school. Doing this, however, requires both initiative and responsiveness.

Discussion questions

1. Use the four guiding principles of invitational leadership – optimism, respect, trust, and intention – to show how you would solve Principal Anderson's dilemma in the vignette.
2. Stoll and Fink suggest that successful invitational leadership creates a "moving school." What are the attributes of a "moving school"? What are the advantages of

this type of school environment, as opposed to a more static model? Are there any disadvantages?

3. Many teachers state that "people skills" are the most important attribute of a successful principal. Think of a leader you admire. How do the leader's people skills manifest themselves? Give three examples.

4. Egley's study of Mississippi schools found that the teacher–principal relationship is of paramount importance in the functioning of a school. What steps can a principal take to make this relationship more invitational?

5. Purkey and Siegel suggest that a school can become more invitational by focusing on the "five P's": policies, programs, places, processes, and people. Describe how your school or a school you attended might become more invitational by making one change in each of these areas.

Activities

1. Using a Venn diagram or radar chart, map the relationships in a school, indicating where power lies and in which direction power flows. Discuss how the invitational model can be used to strengthen relationships in the school context.

2. Role-play a meeting with the characters in the vignette at the beginning of the chapter (Anne Murray, Principal Anderson, and the two other teachers), using the invitational model to strengthen relationships and build solid structures for a successful future.

Selected Readings

Fullan, M. (2009). Leadership development: The larger context. *Educational Leadership, 67*(2), 45–49.

McGuigan, L., & Hoy, W. K. (2006). Principal leadership: Creating a culture of academic optimism to improve achievement for all students. *Leadership and Policy in Schools, 5,* 203–229.

Novak, J.M. (2009). Invitational leadership. In B. Davies (Ed.), *The essentials of school leadership.* London: Sage.

Novak, J.M., Rocca, W., & DiBiase, A.M. (2006). *Creating inviting schools.* San Francisco: Caddo Gap Press.

Chapter 10

Constructivist Leadership
A Framework for Building Sustainable School Improvement

Principal Riley was frustrated. In her weekly staff meetings, she begged her staff to come forward with problems or issues they had, rather than griping behind her back. But almost six months of the school year had passed, and not a single teacher had come forward. Her administrative assistant, however, sometimes dropped hints that the teachers weren't satisfied. He would meet them in informal settings after school, where they'd confide that they were unhappy with Principal Riley's management style.

"Then why don't they come forward?" she raged, banging her desk. "Are they cowards? I ask them in every staff meeting to tell me their problems. Did I say ask? I meant beg! *But they just sit there looking at their hands."*

Finally, Principal Riley approached a school commissioner about her communication problems.

"Think about it from their side," he told her. "You're a powerful, intimidating woman, with a huge voice and a huge intellect. You're standing in front of them, yelling at them to tell you their problems. Obviously, they aren't comfortable in that setting."

Principal Riley realized that she lacked the skills necessary to make the teachers feel comfortable. She asked the school commissioner if he could offer some suggestions, and he agreed to meet with her and provide some tools that would get the information flowing again.

Our children and youth will graduate into a very different future from that of previous generations. This is because of the numerous technological advances and scientific discoveries that are constantly accelerating the amount of knowledge and information available to the public. The U.S. now finds itself in an increasingly interdependent international community, where success or failure in one country has ramifications for many others.

With the flurry of changes, there has been a growing concern that the role of school principal, having been designed for the industrial age, has not yet fully evolved to deal with the complexity of challenges in schools that involve preparing the youth to face the 21st century. Growing expectations of how school leaders should change have redefined the school leadership role (Trunk, Sirca, & Shapiro, 2007). As the vignette showed, a school leader like Principal Riley, who has not adapted to the changing mores and expectations, will fail to generate meaningful interaction among stakeholders.

Changes in the school context give rise to myriad issues that require adjustment of both policy and practice of school leadership. The role of the school leaders is the key for improvement of school outcomes through influencing motivation and capacity of teachers and by affecting the environment in which they work. To achieve this, school leaders need to focus more on instructional leadership by:

- Monitoring and assessing teacher performance.
- Organizing and conducting mentoring and coaching sessions.
- Nurturing teachers' professional development.
- Building teamwork and cooperative learning.

Since pedagogy is changing, success in today's knowledge society requires that students engage in powerful forms of active constructivist learning, which transmits understanding and independence. Increasing individualization and personalization offer inclusive and diverse learning opportunities for students. These new forms of pedagogy can be utilized to monitor and assess teachers' practice. With school principals as the leaders of learning, communities of effective practice can be established where there is continuing professional development that is more sophisticated and embedded into the fabric of daily routine (Trunk et al., 2007).

The other change in the education front is the shift in the centers of autonomy and accountability. We now find that school leaders can only make a meaningful impact on student outcomes if they have sufficient autonomy to make decisions on issues such as the curriculum, teacher recruitment, and development. Again, the main responsibilities left to school leaders are those aimed at improving student learning. There is now more demand for decentralized decision-making, balanced with more methods of assuring accountability, such as standardized testing.

Decentralization has disadvantages as well as benefits. A good example of this is school-level control over available devolved budgets, which creates opportunities for school administrators to allocate resources to high-priority development areas, but this in itself increases the cost of financial administration and leaves the leader with less time to focus on teaching and learning processes. Though school leaders were traditionally only accountable for input into learning processes, they are now held accountable for all learning outcomes for both teachers and students.

Another demand in current school leadership is the need for policy and practice to work better together. This is because government policy that is designed to change practice in schools can only work efficiently where it is synchronized with the school-level processes. Additionally, effective implementation relies heavily on the motivation and initiative of school leaders. This age requires that policymakers engage school leaders in meaningful and ongoing consultation in the area of policy formulation and development, because school leaders who feel connected to the reform process are more likely to influence and involve their staff and students in the implementation process and in sustaining changes (Lambert, 2003).

As noted earlier, schools are now being confronted by an increasingly complex scenario. In these rapidly changing environments, the major problem is that goals and objectives for schools and the means for their achievement are not always clear or static. Another challenge presents itself in the form of external pressure to change. School leaders must induce their teachers and students to handle the processes of change effectively. There is also a need for involvement of parents and the wider community in school processes. Additionally, current school leaders have to seek to improve the wellbeing of students by involving the private sector, sports clubs, faith-based groups, and community-based organizations in school activities.

The need for networking has also become increasingly important, with school leaders finding it wise to collaborate with leaders from other schools and districts in sharing resources and skills so as to deliver a diverse range of learning opportunities. For the above challenges to be sufficiently overcome, three major barriers must be addressed (Lambert et al., 2002):

- **Increase in the roles of principals:** Since the task of leading a school has expanded and become more complex, it is becoming increasingly apparent that the responsibilities placed on principals far exceed their capacity to handle them singlehandedly.
- **The aging profession:** The average age of today's school leader in the U.S. is 51 years, which means that most of the current crop of school leaders will retire over the next five to ten years. Therefore, while schools look toward improving the quality of current leadership, they should also develop clear plans for the future in terms of effective processes for leadership succession.
- **Unattractive working conditions:** In many developed countries (and this is not just confined to the U.S.) there is a remarkable decrease in the numbers of applications for the position of school principal. This is due to the negative connotations attached to the job, which is seen as overburdened, stressful, offering inadequate training and preparation, having a meager salary compared to output, and generally poor working conditions. Most teachers and deputy principals feel that the additional incentives that are offered to principals are just too small to compensate for the burdensome workload.

Having looked at the challenges facing school leadership, we will now provide a review of the historical concepts and practical applications of constructivism in learning. To understand the roots of constructivist leadership, we must first note that the theories of learning and leadership are interlinked and share parallel themes (Lambert et al., 2002). The chapter will also examine various types of constructivism and look at how they are currently used in education.

History of Constructivism

Constructivism is grounded in the early work of Immanuel Kant (1724–1804). Kant was of the opinion that *a priori* knowledge must come before any grasp or understanding of human experience. He argued that there must be some inherent organizing principles within every person's consciousness by which he or she structures, arranges, and understands all data. Therefore, he posited that knowledge is independent of any kind of external reality. It is a product of the mind and the various interpretive processes that go along with it (Burrell & Morgan, 1979).

Wilhelm Dilthey (1833–1911) expanded Kant's hypotheses and attempted to explain the distinction between the natural and cultural sciences. He was of the opinion that each science addressed different subject matters. Natural sciences looked into the external processes in the material world, while the cultural sciences looked into the internal process of the human mind. He further suggested that the outward manifestations of human life needed to be understood and interpreted in terms of the inner experience through *verstehen*, a means of studying human knowledge by reliving or reenacting other peoples' experiences. Max Weber (1864–1920) built on the idea of *verstehen* in his philosophy. He stated that the objective reality of the world was not the main issue, but rather the way the individual interprets it is (Burrell & Morgan, 1979).

Alfred Schutz (1899–1959) built on the works of Kant, Dilthey, and Weber. While he agreed with Weber that the essential function of social science was interpretive, he felt that Weber had failed to properly state the essential characteristics of *verstehen*. Schutz then advanced a phenomenological analysis of meaning in which he argued that consciousness is fundamentally one "unbroken stream of lived experiences" that usually have no meaning by themselves. Meaning is consequently developed through a process of dependency and reflexivity, i.e., the act of turning back on oneself so as to look retrospectively at one's past. He was thus of the opinion that meaning is attached to past experiences, not current ones. Schultz further argued that one could genuinely understand another individual by looking at the person's stream of consciousnesses. This understanding stems from direct interaction (Burrell & Morgan, 1979).

Over time, constructivism has become an established theory, though its definition and uses are still a work in progress. "Constructivism" and "constructionism" as terms can be used interchangeably. However, while the main concern of constructivism is making meaning and constructing social or psychological worlds through processes of individual cognition, constructionism focuses on the notion that social and psychological worlds become a reality through social processes and interactions (Bodner, Klobuchar, & Geelan, 2001). Many researchers believe constructivism is a valid theory, but there are a number of critics. The most common criticism of the constructivism theory is that it is not scientific because it is complex, multifaceted, and somewhat indefinable (Mayer, 2004). In the next part of this chapter we shall look into constructivism in relation to learning and leadership in schools.

Constructivist Leadership

As earlier stated, constructivism refers to the belief that knowledge is actually constructed in the mind of the learner (Bodner et al., 2001). It holds that individuals actively and continuously construct their own meanings and understandings of reality and the world they live in. Knowledge is assumed to be autonomous of the external world and acquired by passive absorption or by simple transfer from one individual to another through interaction. In short, knowledge is made, not acquired. Since we all have different experiences due to diverse upbringing, cultures, and personalities, we all perceive the world differently (Trunk, Sirca, & Shapiro, 2007). The constructivist theory therefore holds that knowledge should not be judged in terms of whether it is "true or false," but in terms of whether or not it works. The only thing that matters is whether the knowledge that is constructed functions properly in the context in which it arises (Bodner et al., 2001).

Constructivist leaders should always consider ways to facilitate the learning process, since they believe that knowledge originates from within the individual. These leaders facilitate learning by posing questions to learners that stimulate self-construction and interaction. However, the biggest hindrance to constructivist leadership is learners who are either unable or unwilling to become autonomous learners. The process of facilitation involves active listening and repetition of what the learner says so as to "hammer in" meaning and understanding (Coe, 2006). Lambert et al. (2002) state that a constructivist leader seeks understanding through a balance of inquiry, paraphrasing, and articulation, such that the learner can seek out cohesion and meaning in various ideas.

Bouck (2004) articulated that leadership is all about learning and is a reciprocal process that enables leaders to engage in making meaning within the context of relationships. Lambert et al. (2002) felt that leaders should stop thinking of roles or of followers as fixed entities and should instead perceive them as interconnected relationships. They add that the reciprocal processes of leadership include such activities as inquiry, reflection, dialogue, and action. Leaders should show a profound respect for the worthiness of each individual, and this should be integrated in daily communication with fellow stakeholders. However, as we saw in the opening vignette, it is imperative that the communication be two-way, and that the leader seek structures that will free the stakeholders to speak their minds.

One of the aspects that separate constructivist leadership from other leadership theories is the insistence on the growth of followers within the institution. Lambert et al. (2002) give the following key points as the founding principles for constructivist leadership:

1. Learning is an active not a passive process.
2. Learning is naturally social and is thus most likely to occur where learners share ideas, practice and appreciate inquiry, and face challenges in a social construct.
3. For learners to go beyond rote learning, they must have opportunities to make sense of newly received knowledge and create meaning for themselves that is based on their individual and shared experiences through the processes of application and experiential activity.
4. Both reflection and meta-cognition contribute positively to the construction of knowledge and the sense-making process.
5. New learning is dependent on prior experience, beliefs and values and beliefs.

Types of Constructivism

1. Psychological Constructivism

Also referred to as Piagetian constructivism, psychological constructivism believes the purpose of education to be educating the child in a manner that supports his or her interests and needs. As a consequence, the child is the subject of study, with individual cognitive development being the main focus. Learning is seen as a primarily individualistic enterprise. This child-centered approach seeks to establish the natural path of cognitive development through scientific processes (Vadeboncoeur, 1997).

In application, this approach is of the assumption that students usually come to classrooms with preconceived beliefs, ideas, and opinions that need alteration or modification by the teacher, who facilitates this by devising several tasks and questions that create dilemmas for students. By working through these dilemmas, knowledge is constructed. The instructional practices that characterize constructive leadership include "discovery learning" and hands-on activities, such as the use of "manipulatives"—student tasks that challenge the existing concepts and schools of thought, and question the techniques that probe into students' preconceived beliefs, encouraging examination and testing of those beliefs (Richardson, 1997).

To some extent, this kind of approach assumes that development is a natural, ingrained, and biological process that is the same for all individuals regardless of the diverse environments in which they learn or live (Vadeboncoeur, 1997). The focus of the teaching environment is internal development. The social and historical context, issues of power and authority, and the impact of formal knowledge in the learning environment are not subjects of focus (Richardson, 1997). Psychological constructivism is essentially a de-contextualized approach to learning and teaching.

This approach is often criticized due to its lack of attention to the influence of classroom culture and the broader social context and also its disregard for power issues especially those related to knowledge production (Richardson, 1997; Vadeboncoeur, 1997).

2. Social Constructivism

Also known as Vygotskian constructivism, social constructivism places an emphasis on education for transforming societies and is essentially a theory of human development that attempts to place the individual within a socio-cultural context. Social interactions beget individual development through internalization of the cultural meanings shared by the group (Richardson, 1997). Richardson notes that individuals construct knowledge in cognizance of their environment, and in the process both the environment and individual are changed. The basic subject of study in social constructivism is the dialectical relationship between the individual and the socio-cultural milieu.

In this case, schools reflect the socio-cultural settings where both teaching and learning take place and where the "cultural tools" of writing, reading, mathematics, and other modes of discourse are utilized (Richardson, 1997). The positive aspect of this approach is its assumption that theory and practice cannot develop in a vacuum; they are influenced and designed by the dominant cultural assumptions (O'Loughlin, 1995). The formal knowledge, subject of instruction, and manner of presentation are all influenced by the historical and cultural environments that produced them.

In order to accomplish the objectives of social transformation or reconstruction, the educational context must be deconstructed. In addition, the cultural domain, power relationships, and historical influences that limit the context must be critiqued, exposed, and, if necessary, changed. The variants of the social constructivist approach include socio-cultural constructivism, socio-historical constructivism, situated constructivism, social re-constructivism, and emancipatory constructivism.

Social Constructivism in Education

As we have seen above, social constructivism holds that social worlds develop out of individuals' interactions with their culture and society (Trunk, Sirca, & Shapiro, 2007). A similar perspective is that of Luddeke (1999), who held that knowledge evolves through the process of social negotiation and evaluation of the viability of individual understanding.

In order to apply social constructivism theories in the education arena, there is need for a shift in perspective for the teachers and school leaders. Both must move from being "people who teach" to being "facilitators of learning." A good constructivist teacher is one who questions students' answers, irrespective of whether they are right or wrong, to make sure the student has a good grasp of the concept. Additionally, instructors should have their students explain the answers they give and not allow students to use words or equations without explanations. They should also encourage students to reflect on their answers (Bodner et al., 2001).

Social constructivism teaches that all knowledge develops as a result of social interaction and language use, and is therefore a shared, rather than an individual, experience. Knowledge is additionally not a result of observing the world, but merely one of many social processes and interactions (Olsen, 1999). We therefore find that constructivist learning attaches as much meaning to the process of learning as it does to the acquisition of new knowledge.

In the words of Olsen (1999), "learning is not the result of development; learning is development." The process of learning requires that the learner actively participate in creative activities and self-organization. Teachers should allow their students to come up with their own questions, make their own hypotheses, and test them for viability. Moreover, constructivists find that disequilibrium facilitates learning, in the sense that contradictions between the learner's current understanding and experiences create a disequilibrium, which leads the learner to inquire into his or her own beliefs and then try out new ideas (Cobern, 1993). Instructors should therefore encourage errors resulting from the learners' conceptions, instead of minimizing or avoiding them.

Students should also be challenged by their instructors to perform open-ended investigations into realistic and meaningful contexts. This activity enables the learner to explore and come up with either affirming or contradictory possibilities. In particular, contradictions need to be investigated, clarified, and discussed. Through the process of reflective abstraction, learning is given an impetus. A good example of allowing reflection is through journal writing, which usually facilitates reflective abstraction (Olsen, 1999).

Olsen further found that dialogue within a community stimulates new ideas. All school stakeholders should view the classroom as a community for discourse and exchange of ideas. Students in the classroom are responsible for the defense, proof, justification, and communication of their ideas to the community. These ideas can only be accepted as truth if they can make sense to the community. If they do, they become shared knowledge (Olsen, 1999). In summary, learning occurs not through transmission, but primarily through interpretation. Interpretation is shaped by prior knowledge and is further facilitated through discourse (Cobern, 1993).

Social Constructivism and Leadership

While most current literature is directed toward the use of social constructivism in educational organizations, it can be used by leaders of organizations both inside and outside of the educational sphere to bring about organizational growth and communication. One example of this is in the use of metaphors to further the understanding of followers, which allows them to build their own knowledge base as individual learners, and adapt to new and expanding concepts (Wilson, 1995). Early research by Morgan (1998) showed that metaphors are "a force through which people create meaning by use of one element of experience to understand another." Metaphors in this sense include anything symbolic to a person, which can be used to better their understanding and enable them to acquire new ideas or concepts (Tompkins & Lawley, 2000).

The active use of metaphors can also help the leader move the organization toward social constructivism. Early researchers Lakoff and Johnson (1980) stated that "the essence of a metaphor is to promote understanding and experiencing a thing in terms of another." Through the constructive use of language, the leader can explore the communication practices of followers and their individual roles in the construction of meaning through the process of social interaction (Jacobs & Heracleous, 2006). Weick (1979) termed this process "sense-making."

Sense-making occurs when individuals in the organization communicate; that communication is viewed in retrospect, sense is made out of it, and the sense is kept as knowledge and used to achieve organizational effectiveness. The brain normally forms thoughts as image-schemas, prototypes, conceptual metaphors, conceptual frames, and conceptual blends. Consequently, the thinking process is not just algorithmic symbol manipulation; it is the brain's neural computation.

Weick (1976) was of the belief that people find it hard to identify instances of rational practices within the organization, find rational practices that have had beneficial outcomes as predicted, or feel that the existing rational practices explain what goes on in the organization. This is probably why he used the metaphors of collective structure, planning, natural selection, and enactment to define organizational processes. Northouse (2007) stated that making the connection between organizational structure and its processes is done through process leadership. This kind of leadership is defined as that attained by any member of an organization to lead the organization or its parts forward.

A study by Gass and Priest (2006) on a sample of Deutsche Bank workers showed how metaphors can facilitate team-building. The participants used a corporate adventure training program to "experiment" on the use of metaphors in their team-building exercises. Each group received similar corporate training.

While four groups received different kinds of facilitative metaphors in their respective programs, a fifth group—the control group—simply received corporate adventure training without metaphors.

From the study, it was evident that, when isomorphic frames were created through use of metaphors that paralleled the work environment, the training could be conducted in a more effective manner. The results showed that participants who formulated their own metaphoric interpretations and reinforced them with isomorphics retained increasing teamwork measurements from 15% to 30% one year later (Gass & Priest, 2006). Through the use of metaphors to build retention of knowledge or expand current knowledge as determined in constructivist learning, school leaders can replicate the results of the Deutsche Bank study. Jacobs and Heracleous (2006) also suggest that metaphors can facilitate change by providing a bridge from what followers are familiar with to the vision of the leader. They are particularly useful because they represent the existing organizational aspect as seen by individuals within the organization.

Application of Constructivist Leadership in the School Setting

Drawing from the works of Lambert et al. (2002), we find that constructivist leadership involves the various reciprocal processes that enable participants in the school community to construct meanings that lead them toward a common purpose of schooling. Reciprocity here is characterized by the ability to move outside oneself, differentiate one's perceptions from those of others, and practice empathy. It is defined as the mutual and dynamic interaction and exchange of ideas and concerns. Lambert et al. (2002) state that this requires a great deal of maturity, which emerges from the processes of meaning-making in sustainable communities over a period of time.

The researchers state that school stakeholders, if they are to develop their capacities for reciprocity, should engage in the processes of meaning-making continuously as they live and work together in educational communities. As early researcher Paulo Freire (1973) stated, "knowledge is not extended from those who are considered to know to those who do not know, instead it is built up in the relations between people."

Judith Warren Little (1982) observed multiple forms of relationships in schools and identified the differences among congenial, collegial, and individualistic relationships. She found that these relationships usually shift as the collegial nature of professional culture changes over time. Reciprocity is therefore a spiraling experience, which gathers strength the more it is practiced. Wheatley (1992) found further meaning in relationships when she explained that individuals usually generate information during their interactions with each other. This information then becomes feedback, enriching existing information and creating additional information.

As we have learned, the reciprocal process that enables us to construct meaning usually occurs within the context of relationships. Therefore, creation and expansion of the possibilities and capacities for reciprocity only occur in those communities that are rich in relationships. There is thus a need for school leaders to stop thinking of people as fixed entities, but rather as relationships that are part of interconnected patterns.

A relationship pattern can be seen in the governance structures in most schools. Many such schools and districts have formed separate and fragmented governance processes, e.g., leadership teams, school curriculum committees, PTAs, and professional development committees. These kinds of fragmented processes tend to be autonomous, neither involving nor connecting with each other. Consequently, the process of decision-making becomes time-consuming, redundant, and disengaged from the other important information and feedback systems. These processes also deny coherence of practice and building of effective school communities.

However, the above governance groups can be controlled and coordinated so as to connect them via information, people, and products. These integrated structures are essential to the building and connecting of relationships. Such connectedness brings about opportunities for conversations and meaning-making in the long run (Lambert et al., 2002).

A study by Claremont Graduate Schools' Institute for Education in Transformation found that the most important factor in schools is relationships (Poplin & Weeres, 1993). The study was unique in that it was carried out by teachers and was conducted as a series of dialogues. The teachers wrote:

> For it is in the coming to know that we came to want to act. It is in the listening that we changed. It is in the hearing our own students speak, as if for the first time, that we came to believe. This is what we heard . . . Relationships dominated all participant discussions about issues of schooling. No group inside the schools felt adequately respected, connected, or affirmed.
>
> (p. 19)

The participants in the Claremont study, which involved parents, students, teachers, administrators, and support staff, felt that there was an absence of authentic relationships in which they were trusted, entrusted with responsibility, spoken to warmly and in an honest manner, and treated with dignity and respect. However, the perceptions of caring seemed to vary among groups, with teachers viewing dedication to their work as an indication of caring. Students, on the other hand, saw caring from teachers in the form of direct and personal touch, using of their names, being asked or told personal things, and shared laughter. One teacher observed:

> Our data is contrary to the way most of us traditionally have thought about schooling in which curriculum is at the center of the model and measures of school productivity are there. And here we're saying we have to put relationships at the core of what we're doing.

The study made teachers and school administrators realize that their relationships were usually dominated by rules, regulations, and, often, contractual agreements. School leaders admitted that changes were often unsuccessful because they rushed preliminary dialogue. Those participants who survive in arid and impersonal environments devoid of meaningful relationships stated that they often went elsewhere to get what they needed. This was echoed by a student, who said:

If I talk to my parents sometimes they get mad at me because of what I say to them. Or maybe they're too busy. If I talk to teachers I can't tell them that I said a word or something because they will suspend me. So I guess the only people that understand are gangsters. They always understand and they always help me solve it too.

Reciprocal relationships form the basis by which we as human beings make sense of our world through continually defining ourselves and "coevolving," or growing together. Lambert et al. state that, through relationships, predictability becomes potential. Potential is defined as those possibilities that develop within us; they are the personal passions and schemas that enable us to construct meaning and knowledge. Potential is unpredictable, limitless, built on relationships, dynamic, paradoxical, and continuously renewing itself. For it to develop, it must be evoked or provoked (Wheatley, 1992), since it does not appear on command or through persuasion, enlistment, or recruitment.

Reciprocal processes include:

1. Those processes that evoke potential within a trusting environment. These are the processes that enable the individuals to bring out memories, perceptions, and assumptions that they rely on or that inform their work. The recollections may be in the form of discussions, stories, brainstorming, writing, or even reenactment. Through these evoked ideas, an individual can create a good foundation for constructing both meaning and knowledge and that enable him or her to understand how others make sense of the world.
2. Those processes that reconstruct or break away from old assumptions and myths. These necessitate a thorough reexamination of the accepted ideas and traditional interpretations. They involve gathering of new data, posing questions that bring about dissonance and disequilibrium between preexisting beliefs and the new information, and re-conceptualizing or redesigning those ideas.
3. Those processes that focus on the construction of meaning. These are the same as those described above, e.g., stories, discussion, and writing, and they entail combining or recombining ideas so as make sense of them. "Making sense," which is the same as "constructing meaning," requires creation of new symbols or images, such as patterns or metaphors, so as to form the basis for interpretation.
4. Those processes that frame actions. These embody new kinds of behaviors and purposeful intentions, and involve the most practical aspects of the reciprocal processes. They include establishing new criteria, implementing new actions, planning approaches, identifying emerging goals and objectives, evaluating progress, and redesigning or reframing the actions in response to additional information received from the process.

The above are spiraling processes that involve and build on each other while circling back upon themselves. Through new actions, other potentials are evoked, and new information is consequently generated and deeper meanings constructed.

Principal Lambert at the beginning of this chapter was frustrated because her vociferous, top-down exhortations for feedback and communication were going unheeded. The processes listed above indicate why she is failing to achieve her stated wish. If the power dynamic is such that one party feels threatened by another, the spiraling, building qualities of reciprocal processes will founder, and voices will fall silent.

Acts of Leadership

These acts are distinguished from role leadership and refer to the performance of actions that enable participants in the school to evoke potential within a trusting environment, reconstruct (break set) with old assumptions, focus on the construction of meaning (meaning-making), or frame actions that are based on new behaviors and purposeful intention. Lambert et al. (2002) state that everyone in the school can perform an act of leadership irrespective of who they are, because constructivist leadership is an inclusive field of processes through which leaders do their work.

However, Lambert et al. state that, for one to perform acts of leadership, he or she needs:

- A sense of purpose and ethics, since honesty and trust are fundamental to relationship building.
- Facilitation skills, which are needed because framing the conversations about teaching and learning is fundamental to constructing meaning.
- A solid understanding of constructivist learning in humans.
- A deep understanding of the processes of change and transition, since they are often not what we think they are.
- A proper understanding of context such that memories can be continually drawn and enriched in meaning-making.
- A personal identity that allows for courage and risk, low ego, and a heightened sense of possibilities.

As we saw in the Claremont study, educators generally start their life's work with a sense of purpose and ethics. Poplin and Weeres give an example of a young teacher named Susan, who was in her third year of teaching. When interviewed, Susan stated that she had entered the profession because she wanted to make a difference. Halfway through the second year, she had already begun to question her potential and ability to make a difference. Yet she states that, during an initial meeting to plan for a professional practice school, the feeling of purpose began to resurface. This feeling, as stated, is thus easily lost, easily regained, and hence quite vulnerable.

Poplin and Weeres suggest that perhaps all educators at one point were just like Susan. It is thus apparent that those who initiate acts of leadership are those who have held tight to their purposes or who have reawakened after experiencing a pattern of relationships that has assisted them to resurface and redefine those original compelling purposes into their ethical behavior. For such people, a sense of coherence and authenticity contributes to the establishment of trust in communal relationships.

Facilitation skills developed through relationships are vital for those performing acts of leadership. Lambert et al. give an example of a school leader who stated:

> When I entered my third year of teaching, I discovered in the interview that all teachers and administrators in my new school were expected to participate in 30 hours of training in open communication, shared decision-making, problem-solving, and accountability. The school was genuinely founded on these four principles, and everyone was a leader expected to facilitate the processes. What a phenomenal experience! One that influenced me dramatically later as a principal and one that helped me to negotiate the next 25 years of educational experience through a unique lens.

We find that an understanding of constructivist learning enables leaders to pose questions and frame actions that lead to self-construction and collegial interaction, which are important in the design of a constructivist curriculum, assessment, and instruction. Constructivism is therefore a uniquely different paradigm that does not emerge naturally from our training and experiences in behaviorism. It enables the school leader to frame new questions that help him or her to create learning environments based on passion, unique learning gifts and perceptions, the community, and authentic work and assessment (Lambert et al., 2002).

Leaders also need to have a deep understanding of change and transition, which assists them in the design of the timing, sequencing, and duration of reciprocal processes. These leaders are most likely to find that change that is constructivist in nature and emerges from the meaning-making process can be unpredictable. However, the use of preset objectives and predetermined strategies and techniques that are tightly drawn violates the nature of constructivism. Though constructivist leaders may have goals, outcomes, and various change strategies that are aimed at focusing talent and resources toward a common purpose, their main aim is to harness real change that is pulled by intention, not prediction. Lambert et al. state that this change process is so complex that it can only be understood through dialogue among co-leaders in the learning community.

The change context is understood through "communities of memories," which, as we saw earlier, must be drawn forth, enriched, and reinterpreted. Bellah (1985) found that communities are important in the sense that they are constituted by their past, and it is for this reason that we speak of a real community as being a "community of memory," i.e., one that does not forget its past. So as not to forget their past, communities are constantly involved in retelling their story or constitutive narrative.

These memories bear meaning when shared, and constitute a vital part of the construction or reconstruction of meaning in schools. When a new principal joins a school, for example, he or she is advised to talk to people so as to find out about the memories, which are mostly about the men and women who had previously embodied and exemplified the meaning of the community. Also, the new principal learns the values and intentions that drive work in the school, fears and lost hopes that may form barriers to creativity and innovation. Through the sharing of memories, it is easier to conceptualize work, a process that entails sketching out memories, assumptions, values, and promises that create a forum for dialogue and a launching pad for action.

Constructivist leaders also attempt to construe and interpret themselves as they construct meaning and knowledge with other stakeholders. This sense of personal identity helps to grow courage and risk-taking ability, lower ego needs, and increase the sense of possibilities. Personal identity is formed through reflective interactions with others. Leaders who are constructivist seek not only to explain, but also to listen and understand. These leaders have outgrown the need to "win," as was common in the traditional sense, and understand that reciprocity and high personal regard are better than "winning," since they are more crucial for moving toward a common purpose.

Due to their growing clarity and confidence in the values that guide their lives, these leaders are able to ask essential questions. Because personal efficacy evolves a trusting environment, these leaders work with other stakeholders to create possibilities for all students and teachers. The possibilities created are as diverse as the web of their relationships, since, as we have seen, diversity stems from multiple perspectives and multiple framing.

With the above in mind, the vision of educational leaders' potential not only seems ideal but possible. Constructivist leadership therefore enables human growth that was previously reserved for a select few. Previously, other persons in the school community were seen as followers and relegated to second-class citizenship, but since constructivist leadership sees growth as a limited resource in ecological communities, interdependence and reciprocity require equal partners.

Who Can Lead in Constructivism?

Lambert et al. state that leadership represents a possible set of actions for everyone in the school community and, therefore, anyone can lead. Constructivism calls for "participantship" and not followership through full engagement. As Wheatley (1992) stated, "we need a different pattern in which we engage fully, evoking multiple meanings. The more the participants we engage in this participative universe, the more the potential we access and the wiser we can become (p. 65)."

It is through full participation that acts of leadership are done, mainly because being fully engaged in meaning usually activates one's drive toward a purpose in the community. The responsibility toward oneself and others comes up as an essential developmental process. Early work by Freire (1973) states that "people emerge from their submersion and acquire the ability to intervene in reality as it is unveiled." Intervention and re-intervention help in the construction of realities, especially when staff-members emerge into the leadership arena. It is essential that the participation processes form the basis of creating meaning and understanding that people commit to. This is because, without these participatory opportunities, only obedience, and not commitment from the stakeholders, is possible.

While it may not be fitting that students, teachers, parents, and administrators are leaders according to the old adage "too many cooks spoil the broth," new paradigms in leadership are making a different "broth." This is because the patterns of relationships in this new "broth" connect synergistically, creating rich possibilities that exist outside traditional lines of authority, roles, norms, rules, and policies. In summary, constructivist leadership provides a system of meaning making for leadership actions.

Constructivism as Leadership

While the kinds of educational communities described above are quite rare, the knowledge, understandings, and practices suggested are not unique. This is because many learning centers, networks, projects, and partnerships already function on notions of reciprocity, community, and purpose. Schools are beginning to focus more on student outcomes and collegiality. However, some researchers have questioned constructivist leadership and have dismissed it as "community work," restructuring, or re-culturing.

The case for constructivist leadership is that these noble conceptions are isolated and fragmented. While these processes are happening, there is something missing that can act as glue, integration, or unity of spirit. Constructivist leadership entails reciprocal processes that enable participants in the school to construct meanings that lead toward a common purpose of schooling.

The Case for a Constructivist Approach

The question remains as to what roles leaders, teachers, and researchers should play in translating reform policies into the reality of best practices within school cultures. Lambert and Walker (1995) and Lambert (2003) suggest a constructivist framework for educational leadership as a means of supporting teacher development and facing these new challenges. A constructivist approach to teacher leadership argues that teachers need to be allowed to develop their capacity to use reciprocity in problem-solving through collaborative inquiry. The approach promotes the development of teachers' use of reciprocity in thinking, solving problems, and engaging in action research in their schools. The purpose of the model suggested by Lambert (2003) is to track the thinking of teachers about collaboration and inquiry as they participate in inquiry-based learning. This kind of learning describes a wide range of curricular, philosophical, and pedagogical approaches to teaching. Its most profound requirement is that learning should be based around student questions. Collaborative learning is another term under constructivist leadership in education that involves joint intellectual effort among students and their teachers. It also refers to the methodologies and environments in which learners engage in common tasks and dialogue within a sustained community of inquirers and the way they impact reciprocity in teachers' thinking.

Current policies guiding educational reform on a national level reflect the tendency in most people to oversimplify the change process by emphasizing large-scale uniform mandates instead of supporting ongoing and locally responsive research that encourages professional teacher development and teacher-driven inquiry. Earlier research by Wheatley (1999) and Senge (2000) had already dispelled the notion that change is a linear top-down process, instead of a more realistic understanding that change is a complex process.

Constructivism teaches that change occurs by creating the right conditions for stakeholders to engage in dialogue and collaborative inquiry and allowing them to develop the capacity to use their own ideas to create locally transformative solutions to problems. In the reform process in education, Fullan (2001), Barth (2001), and Lambert (2003) state that school leaders need to move beyond top-down, quick-fix, or one-size-fits-all models of reform. They add that if meaningful reforms are to be realized, contextually sensitive inquiries by teacher leaders need to be engaged in the complex process of developing effective teaching practices so as to bring about change. This finding is consistent with earlier research by Dufour and Eaker (1998), who articulated that teacher inquiry/action research within schools needs to be systematic and ongoing if continuous improvement is to be achieved.

Lambert et al. posit that if systematic and continuous inquiry is to become part of school cultures, a theoretical approach that embraces constructivist premises needs to be applied to teacher leadership so as to offer a promising framework for the development of school communities where dialogue and collaborative inquiry thrive and transform thinking among individual actors to form a collective school culture. The researchers state that "today, the mission of one institution can be accomplished only by recognizing that it lives in an interdependent world with conflicts and overlapping interests." The assumption here is that engaging teachers in ongoing processes of professional development involving a shared vision, dialogue, collaboration, contextually sensitive inquiry, and shared learning for a common goal, develops the capacity and passion for the growth of sustainable change.

Context and Process

Most of the research in the Lambert et al. study was conducted as part of an ongoing study of a professional development program involving approximately one thousand teachers that was designed to facilitate the development of reciprocity and interdependence in the teachers' way of thinking, problem-solving, and inquiry. It was structured as a two-year program in which teachers were to employ a shared vision, dialogue, collegiality, and collaboration.

In order to observe how teachers in the program were experiencing and developing professionalism, the researchers gathered data from learner-generated written documents. This approach was used in order to promote trustworthiness. Data gathered from the study were categorized into six emergent dimensions of constructivist or inquiry-based dialogue:

1. Awareness and sensitivity to context.
2. Empowerment and giving voice.
3. Finding common points and building on diversity.
4. Dynamic feedback processes.
5. Learning and development of coherent frameworks that guide decision-making.
6. Construction of a caring and interdependent institution.

Emergent Dimensions in Teacher-Leader Thinking

As we saw above, the six themes frame changes in learners' use of reciprocity and in teacher-leader thinking. These dimensions demarcate developmental changes in participant thinking that are related to the problem-solving acts of leaders.

1. Teacher Awareness and Sensitivity to Their Context as a Place for Inquiry

Participant teachers, during their reflections, spoke extensively about the context and the dynamics in which they often find themselves embedded. Across the two years, there was a shift from their initial views of their context. Through the processes of inquiry and dialogue into their daily routines, teacher-leaders seemed to be stimulated, and developed an ability to balance the need for routine with intentional acts of collection, observation, meaning-making, and sharing.

2. Empowering and Giving Voice

Participant teachers in their reflections also showed a dimension embodied in the theme of empowerment and giving voice. In this case, the thinking of participant teachers across the two years shifted from their initial understandings that sharing one's "voice" or opinions played little or no role in bringing about change in oneself or others toward a confident understanding of the value and role of personal voice as an important tool for bringing into being opportunities and possibilities for collaborative change. It was apparent that, after two years of being in a sustained community, teachers mutually giving value to each others' voices appeared to provide a growing context for ongoing use of reciprocity in the development of "legitimacy of voice" as a pathway for ideas to turn to action.

3. Finding Commonalities and Building on Diversity of Understandings

The third emergent dimension from teacher reflections was the development of the ability in teacher leaders to find commonalities in thinking and to build upon personal understandings through the diversity in thought that others bring to sustained groups, when engaged in dialogue. The reflections of participants seemed to shift slowly from initially seeking to have one's perspective accepted as a condition for mutual discussion toward leaders being able to balance the differences and commonalities in perspective as mutually useful tools that enrich one's professional thinking. Though the process was slow and tedious, eventually, after the two years of engaging in sustained community dialogue, it was apparent that this was necessary to improve the conditions for professional development. However, it was noticed that participants put in real investments in their personally developed views of teaching. Still, it became evident that a trusting relationship is needed to help participants become open to alternative points of view. This suggested that the unwillingness to suspend judgment and risk being open among teachers was caused by the climate in their schools, which was largely hostile toward the sharing of different points of view.

4. Dynamic Feedback Processes Guiding Change

Another theme involved the change in the understanding of feedback processes and assessment of tools for learning, planning, and processes of decision-making. The teachers' way of thinking across the two years moved from their initial understanding of data as being mainly an external evaluation resource toward an inclusive understanding of the role of feedback as an assessment and data-gathering tool. All feedback that is framed for learning purposes is understood as a tool for the generation of new knowledge. The participants consequently developed abilities to use authentic assessments, which are defined as the measurements of intellectual accomplishments that are considered to be significant and meaningful, instead of multiple choice standardized tests. The teachers also learned how to gather data in ways that make students aware of their own thinking. Teachers' reflections showed that there was a shift in the understanding of how feedback can be harnessed and utilized in the knowledge construction process. Feedback tools are therefore seen as empowering and iterative.

5. Learning and Development of Coherent Frameworks to Guide Decision-Making

The fifth emergent dimension in the study involved the grounding of teachers' thinking in research. Throughout the two years of sustained research reading and the implementation of action research, there was a remarkable shift in teacher understanding of the meaning of principles, standards, and concepts that relate to educational reform. This means that there was a developing capacity among teachers to balance and integrate their personal beliefs and principles with the expectations of policymakers. This comes from the constructivist shift from externalizing and blaming those in charge to the use of available educational research to analyze the expectations of educational policies and inform and reinforce teachers' personal beliefs. It was evident that research literature has shifted from being valued for its tricks and techniques toward teachers valuing it for its ability to help frame their coherence and serve as an aid for discerning.

6. Constructing a Caring and Interdependent Sense of Community

The last dimension involved participants' understanding of mutuality and the importance of initiating learning conversations as steppingstones for personal growth and mentoring others. It was observed that, over the two years, teacher thinking shifted gradually from an understanding of the learning community as the source of mutual affirmation and emotional support, toward a perspective of the community as a place for generative commitment toward facilitating other people's development. There was a seemingly emerging expectation in participants' reflections of the learning community conversations serving as a source for valued critique and opportunity for low-risk strategies being introduced as new teaching practices. This was indicative of participants' heavy reliance on the learning community as a "safe haven" for caring. Through this perception, the learning community becomes a hothouse for development of creative work. From the descriptive reflections of teachers, a shift from a focus on inward security toward an outward-looking posture that is more understanding of a community as an interdependent network for sharing, generating, and testing strategies could be detected.

As we can see, Principal Riley in the opening story, by her top-down, heavy-handed approach, failed in almost every one of these areas. In particular, her inability to achieve a satisfactory feedback process hampered the development of the school. The school commissioner might encourage her to try out different formats for staff meetings, including circular seating arrangements or meetings led by other staff members, in which Principal Riley would sit among the teachers and take notes. The commissioner might encourage Principal Riley to have more one-on-one sessions with teachers, in less formal situations, and to make a genuine effort to listen to and learn from them. It would require a shift in thinking and tone, but could have a dramatic effect on the school environment.

Summary

From this study, we see how constructivist leadership facilitates the development of sustainable, collaborative, inquiry-based problem-solving, and the conditions that activate teachers' cognitive development. Additionally, the construction of creative solutions to the issues of teaching and learning through leadership activity appears to help stakeholders in the school (previously referred to as followers) to construct an understanding of themselves as agents of change that contribute to the wellness of the learning community to which they belong.

Through the programmatic use of processes that promote focused conversation around mutual problem-solving, sharing of visions, collaborative learning, collegiality, and shared work, there is facilitation of the development of teacher thinking across the above-mentioned dimensions of dialogue. In the two years of the program (study), the participants' ability to use reciprocal thinking to bring about development reflects an increasingly differentiated and balanced consideration of the various dimensions of issues and demands that teachers face as they engage in the performance of their leadership activities.

The transformations in thinking identified in the study suggest that there is strong promise for significant development of teacher thinking along the dimensions that are required to meet the inherent challenges that teachers face today. The use of processes that support varied dimensions of dialogue, interdependent problem-solving abilities, and sustained inquiry, as was practiced in the study, suggests that these conditions are evidence of the development capability in teacher thinking on matters that are central to teacher leadership activities. Since the findings in the study show consistency with the constructivist premise that meaningful development requires sustained levels of thoughtful interaction around areas of significance, it is the opinion of the researchers that teacher inquiry and collaborative problem-solving merit an expanded and normative role in professional teacher development and also in shared school decision-making.

However, there is still a great deal of research needed in order for us to fully understand how teachers contextualize leadership. We need to ascertain the length of time that is required to bring about these transformational shifts in thinking, as observed in the study. Another area of concern is that of individual variability in the changes in thinking, which suggests that a great deal remains to be learned about how to most effectively facilitate the development of thinking in teachers and leaders. Nevertheless, there is confidence in the knowledge that sustained teacher interactions with their colleagues and with other stakeholders in solving real-life problems using inquiry and research-based decision-making can play a major role in bringing about sustainable educational reform.

Constructivist leadership therefore seems to be a valid way forward in bringing about real change in schools. This is because it focuses on what is authentic and real in the school setting. Constructivism teaches us that knowledge or change in our schools should not come from outside; instead, it should sprout from within the institutions themselves, since only the stakeholders are conversant with the unique problems in their schools. Constructivist leadership also holds that no one has a monopoly of knowledge and thus all stakeholders in the school should come together to bring about real sustainable change.

Discussion Questions

1. Constructivism, as defined by Bodner et al., holds that individuals "actively and continuously construct their own meanings and understandings of reality." According to arguments developed in this chapter, what implications does this have for teaching methodology and school leadership?
2. According to social constructivism, formal knowledge, subject of instruction, and manner of presentation are influenced by the historical and cultural environments that produced them. Choose a subject area you received instruction in (e.g., literature, geology, music), and name at least three ways in which the subject was influenced by the historical and cultural environment in which it was taught.
3. In the Claremont study outlined in this chapter, which relationships did the researchers examine? How did the strength of the relationships vary among the participants in the study?
4. Feedback tools are crucial for keeping information flowing in constructivist leadership. What feedback tools have you had experience with in the school setting? Which were the most effective? Which were the least effective? Why?
5. In the vignette at the beginning of the story, the school commissioner offers to describe a few effective feedback tools to get communication flowing. Create two feedback tools that might enable teachers at Principal Riley's school to feel more comfortable sharing information.

Activities

1. In constructivist theory as applied to the school setting, leaders should stop thinking of roles or of followers as "fixed entities" and should instead perceive them as "interconnected relationships." Make a hierarchical list of the stakeholders in your present school or one you attended. Now redraw the list, using colors or other visual textures to demonstrate the interconnections among the various parties.
2. In order to create sustainable change, according to Lambert et al., teachers must engage in ongoing processes involving a shared vision, dialogue, and shared learning for a common goal. Together with one or more class members, design such a process, keeping sustainability in mind.

Selected Readings

Galloway, C (2007). *Vygotsky's constructivism.* Retrieved from http://projects.coe.uga.edu/epltt/index.php?title=Vygotsky's_constructivism

Lambert, L. (2009). Constructivist leadership. In B. Davies (Ed.), *The essentials of school leadership.* London: Sage.

Northouse, P. G. (2007). *Leadership: Theory and practice* (4th ed.). Thousand Oaks: Sage Publications, Inc.

Sergiovanni, T. J. (2009). *The principalship: A reflective practice perspective.* Boston, MA: Allen & Bacon.

References

Chapter 1: Transformational Leadership

Aarons, G. A. (2006). Transformational and transactional leadership: Association with attitudes toward evidence-based practice. *Psychiatric Services, 57*(8), 1162–1169.

Avey, J. B., Hughes, L. W., Norman, S. M., & Luthans, K. W. (2008). Using positivity, transformational leadership and empowerment to combat employee negativity. *Leadership and Organization Development Journal, 29*(2), 110–126.

Avolio, B. J., Bass, B. M. & Jung, D. I. (1999). Re-examining the components of transformational and transactional leadership using the Multifactor Leadership Questionnaire. *Journal of Occupational and Organizational Psychology, 72*, 441–462.

Barling, J., Weber, T., & Kelloway, E. K. (1996). Effects of transformational leadership training on attitudinal and financial outcomes: A field experiment. *Journal of Applied Psychology, 81*, 827–832.

Bass, B. M. (1985). *Leadership and performance beyond expectations.* New York, NY: Free Press.

Bass, B. M. (2005). *Transformational leadership.* New York, NY: Free Press.

Bass, B. M., & Riggio, J. (2006). *Transformational leadership: Second edition.* New York, NY: Free Press.

Boehnke, K., Bontis, N., DiStefano, J. J., & DiStefano, A. C. (2002). Transformational leadership: An examination of cross-national differences and similarities. *Leadership and Organization Development Journal, 32*, 244–298.

Bono, J. E., & Judge, T. A. (2003). Self-concordance at work: toward understanding the motivational effects of transformational leaders. *Academy of Management Journal, 46*, 554–571.

Clements, C., & Washbush, J. B. (1999). The two faces of leadership: considering the dark side of leader-follower dynamics. *Journal of Workplace Learning, 11*(5), 170–176.

Conger, J. A. (1990). The dark side of leadership, *Organizational Dynamics, 4*, 44–45.

Crossley, C. D., Bennett, R. J., Jex, S. M., & Burnfield, J. L. (2007). Development of a global measure of job embeddedness and integration into a traditional model of voluntary turnover. *Journal of Applied Psychology, 92*, 1031–1042.

Dvir, T., Eden, D., Avolio, J. B., & Shamir, B. (2002). Impact of transformational leadership on follower development and performance: A field experiment. *The Academy of Management Journal, 45*(4), 735–744.

Gramling, J. (2010). African centered education initiative at the Madison Metropolitan School District: Culturally relevant education for all. *Capital City Hues, 5*, 22.

Hackman, J. R., & Oldham, G. R. (1980). *Work redesign.* Reading, MA: Addison-Wesley.

Judge, T. A., & Ilies, R. (2004). Affect and job satisfaction: a study of their relationship at work and at home. *Journal of Applied Psychology, 89*, 661–673.

Judge, T. A. & Piccolo, R. F. (2004). Transformational and transactional leadership: A meta-analytic test of their relative validity. *Journal of Applied Psychology, 89*, 755–768.

Khunert, K. W., & Lewis, P. (1987). Transactional and transformational leadership: A constructive/developmental analysis. *The Academy of Management Review, 12*, 648–656.

Northouse, P. (2009). *Introduction to leadership: Concepts and practice.* Thousand Oaks, CA: Sage.

Piccolo, R. F., & Colquitt, J. A. (2006). Transformational leadership and job behaviors: The mediating role of core job characteristics. *Academy of Management Journal, 49,* 327–340.

Russell, R. F., & Stone, A. G. (2002). A review of servant leadership attributes: Developing a practical model. *Leadership and Organization Development Journal, 23,* 145.

Sergiovanni, T. (1984). Leadership and excellence in schooling. *Educational Leadership, 7,* 4–3.

Smircich, L., & Morgan, G. (1982). Leadership: The management of meaning. *Journal of Applied Behavioral Science, 18,* 257–273.

Spreitzer, G., & Mishra, A. (2002). To stay or go: Voluntary survivor turnover following an organizational downsizing. *Journal of Organizational Behavior, 23,* 707–729.

Yukl, G. (2009). Leading organizational learning: Reflections on theory and research. *The Leadership Quarterly, 20,* 49–53.

Chapter 2: Instructional Leadership

Andrews, R., & Soder, F. (1987). Principal instructional leadership and school achievement. *Instructional Leadership, 44,* 9–11.

Antonakis, J., Cianciolo, A. T., & Sternberg, R. J. (2004). *The nature of leadership.* Thousand Oaks, CA: Sage Publications.

Bayne, R. (2005). *Ideas and evidence: Critical reflections on MBTI theory and practice.* Gainesville, FL: Center for the Applications of Psychological Type.

Beatty, B. (2007, November). Going through the emotions: Leadership that gets to the heart of school renewal. *Australian Journal of Education, 51,* 328–340.

Bernhardt, V. (1998). *Data analysis for comprehensive schoolwide improvement.* Larchmont, NY: Eye on Education.

Blasé, J., & Blasé, J. (2004). *Handbook of instructional leadership: How successful principals promote teaching and learning* (2nd ed.). Thousand Oaks, CA: Corwin Press.

Bolman, L. G., & Deal, T. E. (2003). *Reframing organizations: Artistry, choice, and leadership.* San Francisco, CA: Jossey-Bass.

Brewer, D. J. (1993). Principals and student outcomes: Evidence from U.S. High Schools, *Economics of Education Review, 12*(4), 281–292.

Bryk, A. S., & Schneider, B. (2002). *Trust in schools: A core resource for improvement.* New York: Russell Sage Foundation.

Burch, P. E. (2005). The new educational privatization: Educational contracting and high stakes accountability. *Teachers College Record.* Retrieved from www.tcrecord.org/content. asp?contentid=12259

Burns, J. M. (1978). *Leadership.* New York: Harper & Row.

Copland, M. A. (2003). Leadership of inquiry: Building and sustaining capacity for school improvement. *Educational Evaluation and Policy Analysis, 25*(4), 375–395.

Cuban, L. (1984). Transforming the frog into a prince: Effective schools research, policy, and practice at the district level. *Harvard Educational Review, 54*(2), 129–151.

Cuban, L. (1988). *The managerial imperative and the practice of leadership in schools.* Albany, NY: State University of New York Press.

Drago-Severson, E. (2007). Helping teachers learn: Principals as professional development leaders. *Teachers College Record, 109*(1), 70–125.

Dwyer, D. C. (1986). Understanding the principal's contribution to instruction. *Peabody Journal of Education, 63*(1), 3–18.

Dwyer, D. (2007). Understanding the principal's contribution to instruction. *Peabody Journal of Education, 63*(1), 3–18.

Edmonds, R. (1979). Effective schools for the urban poor. *Educational Leadership, 37,* 15–24.

Etzioni, A. (1988). *The moral dimension: Towards a new economics.* New York: The Free Press.

Firestone, W. A., & Shipps, D. (2005). How do leaders interpret conflicting accountabilities to improve student learning? In W. A. Firestone & C. Riehl (Eds.), *A new agenda for research in educational leadership* (pp. 81–100). New York: Teachers College Press.

Friedkin, N. E., & Slater, M. R. (1994). School leadership and performance: A social network approach. *Sociology of Education, 67*(2), 139–157.

Fullan, M. (2007). *The new meaning of educational change* (4th ed.). New York: Teachers College Press.

Gewertz, C. (2003, January, 8). N.Y.C. Chancellor Aims to Bolster Instructional Leadership. *Education Week, 22*(7), 12–15.

Hallinger, P. (2003). School leadership development: Global challenges and opportunities. In P. Hallinger (Ed.), *Reshaping the landscape of school leadership development: A global perspective* (pp. 45–78). Lisse, Netherlands: Swets & Zeitlinger.

Hallinger, P. (2005). Instructional leadership and the school principal: A passing fancy that refuses to fade away. *Leadership and Policy in Schools, 4*, 221–239.

Hallinger, P. H., & Heck, R. H. (1996a). Reassessing the principal's role in school effectiveness: A review of the empirical research, 1980–1995. *Educational Administration Quarterly, 32*(1), 5–44.

Hallinger, P., & Heck, R. (1996b). The principal's role in school effectiveness: A review of methodological issues, 1980–95. In K. Leithwood et al. (Eds.), *The international handbook of educational leadership and administration* (pp. 723–784). Dordrecht, Netherlands: Kluwer.

Hallinger, P., & Murphy, J. (1985). What's effective for whom? School context and student achievement. *Planning and Changing, 16*(3), 152–160.

Hallinger, P., & Murphy, J. (1986). The social context of effective schools. *American Journal of Education, 94*(3), 328–355.

Hallinger, P., & Wimpelberg, R. (1992). New settings and changing norms for principal development. *The Urban Review, 67*(4), 1–22.

Halverson, R., Grigg, J., Prichett, R., & Thomas, C. (2006). The new instructional leadership: Creating data-driven instructional systems in schools. *Journal of School Leadership, 64*, 284–98.

Halverson, R., Grigg, J., Prichett, R., & Thomas, C. (2007). The new instructional leadership: Creating data-driven instructional systems in school. *Journal of School Leadership, 17*(2), 159–194.

Heck, R. H., & Hallinger, P. (2005). The study of educational leadership and management: Where does the field stand today? *Educational Management Administration & Leadership, 33*(2), 229–244.

Hogan, R. (2004). Personality Psychology for Organizational Researchers. In B. Schneider & D. B. Smith (Eds.), *Personality and organizations* (pp. 3–23). Mahwah, New Jersey: Lawrence Erlbaum Associates.

Holcomb, E. L. (1999). *Getting excited about data: How to combine people, passion, and proof.* Thousand Oaks, CA: Corwin Press.

Johnson, J. R. (2002). Research and the MBTI. *Bulletin of Psychological Type, 25*, 28–29.

Kise, J. A. G., & Russell, B. (2008). *Differentiated school leadership: Effective collaboration, communication, and change through personality type.* Thousand Oaks, CA: Corwin Press.

Leithwood, K., & Jantzi, D. (2005, September). A review of transformational school leadership research 1996–2005. *Leadership and Policy in Schools, 4*(3), 177–199.

Leithwood, K., & Montgomery, D. (1982). The role of the elementary principal in program improvement. *Review of Educational Research, 52*(3), 309–339.

Leithwood, K., Begley, P., & Cousins, B. (1990). The nature, causes and consequences of principals' practices: An agenda for future research. *Journal of Educational Administration, 28*(4), 5–31.

Leithwood, K., Harris, A., & Hopkins, D. (2008, February). Seven strong claims about successful school leadership. *School Leadership & Management, 28*(1), 27–174.

Love, N. (2002). *Using data/getting results: A practical guide for school improvement in mathematics and science*. Norwood, MA: Christopher-Gordon.

Macdaid, G. P., McCaulley, M. H., & Kainz, R. I. (2007). *Myers-Briggs type indicator (R) atlas of type tables* (Sixth ed.). Gainesville, FL: Center for Applications of Psychological Type (Original work published 1986) 175.

Marks, H., & Printy, S. (1992). Principal leadership and school performance: An integration of transformation and instructional leadership. *Educational Administration Quarterly, 9*(1), 45–56.

Marsh, D. (1992). School principals as instructional leaders: The impact of the California School Leadership Academy. *Education and Urban Society, 24*(3), 386–410.

Marshall, K. (1996). How I confronted HSPS (Hyperactive Superficial Principal Syndrome). *Phi Delta Kappan, 77*(5), 336–345.

Meier, S. R. (2010). *An investigation into the relationship between instructional leadership practices preferences and personality*. New York: University of Rochester Press.

Murphy, J., & Shipman, N. (2003). Developing standards for school leadership development: A process and rationale. In P. Hallinger (Ed.), *Reshaping the landscape of school leadership development: A global perspective* (pp. 23–41). Lisse, Netherlands: Swets & Zeitlinger.

Ozer, D. J., & Benet-Martínez, V. (2006, January). Personality and the prediction of consequential outcomes. *Annual Review of Psychology, 57*, 401–421. doi:10.1146/annurev.psych.57.102904.190127

Purkey, S., & Smith, M. (1983). Effective schools: A review. *Elementary School Journal, 83*, 427–452.

Reeves, D. B. (2006). *The learning leader: How to focus school improvement for better results*. Alexandria, Virginia: Association for Supervision and Curriculum Development.

Reynolds, D. (2006). World class schools: Some methodological and substantive findings and implications of the International School Effectiveness Research Project (ISERP). *Educational Research and Evaluation, 12*(6), 535–560.

Rowe, W. G. (2007). *Cases in leadership*. Thousand Oaks, CA: Sage Publications.

Stein, M. K., & Spillane, J. (2005). What can researchers on educational leadership learn from research on teaching? Building a bridge. In W. A. Firestone & C. Riehl (Eds.), *A new agenda for research in educational leadership*. Columbia University: Teachers College.

Sternberg, R. J. (2002). Successful intelligence: A new approach to leadership. In R. E. Riggio, S. E. Murphy, & F. J. Pirozzolo (Eds.), *Multiple intelligences and leadership* (pp. 9–28). Mahwah, NJ: Lawrence Erlbaum.

Weick, K. (1982). Administering education in loosely coupled schools. *Phi Beta Kappan, 63*(10), 673–676.

Wilson, M. (Ed.). (2004). *Towards coherence between classroom assessment and accountability*. Chicago: University of Chicago Press.

Chapter 3: Distributed Leadership

Alvesson, M., & Thompson, P. (2005). Post-bureaucracy? In *The Oxford handbook of work and organization*. Oxford: Oxford University Press.

Avolio, B. J., Kahai, S., Dumdum, R., & Sivasubramaniam, N. (2001). Virtual teams: Implications for e-leadership and team development. In M. London (Ed.), *How People Evaluate Others in Organizations* (pp. 337–358). Mahwah, NJ: Erlbaum.

Bennett, N., Wise, C., Woods, P., & Harvey, J. (2003). *Distributed Leadership: full report*. Nottingham: NCSL.

Camburn, E., Rowan, B., & Taylor, J. E. (2003). Distributed leadership in schools: the case of elementary schools adopting comprehensive school reform models. *Educational Evaluation and Policy Analysis, 25*(4), 347–373.

Copland, M. A. (2003). Leadership of inquiry: building and sustaining capacity for school improvement. *Educational Evaluation and Policy Analysis, 25*(4), 375–395.

Day, C. & Harris, A. (2002). Teacher leadership, reflective practice, and school improvement. In K. Leithwood and P. Hallinger (Eds), *Second International Handbook of Educational Leadership and Administration* (pp. 957–977). Dordrecht, The Netherlands: Kluwer.

Dean, D. R. (2006). Thinking globally: The National College of School Leadership. A case study in distributed leadership development, *Journal of Research on Leadership Education, 1*(2).

Elmore, R. F. (2002). *Bridging a new structure for school leadership*. Washington, DC: Albert Shanker Institute. Retrieved from www.shankerinstitute.org/education

Engeström, Y. (2001). Expansive learning at work: Toward an activity theoretical reconceptualisation. *Journal of Education and Work, 41*(1), 133–156.

English, F. (2006). The unintended consequences of a standardised knowledge base in advancing educational leadership preparation. *Educational Administration Quarterly, 42*(3), 461–472.

Etzioni, A. (1965). Dual leadership in complex organizations, *American Sociological Review, 30*(5), 688–698.

Fay, B. (1987). *Critical social science: Liberation and its limits*. Cambridge, MA: Polity.

Friedkin, N.E., & Slater, M. S. (1994). School leadership and performance: A social network approach. *Sociology of Education, 67*, 139–157.

Goldstein, J. (2003). Making sense of distributed leadership: The case of peer assistance and review. *Educational Evaluation and Policy Analysis, 25*(4). Retrieved from www.jstor.org/stable/3699584

Gordon, R. D. (2002). Conceptualizing leadership with respect to its historical-contextual antecedents to power. *Leadership Quarterly, 13*(2), 151–167.

Grace, G. (2000). Research and the challenges of contemporary school leadership: the contribution of critical scholarship. *British Journal of Educational Studies, 48*(3), 231–247.

Gronn, P. (2000). Distributed properties: a new architecture for leadership. *Educational Management and Administration, 28*(3), 317–338.

Gronn P, & Rawlings-Sanaei, F. (2003) Principal recruitment in a climate of leadership disengagement. *Australian Journal of Education, 47*(2), 172–184.

Harris, A. (2005). Distributed leadership. In B. Davies(Ed.), *The essentials of school leadership*, London: Paul Chapman.

Hartley, D. (2007). The emergence of distributed leadership in education: Why now? *British Journal of Educational Studies, 55*(2), 202–214.

Hatcher, R. (2005). The distribution of leadership and power in schools. *British Journal of Sociology of Education, 26*(2), 253–267.

Hosking, D. M. (1988). Organizing, leadership and skilful process. *Journal of Management Studies, 25*(2), 147–166.

Hosking, D.M. (1991). Organization and organizing. In M. Smith (Ed.), *Analysing organizational behaviour* (pp. 56–76). Aldershot: Macmillan.

Ingvarson, L., Anderson, M., Gronn, P., & Jackson, A. (2006). *Standards for school leadership: A critical review of literature*. Acton: Australian Institute for Teaching and School Leadership.

Kempster, S. (2009). *How managers have learnt to lead: Exploring the development of leadership practice*. Basingstoke, UK: Palgrave MacMillan.

Kempster, S., Cope, J., & Parry, K. (2010). *Dimensions of distributed leadership in the SME context*. Carlisle: University of Cumbria.

Kouzes, J. M., & Posner, B. Z. (1993). *Credibility: How leaders gain and lose it, why people demand it*. San Francisco: Jossey-Bass.

Leadbeater, C. (2004). *Personalisation through participation: A new script for public service*. London: DEMOS.

Leithwood, K., & Levin, B. (2005). *Assessing school leader and leadership programme effects on pupil learning (Report No. RR662)*. London, UK: Department for Education and Skills.

Leithwood, K., & Riehl, C. (2005). What we know about successful school leadership. In W. Firestone and C. Riehl (Eds.), *A new agenda: Directions for research on educational leadership* (pp. 12–27). New York: Teachers College Press.

Leithwood, K., Day, C., Sammons, P., Harris, A., & Hopkins, D. (2006). *Seven strong claims about successful school leadership.* Nottingham: NCSL/DfES.

Levacic, R. (2005). Educational leadership as a causal factor: Methodological issues in research on leadership "effects." *Educational Management Administration and Leadership, 33*(2), 197–210.

MacBeath, J. (2005). Leadership as distributed: a matter of practice, *School Leadership and Management, 25*(4), 349–366.

Manz, C. C., & Sims, H. P., Jr. (1991). Super Leadership: Beyond the myth of heroic leadership. *Organ. Dynamics, 19*(4): 18–35.

Ogawa, R. T. (2005). Leadership as a social construct: the expression of human agency within organizational constraint. *The Sage Handbook of Educational Leadership: Advances in Theory, Research and Practice.* Thousand Oaks: Sage.

O'Hair, M. J., & Bastian, K. (1993, October). Physiological measures of principal vocal stress in urban settings. Paper presented at the University Council of Educational Administration, Houston.

Page, B. (2006). *Issues to Consider: Social Demographic and Organizational Trends.* London: Ipsos MORI Social Research Institute.

Parry, K.W., & Bryman, A. (2006). Leadership in organizations. In S. Clegg, C. Hardy, T. Lawrence and W. Nord (Eds), *Sage handbook of organization studies.* Thousand Oaks, CA: Sage.

Pricewaterhouse-Coopers (2007). *Independent Study into School Leadership.* Available online: www.dfes.gov.uk/research/data/uploadfiles/RR818A.pdf

Robinson, V. M. (2008). Forging the links between distributed leadership and educational outcomes. *Journal of Educational Administration, 46*(2), 241–256.

Sergiovanni, T. J. (1984). Leadership as cultural expression. In T. J. Sergiovanni and J. E. Corbally (Eds.), *Leadership and Organizational Culture: New Perspectives on Educational Theory and Practice* (pp. 105–184). Urbana, IL; University of Illinois Press.

Sergiovanni, T. J. (1993). *Moral leadership.* San Francisco: Jossey-Bass.

Sims Jr., H. P. & Lorenzi, P. (1992). *The new leadership paradigm.* Newbury Park, CA: Sage Publications.

Spillane, J. P. (2006). *Distributed leadership.* San Francisco: Jossey-Bass.

Spillane, J., Camburn, E., & Pareja, A. (2007). Taking a distributed perspective to the school principal's work day. *Leadership and Policy in Schools, 6*(1), 103–125.

Spillane, J. P., Halverson, R., & Diamond, J. B. (2004). Towards a theory of leadership practice: a distributed perspective. *Journal of Curriculum Studies, 36*(1), 3–34.

Spillane, J. P., Reiser, B. J., & Reimer, T. (2002). Policy implementation and cognition: reframing and refocusing implementation research. *Review of Educational Research, 72*(3), 387–431.

Storey, A. (2004). The problem of distributed leadership in schools. *School Leadership and Management, 24*(3), 249–265.

Tabberer, R. (2005). People development. Presentation to the TDA Stakeholder 2005 Day, 17 October. London: TDA.

Thorpe, R., Gold, J., Anderson, L, Burgoyne, J. G., Wilkinson, D., & Malby, B. (2008). *Towards 'leaderful' communities in the north of England.* Cork, UK: Oak Tree Press.

Timperley, H. S. (2005). Distributed leadership: Developing theory from practice. *Journal of Curriculum Studies, 37*(4), 395–420.

Timperley, H. & Alton-Lee, A. (2008). Reframing teacher professional learning: An alternative policy approach to strengthening valued outcomes for diverse learners. In G. Kelly, A. Luke & J. Green (Eds), *Disciplines, knowledge and pedagogy. Review of Research in Education* (pp. 32–45). Washington DC: Sage Publications.

Uhl-Bien, M. (2006). Relational leadership theory: Exploring the social processes of leadership and organizing. *The Leadership Quarterly, 17*(6), 654–676.

Woods, P. A. (2004). Democratic leadership: drawing distinctions with distributed leadership. *International Journal of Leadership in Education, 7*(1), 3–26A.

Yukl, G. (1994). *Leadership in organizations* (3rd ed.). Englewood Cliffs, NJ: Prentice-Hall.

Chapter 4: Ethical Leadership

Beckner, W. (2004). *Ethics for educational leaders.* Boston: Pearson Education.

Benninga, J. S. (2003). Moral and ethical issues in teacher education. ERIC Clearinghouse on Teaching and Teacher Education. Retrieved from www.ericdigests.org/2004-4/moral.htm

Board of Education vs. Rowley, 458 U.S. 176 (1982).

Bolman, L. G., & Deal, T. (2003). *Reframing organizations,* 3rd ed. San Francisco: Jossey-Bass.

Crockett, J. B. (2005). IEPs, Least Restrictive Environment, and placement. In Lane, K. E., Connelly, M. J., Mead, J. F., Gooden, M. A., & Eckes, S. (Eds.), *The principal's legal handbook* (pp. 197–223). Dayton, OH: Education Law Association.

Fullan, M. (2003). *The moral imperative of school leadership.* Thousand Oaks, CA.

Ghere, G. S., Montie, J., Sommers, W. A., & York-Barr, J. (2006). *Reflective practice to improve schools: An action guide for educators.* Thousand Oaks, CA: Corwin Press.

Heck, R. H., & Hallinger, P. (2005). The study of educational leadership and management: Where does the field stand today? *Educational Management Administration and Leadership, 33*(2), 229–244.

Harvard, A. (2010). *Virtuous Leadership—An agenda for personal excellence.* New York: Sage.

Hinman, L. M. (2003). *Ethics: A pluralistic approach to moral theory.* Belmont, CA: Wadsworth.

Ilgenfritz, R. (2010). Suit: Lower Merion schools spied on students via laptops. *Delaware County Daily Times.* Retrieved from www.delcotimes.com/articles/2010/02/18/news/doc4b7d83e268b47504369176.txt

Josephson Institute of Ethics (2006). *The seven-step path to better decisions.* Retrieved from www.josephsoninstitute.org/MED/MED-4sevensteppath.htm

Kant, I. (1785). *The groundwork of the metaphysics of morals.* New York: Routledge Classics.

Lashley, C. (2007). Principal leadership for special education: An ethical framework. *Exceptionality, 15*(3), 177–187.

Maesschalck, J. (2004). The impact of new public management reforms on public servants' ethics: Towards a theory. *Public Administration, 82*(2), 465–489.

Martin, J. P. (2010). Lower Merion district's laptop saga ends with $610,000 settlement. *The Philadelphia Inquirer.* Retrieved from http://articles.philly.com/2010-10-12/news/24981536_1_laptop-students-district-several-million-dollars

McLaughlin, M., & Nolet, V. (2004). *What every principal needs to know about special education.* Thousand Oaks, CA: Corwin Press.

Patton, M. C. (2008). Principles for principals: Using the realms of meaning to practice ethical leadership—national recommendations. *National Forum of Applied Educational Research Journal, 21*(3).

Pops, G. (2006). The ethical leadership of George C. Marshall. *Public Integrity, 8*(2), 165–185.

Rachels, J. (2007). *The elements of moral philosophy.* New York: McGraw-Hill.

Reilly, A. (2006). *From the tangible to the intangible: An experiential exercise for learning about organizational culture.* 20th Annual Mid-Atlantic Organizational Behavior Teaching Conference, LaSalle University, Philadelphia, Pennsylvania.

Reinhartz, J., & Beach, D. M. (2004). Educational leadership: Changing school. *Leadership and Policy in Schools, 4,* 177–199.

Robinson, D. A. & Harvey, M. (2008). Global leadership in a culturally diverse world. *Business papers.* Retrieved from: http://works.bepress.com/david_robinson/22

Santa Clara University, Markkula Center for Applied Ethics (2006). *A framework for thinking ethically*. Retrieved from www.scu.edu/ethics/practicing/decision/framework.html

Savra, J. (2007). *The ethics primer for public administrators in government and non-profit organizations*. Sudbury, MA: Jones and Bartlett Publishers.

Shapiro, J. P., & Stefkovich, J. A. (2005). *Ethical leadership and decision making in education: Applying theoretical perspectives to complex dilemmas* (2nd ed.). Mahwah, NJ: Erlbaum.

Singer, P. (2006). "What Should a Billionaire Give and What Should You?" *New York Times*.

Vance, N. R., & Trani, V. B. (2008). The ethical grounding to 21st Century public leadership. *International Journal of Organizational Theory and Behavior, 11*(3), 371–383.

Chapter 5: Emotional Leadership

Ackerman, R., & Maslin-Ostrowski, P. (2004). The wounded leader and emotional learning in the schoolhouse. *School Leadership and Management, 24*(3).

Anderson, R., Greene, M., & Loewen, P. (1988). Relationships among teachers' and students' thinking skills, sense of efficacy, and student achievement, *Alberta Journal of Educational Research 34*(2): 145–165.

Ashkanasy, N. M., & Dasborough, M. T. (2003). Emotional awareness and emotional intelligence in leadership teaching. *Journal of Education for Business, 79*, 18–22.

Barbuto, J. E., & Burbach, M. E. (2006). The emotional intelligence of transformational leaders: A field study of elected officials. *The Journal of Social Psychology, 146*(1), 51–64.

Barchard, K. A. (2003). Does emotional intelligence assist in prediction of academic success? *Educational and Psychological Measurement, 63*(5), 840–858.

Bardzill, P., & Slaski, M. (2003). Emotional intelligence: Fundamental competencies for enhanced service provision. *Managing Service Quality, 13*(2), 97–104.

Barling, J., Slater, F., & Kelloway, E. K. (2000). Transformational leadership and emotional intelligence: An exploratory study. *Leadership and Organization Development Journal, 21*(3), 157–161.

Beatty, B. (2000). Teachers leading their own professional growth: Self-directed reflection and collaboration and changes in perception of self and working secondary schoolteachers. *Journal of In-Service Education, 26*(1), 3–97.

Beatty, B. (2002a). *Emotion Matters in Educational Leadership: Examining the unexamined* (Unpublished doctoral dissertation). Ontario Institute for Studies in Education, University of Toronto, Ontario.

Beatty, B. (2002b, April) *Emotional Epistemologies and Educational Leadership: A conceptual framework*. Paper presented at the American Educational Research Association, New Orleans, (ED468293).

Beatty, B. (2005). Emotional leadership, in B. Davies (ed.), *The essentials of school leadership*. Thousand Oaks, CA: Sage, 122–144.

Beatty, B. (2007a). Feeling the future of school leadership: Learning to lead with the emotions in mind. *Leading and Managing, 13*(2): 44–65.

Beatty, B. (2007b). Going through the emotions: Leadership that gets to the heart of school renewal. *Australian Journal of Education, 51*(3): 328–340.

Beatty, B., & Brew, C. (2004). Trusting relationships and emotional epistemologies: A foundational leadership issue. *School Leadership and Management, 24*(3): 329–356.

Beatty, B. & Brew, C. (2005) Measuring student sense of connectedness with school. The development of an instrument for use in secondary schools. *Leading and Managing, 11*(2), 103–118.

Blasé, J. J., & Greenfield, W. (1985). How teachers cope with stress: How administrators can help. *The Canadian Administrator, 25*(2): 1–5.

Bono, J. E., & Ilies, R. (2006). Charisma, positive emotions, and mood contagion. *Leadership Quarterly, 17*, 317–334.

Brown, K. D. (2005). *Relationship between emotional intelligence of leaders and motivational behavior of employees.* D.M. dissertation, University of Phoenix, United States – Arizona. Retrieved from Dissertations & Theses: A&I. (Publication No. AAT 3183509).

Brown, F. W., Bryant, S. E., & Reilly, M. D. (2006). Does emotional intelligence–as measured by the EQI–influence transformational leadership and/or desirable outcomes? *Leadership and Organizational Development Journal, 27*(5), 330–351.

Byrne, B. M. (1991). Burnout: Investigating the impact of background variables for elementary, intermediate, secondary, and university educators. *Teaching and Teacher Education, 7*(2): 197–209.

Caruso, D., Mayer, J., & Salovey, P. (2002). Relation of an ability measure of emotional intelligence to personality. *Journal of Personality Assessment, 79*(2), 306–320.

Coetzee, C., & Schaap, P. (2004). The relationship between leadership styles and emotional intelligence. Paper presented at the 6th Annual Conference of the Society of Industrial and Organizational Psychology.

Costanzo, M. (1992). Training students to decode verbal and nonverbal cues: Effects on confidence and performance. *Journal of Educational Psychology, 84*, 308–313.

Costanzo, M., & Archer, D. (1989). Interpreting the expressive behavior of others: The Interpersonal Perception Task. *Journal of Nonverbal Behavior, 13*, 225–245.

Day, C., & Leithwood, K. (2007). *Successful principal leadership in times of change: An international perspective.* Dordrecht: Springer, 189–203.

Denzin, N. (1984). *On understanding emotion.* San Francisco, CA: Jossey-Bass.

Dibbon, D. (2004). *It's about time: A report on the impact of workload on teachers and students.* St John's: Memorial University of Newfoundland.

Downey, L. A., Papageorgiou, V., & Stough, C. (2006). Examining the relationship between leadership, emotional intelligence and intuition in senior female managers. *Leadership and Organization Development Journal, 27*(4), 250.

Dulewicz, V., & Higgs, M. (2003). Leadership at the top: The need for emotional intelligence in organizations. *The International Journal of Organizational Analysis, 11*(3), 193–210.

Dworkin, A. G. (1987). *Teacher burnout in the public schools: Structural causes and consequences for children.* Albany: State University of New York Press.

Dworkin, A. G. (1997). Coping with reform: The intermix of teacher morale, teacher burnout, and teacher accountability, in B. J. Biddle, T. L. Good, & I. F. Goodson. *International Handbook of Teachers and Teaching.* Dordrecht: Kluwer, 459–498.

Ekman, P., & Friesen, W. V. (1974). Detecting deception from the body or face. *Journal of Personality and Social Psychology, 29*(3), 288–298.

Ekman, P., & O'Sullivan, M. (1991). Facial expression: Methods, means, and modes. In: R. S. Feldman & B. Rime (Eds.), *Fundamentals of nonverbal behavior* (pp. 163–199). Cambridge, NY: Cambridge University Press.

Elfenbein, H. A. & Ambady, N. (2002). Predicting workplace outcomes from the ability to eavesdrop on feelings. *Journal of Applied Psychology, 87*, 963–971.

Esselman, M., & Moore, W. (April, 1992). *In search of organizational variables which can be altered to promote an increased sense of teacher efficacy.* Paper presented at the annual meeting of the American Educational Research Association, San Francisco, CA.

Farber, B., & Miller, J. (1981). Teacher burnout: A psycho-educational perspective. *Teachers College Record, 83*(2): 235–243.

Friedman, E. H. (1985). *Generation to generation.* New York: The Guilford Press.

Gardner, L., & Stough, C. (2002). Examining the relationship between leadership and emotional intelligence in senior level managers. *Leadership and Organizational Development Journal, 23*(2), 68–78.

Gecas, V., & Schwalbe, M. L. (1983). Beyond the looking-glass self: Social structure and self-efficacy based self-esteem. *Social Psychology Quarterly, 46*(2): 77–88.

Goddard, R. D., & Goddard, Y. L. (2001). A multilevel analysis of the relationship between teacher and collective efficacy in urban schools. *Teaching and Teacher Education, 17*(7): 807–818.

Goleman, D. (1998). *Working with emotional intelligence.* New York: Bantam Books.

Goleman, D., Boyatzis, R., & McKee, A. (2002). *Primal leadership: Realizing the power of emotional intelligence.* Boston: Harvard Business School Press.

Groves, K. (2006). Leader emotional expressivity, visionary leadership, and organizational change. *Leadership and Organization Development Journal, 27*(7), 565–582.

Hackman, J., & Oldham, G. (1975). Development of the job satisfaction survey. *Journal of Applied Psychology, 60*(2): 159–170.

Harvey, A., & Spinney, J. (2000), *Life on & off the job: A time study of Nova Scotia teachers.* Halifax, NS: Saint Mary's University Time-Use Research Program.

Hirsch, E. (2004a). *Listening to the experts: A report on the 2004 South Carolina teacher working conditions survey.* Chapel Hill, NC: The Southeast Center for Teaching Quality.

Hirsch, E. (2004b). *Teacher working conditions are student learning conditions: A report to Governor Mike Easley on the 2004 North Carolina teacher working conditions survey.* Chapel Hill, NC: Southeast Center for Teaching Quality.

Kerr, R., Gavin, J., Heaton, N., & Boyle, E. (2005). Emotional intelligence and leadership effectiveness. *Leadership and Organization Development Journal, 27*(4), 265–279.

Leban, W., & Zulauf, C. (2004). Linking emotional intelligence abilities and transformational leadership styles. *The Leadership and Organization Development Journal, 25*(7), 554–564.

Leithwood, K., & Beatty, B. (2007). *Leading with teacher emotions in mind.* Thousand Oaks, CA: Corwin.

Leithwood, K., & Jantzi, D. (2005). A review of transformational school leadership research: 1996–2005, *Leadership and Policy in Schools, 4*(3): 177–199.

Leithwood, K., & Riehl, C. (2005). What we know about successful school leadership, in W. Firestone & C. Riehl (Eds.), *A new agenda: Directions for research on educational leadership.* New York: Teachers College Press.

Loucks-Horsley, S., Hewson, P. W., Love, N., & Stiles, K. E. (1998). *Designing professional development for teachers of science and mathematics.* Thousand Oaks, CA: Corwin Press.

Lubit, R. (2004). The tyranny of toxic managers: Applying emotional intelligence to deal with difficult personalities. In J. Osland, D. Kolb, & I. Rubin (Eds.), *The organizational behavior reader* (8th ed.) (pp. 64–77). New Jersey: Prentice Hall.

Maslach, C., & Jackson, S. E. (1981). A scale measure to assess experienced burnout: The Maslach burnout inventory, *Journal of Occupational Behaviour, 2*(2): 99–113.

Mayer, J., & Salovey, P. (1990). Emotional intelligence. *Imagination, Cognition, and Personality, 9*: 185–211.

Mills, L. B. (2009). A meta-analysis of the relationship between emotional intelligence and effective leadership. *Journal of Curriculum and Instruction, 3*(2), 22–38.

Modassir, A., & Singh, T. (2008). Relationship of emotional intelligence with transformational leadership and organizational citizenship behavior. *International Journal of Leadership Studies, 4*(1), 3–21.

Moos, L., Krejsler, J., Kofod, K. K., & Jensen, B. B. (2007). Communicative strategies among successful Danish school principals, in C. Day & K. Leithwood (eds.), *Successful principal leadership: An international perspective.* Dordrecht: Springer.

Naylor, C., & Schaeffer, A. (2003). *Worklife of BC teachers: A compilation of BCTF research reports on working and learning conditions in 2001.* Vancouver, BC: Teachers' Federation.

Nowicki, S., & Duke, M. (1994). Individual differences in the nonverbal communication of affect. *Journal of Nonverbal Behavior, 18,* 9–36.

Nowicki, S. & Duke, M. (2001) Nonverbal receptivity. In J. Hall & F. Bernieri (Eds.) *Current perspectives on research on nonverbal communication* (pp. 183–200). Mahwah, NJ: Erlbaum.

O'Sullivan, M., & Guilford, J. P. (1976). *Four factor tests of social intelligence: Manual of instructions and interpretations*. Orange, CA: Sheridan Psychological Services.

Oatley, K., Keltner, D., & Jenkins, J. M. (2006). *Understanding emotions* (2nd ed.). Malden, MA: Blackwell.

Palmer, B., Walls, M., Burgess, Z., & Stough, C. (2001). Emotional intelligence and effective leadership. *Leadership and Organization Development Journal, 22*(1), 5–10.

Parkay, F., Greenwood, G., Olejnik, S., & Proller, N. (1988). A study of the relationship among teacher efficiency, locus of control, and stress. *Journal of Research and Development in Education, 21*(4): 13–22.

Perez, M., Anand, P., Speroni, C., Parrish, T., Esra, P., Socias, M., & Grubbins, P. (2007). *Successful California schools in the context of educational adequacy*. Washington, DC: American Institutes for Research.

Reichard, R.J. & Riggio, R. E. (2008). An interactive, process model of emotions and leadership. In C. Cooper & N. E. Ashkanasy (Eds.), *Research companion to emotion in organizations*. Northampton, MA: Edward Elgar.

Riggio, R.E. (2008). *Introduction to industrial/organizational psychology* (5th ed.). Upper Saddle River, NJ: Prentice-Hall.

Riggio, R. E., & Carney, D. R. (2003). *Social skills inventory manual* (2nd ed.). Redwood City, CA: Mind Garden.

Riggio, R. E., & Reichard, R. J. (2008). The emotional and social intelligences of effective leadership: An emotional and social skill approach. *Journal of Managerial Psychology, 23*(2), 169–185.

Riggio, R. E., & Riggio, H. R. (2005). Self-report measures of emotional and nonverbal expressiveness. In V. Manusov (Ed.), *The sourcebook of nonverbal measures: Going beyond words* (pp. 105–111). Mahwah, NJ: Erlbaum.

Rinderle-Tessa, A. (1999). When angry "teacher-talk" affects the student's performance. Retrieved from www.eftuniverse.com/index.php?option=com_content&view=article&id=318:when-angry-qteacher-talkq-affects-the-students-performance&catid=9:children-adolescents&Itemid=235

Rosenthal, R., Hall, J. A., DiMatteo, M. R., Rogers, P. L., & Archer, D. (1979). *Sensitivity to nonverbal communications: The PONS test*. Baltimore, MD: The Johns Hopkins University Press.

Rosete, D., & Ciarrochi, J. (2005). Emotional intelligence and its relationship to workplace performance outcomes of leadership effectiveness. *Leadership and Organization Development Journal, 26*(5), 388–399.

Ross, J. A. (1992). Teacher efficacy and the effect of coaching on student achievement. *Canadian Journal of Education, 17*(1), 51–65.

Rubin, R., Munz, D., & Bommer, W. (2005). Leading from within: The effects of emotion recognition and personality on transformational leadership behavior. *Academy of Management Journal, 48*(5), 845–858.

Salovey, P., & Mayer, J.D. (1990). Emotional intelligence. *Imagination, Cognition, and Personality, 9*, 185–211.

Schulte, M. J. (2002). *Emotional intelligence: A predictive or descriptive construct in ascertaining leadership style or a new name for old knowledge?* (Doctoral dissertation). Retrieved from Dissertations & Theses: A&I.

Sivanathan, N., & Fekken, G. C. (2002). Emotional intelligence, moral reasoning, and transformational leadership. *Leadership Organization Development Journal, 23*(4), 198–204.

Srivastava, K. B., & Bharamanaikar, S. R. (2004). Emotional intelligence and effective leadership behaviour. *Psychological Studies, 49*(2–3), 107–113.

Stacey, R.D. (1996). *Complexity and creativity in organizations*. San Francisco: Berrett Koehler.

Stein, M., & Spillane, J. (2005). What can researchers on educational leadership learn from research on teaching: Building a bridge, in W. Firestone & C. Riehl (eds.), *A new agenda for research in educational leadership*. New York: Teachers College Press: 28–45.

Taylor, D. (2002). *The naked leader*. London, Bantam Books.

Teacher removed from classroom on a stretcher after throwing chairs and tables while pupils taunt him. (2010). *Daily Mail*. Retrieved from www.dailymail.co.uk/news/article-1319521/Teacher-suspended-throwing-tables-pupils-taunt-Nashville-school.html

Turner, B. (2004). *Servant leadership. Pastoral forum*. Retrieved from www.pilink.org/downloads/billturner.pdf

Vakola, M, Tsaousis, I., & Nikolaou, I. (2004). The role of emotional intelligence and personality variables on attitudes toward organisational change. *Journal of Managerial Psychology, 19*, 88–110.

Weinberger, L. A. (2003). *An examination of the relationship between emotional intelligence, leadership style, and perceived leadership effectiveness* (Doctoral dissertation). Retrieved from Dissertations & Theses: A&I.

Welch, J. (2003). The best teams are emotionally literate. *Industrial and Commercial Training, 35*(4), 168–170.

Wong, C., & Law, K. S. (2002). The effects of leader and follower emotional intelligence on performance and attitude: An exploratory study. *The Leadership Quarterly, 13*(3), 243–274.

Wong, C. S., Law, K.S., & Wong, P. M. (2004). Development and validation of a forced choice emotional intelligence measure for Chinese respondents in Hong Kong. *Asia Pacific Journal of Management, 21*, 535–559.

Chapter 6: Entrepreneurial Leadership

Akerlof, G. A., & Kranton, R. E. (2002). Identity and schooling: Some lessons for the economics of education. *Journal of Economic Literature, 40*, 1167–1201.

Aldrich, H., Renzulli, L. A., & Langton, N. (1998). Passing on privilege: Resources provided by self-employed parents to their self-employed children. *Research in Social Stratification and Mobility, 16*, 291–317.

Amason, A. C. (1996). Distinguishing the effects of functional and dysfunctional conflict on strategic decision making: Resolving a paradox for top management teams. *Academy of Management Journal, 39*, 123–148.

Ashour, A. S. (1973). Further discussion of Fiedler's contingency model of leadership effectiveness: An evaluation. *Organizational Behavior and Human Performance, 9*, 339–355.

Bandura, A. (1977). *Social learning theory*. Englewood Cliffs, NJ: Prentice Hall.

Bantel, K. A. & Jackson, S. E. (1989). Top management and innovations in banking: Does the composition of the top team make a difference? *Strategic Management Journal, 10*, 107–124.

Baum, J. R., & Wally, S. (2003). Strategic decision speed and firm performance. *Strategic Management Journal, 24*, 1107–1129.

Baum, J. R., Locke, E. A., & Kirkpatrick, S. A. (1998). A longitudinal study of the relation of vision and vision communication to venture growth in entrepreneurial firms. *Journal of Applied Psychology, 83*, 43–54.

Baumol, W. B. J. (1968). Entrepreneurship in economic theory. *American Economic Review, 58*(2), 64–71.

Bryant, T. A. (2004). Entrepreneurship. In G. R. Goethals, G. J. Sorenson, & J. M. Burns (Eds.), *Encyclopedia of leadership* (Vol. 1, pp. 442–448). Thousand Oaks, CA: Sage.

Cogliser, C. C., & Brigham, K. H. (2004). The intersection of leadership and entrepreneurship: Mutual lessons to be learned. *Leadership Quarterly, 15*, 771–799.

Conger, J. A. (1989). Leadership: The art of empowering others. *Academy of Management Executive, 3*, 471–482.

Covin, J. G., & Slevin, D. P. (2002). The entrepreneurial imperatives of strategic leadership. In M. A. Hitt, R. D. Ireland, S. M. Camp, & D. L. Sexton (Eds.), *Strategic entrepreneurship* (pp. 309–327). Oxford: Blackwell Publishers.

Covin, J. G., & Slevin, D. P. (2004). The concept of entrepreneurial leadership. In M. A. Hitt, & R. D. Ireland (Eds.), *Entrepreneurship encyclopedia.* Malden, MA: Blackwell Publishing.

Cruz, M. G., Henningsen, D. D., & Smith, B. A. (1999). The impact of directive leadership on group information sampling, decisions, and perceptions of the leader. *Communications Research, 26,* 349–369.

Davidsson, P., & Wiklund, J. (2001). Levels of analysis in entrepreneurship research: Current research practice and suggestions for the future. *Entrepreneurship Theory & Practice, 25,* 81–100.

Dunn, T., and D. Holtz-Eakin (2000). Financial capital, human capital, and the transition to self-employment: Evidence from intergenerational links. *Journal of Labor Economics, 18,* 282–305.

Eisenhardt, K. M. (1989). Making fast strategic decisions in high-velocity environments. *Academy of Management Journal, 32,* 543–576.

Elenkov, D. S., Judge, W., & Wright, P. (2005). Strategic leadership and executive innovation influence: An international multi-cluster comparative study. *Strategic Management Journal, 26,* 665–682.

Ensley, M. D., Pearce, C. L., & Hmieleski, K. M. (2006). Environmental dynamism: A moderator of the entrepreneur leadership behavior—new venture performance linkage. *Journal of Business Venturing, 21,* 243–263.

Ensley, M. D., Pearson, A., & Pearce, C. L. (2003). Top management team process, shared leadership, and new venture performance: A theoretical model and research agenda. *Human Resource Management Review, 13,* 329–346.

Fairlie, R. W., & Robb, A. (2007). Families, human capital, and small business: Evidence from the characteristics of business owner's survey. *Industrial and Labor Relations Review, 60,* 225–245.

Falck, O., S. Heblich, & Luedemann, E. (2009). *Identity and entrepreneurship: Do peers at school shape entrepreneurial intentions?* PEPG 09–05 Working Paper, Program of Education.

Gebert, D., & Boerner, S. (1999). The open and the closed corporation as conflicting forms of organization. *Journal of Applied Behavioral Science, 35*(3), 341–359.

Gebert, D., Boerner, S., & Lanwehr, R. (2003). The risk of autonomy: Empirical evidence for the necessity of a balance management in promoting organizational innovativeness. *Creativity and Innovation Management, 12,* 41–49.

Gold, R., Falck, O., & Heblich, S. (2010). *Entrepreneurship education.* Entrepreneurship, Growth, and Public Policy Group. Jena: Max Planck Institute of Economics.

Griffin, M. A., & Mathieu, J. E. (1997). Modeling organizational processes across hierarchical levels: Climate, leadership, and group process in work groups. *Journal of Organizational Behavior, 18,* 731–744.

Gupta, V., MacMillan, I. C., & Surie, G. (2004). Entrepreneurial leadership: Developing and measuring a cross-cultural construct. *Journal of Business Venturing, 19,* 241–260.

Herzberg, F. (1974). *Work and the nature of man.* Crosby, St Albans: Signet.

Heskett, J. L., Sasser, W. E., Jr., & Hart, C. W. L. (1990). *Service breakthroughs, Changing the rules of the game.* New York: Free Press.

Heskett, J. L., Sasser, W. E., Jr., & Schlesinger, L. A. (1997). *The service profit chain.* New York: The Free Press.

Hmieleski, K. M., & Ensley, M. D. (2007). A contextual examination of new venture performance: entrepreneur leadership behavior, top management team heterogeneity, and environmental dynamism. *Journal of Organizational Behavior, 28*(7), 865–889.

Homburg, C., & Stock, R. (2001). The link between sales people's job satisfaction and customer satisfaction in a business-to-business context: A dyadic analysis. *Journal of the Academy of Marketing Science, 32*(2), 144–158.

House, R. J., & Aditya, R. N. (1997). The social scientific study of leadership: Quo vadis? *Journal of Management, 23*, 409–473.

Hout, M., & Rosen, H. S. (2000). Self-employment, family background, and race. *Journal of Human Resources, 35*(4), 670–692.

Hu, W. (2010). Ambitious new model for 7 Newark schools. *The New York Times.* Retrieved from www.nytimes.com/2010/07/26/education/26newark.html

Ireland, R. D., Hitt, M. A., & Sirmon, D. G. (2003). A model of strategic entrepreneurship: The construct and its dimensions. *Journal of Management, 29*, 963–989.

Kahai, S. S., Sosik, J. J., & Avolio, B. J. (1997). Effects of leadership style and problem structure on work group process and outcomes in an electronic meeting system environment. *Personnel Psychology, 50*, 121–146.

Katz, J. A. (2003). The chronology and intellectual trajectory of American entrepreneurship education. *Journal of Business Venturing, 18*(2), 283–300.

Kerr, S., & Jermier, J. (1978). Substitutes for leadership: Their meaning and measurement. *Organizational Behavior and Human Performance, 22*, 375–403.

Kotter, J. P. & Heskett, J. L. (1992). *Corporate culture and performance.* New York: The Free Press.

Laband, D., & Lentz, B. F.(1990). Entrepreneurial success and occupational inheritance among proprietors. *Canadian Journal of Economics, 23*(3), 101–117.

Lam, T., Zhang, H., & Baum, Th. (2001). An investigation of employee's job satisfaction: the case of hotels in Hong Kong. *Tourism Management, 22*(2) 34–51.

Langer, E. J., & Sviokla, J. (1988). *Charisma from a mindfulness perspective.* Cambridge, MA: Harvard University.

Larson, J. R., Foster-Fishman, P. G., & Franz, T. M. (1998). Leadership style and the discussion of shared and unshared information in decision-making groups. *Personality and Social Psychology Bulletin, 24*, 482–495.

Lazear, E. P. (2005). *Personal economics for managers.* New York: John Wiley & Sons.

Leithwood, K. & Beatty, B. (2008). *Leading with teacher emotions in mind.* Thousand Oaks, CA: Corwin Press.

Lok, P., & Crawford, J. (1999). The relationship between commitment and organizational structure, subculture, leadership style and job satisfaction in organizational change and development. *Leadership and Organizational Development Journal, 20*, 34–65.

Low, M., & MacMillan, I. (1988). Entrepreneurship: Past research and future challenges. *Journal of Management, 14*, 139–161.

Marion, R., & Uhl-Bien, M. (2001). Leadership in complex organizations. *Leadership Quarterly, 14*, 389–418.

Marshall, A. (1920). *Principles of economics* (8th ed.). London: MacMillan.

McGrath, R., & MacMillan, I. (2000). *The entrepreneurial mindset.* Cambridge, MA: Harvard Business School Press.

Montanari, J. R., & Moorhead, G. (1989). Development of the Groupthink Assessment Inventory. *Educational and Psychological Measurement, 49*, 209–219.

Mumford, M. D., Feldman, J. M., Hein, M. B., & Nagao, D. J. (2001). Tradeoffs between ideas and structure: Individual versus group performance in creative problem solving. *Journal of Creative Behavior, 35*, 1–23.

Nicholls-Nixon, C. L. (2005). Rapid growth and high performance: The entrepreneur's "impossible dream?" *Academy of Management Executive, 19*, 77–89.

Nicolaou, N., & Shane, S. (2009). Born Entrepreneurs? The genetic foundations of entrepreneurship. *Journal of Business Venturing, 30*, 45–67.

Nicolaou, N., Shane, S., Cherkas, L., Hunkin, J., & Spector, T. (2008). Is the tendency to engage in entrepreneurship genetic? *Management Science, 54*, 167–179.

Normann, R. (1996). *Service management.* New York, NY: John Wiley & Sons.

Osborn, R. N., Hunt, J. G., & Jauch, L. R. (2002). Toward a contextual theory of leadership. *Leadership Quarterly, 13*, 797–837.

Pearce, C. L. (2004). The future of leadership: Combining vertical and shared leadership to transform knowledge work. *Academy of Management Executive*, *18*, 47–57.

Pearce, C. L., Sims, H. P., Cox, J. F., Ball, G., Schnell, E., Smith, K. A., et al. (2003). Transactors, transformers and beyond: A multi-method development of a theoretical typology of leadership. *Journal of Management Development*, *22*, 273–307.

Pennigton, P., Townsend, C. & Cummins, R. (2003). The relationship of leadership practices to culture. *Journal of Leadership Education*, *2*(1), 1–18.

Peters, M. (2005). Entrepreneurial skills in leadership and human resource management evaluated by apprentices in small tourism businesses. *Education and Training*, 47, 575–591.

Peters, M. & Buhalis, D. (2004). Family hotel businesses: strategic planning and the need for education and training. *Education Training*, *46*(9), 6–15.

Peters, M., Weiermair, K. & Leimegger, R. (2004). Employees' evaluation of entrepreneurial leadership in small tourism businesses. In P. Keller, & T. Bieger (Eds.), *The future of small and medium sized enterprises in tourism* (pp. 315–333). London: World Tourism Organisation.

Pfeffer, J. (1983). Organizational demography. *Research in Organizational Behavior*, *5*, 299–357.

Robinson, V. M. J. (2008). Fit for purpose: An educationally relevant account of distributed leadership. In A. Harris (Ed.), *Distributed leadership: Different perspectives* (pp. 219–240). Berlin: Springer.

Schriesheim, C.A., & Kerr, S. (1977). Theories and measures of leadership: a critical appraisal of current and future directions. In J. G. Hunt & L. L. Larson (Eds.), *Leadership: the cutting edge* (pp. 9–45). Carbondale: Southern Illinois University Press.

Schumpeter, J. A. (1912). *The theory of economic development*. New York: Oxford University Press.

Shalley, C. E., & Gilson, L. L. (2004). What leaders need to know: A review of social and contextual factors that can foster or hinder creativity? *Leadership Quarterly*, *15*, 33–53.

Sharpley, R., & Forster, G. (2003). The implications of hotel employee attitudes for the development of quality tourism: the case of Cyprus. *Tourism Management*, *24*(6), 687–697.

Spillane, J. P., Halverson, R. & Diamond, J. B. (2004). Towards a theory of leadership practice: a distributed perspective. *Journal of Curriculum Studies*, *36*(1), 3–34.

Spreitzer, G. M. (1996). Social structural characteristics of psychological empowerment. *Academy of Management Journal*, *39*, 483–504.

Vecchio, R. (2003). Entrepreneurship and leadership: Common trends and common threads. *Human Resource Management Review*, *13*, 303–327.

Wickham, P. A. (2001). *Strategic entrepreneurship: A decision-making approach to new venture creation and management*. Harlow: Prentice Hall.

Williamson, I. O. (2000). Employer legitimacy and recruitment success in small businesses. *Entrepreneurship Theory & Practice*, *25*, 27–42.

Yukl, G. (2002). *Leadership in organizations*. Upper Saddle River, NJ: Prentice Hall.

Chapter 7: Strategic Leadership

Aaker, D. A., & Joachimsthaler, E. (2000). *Brand leadership*. New York: The Free Press.

Abdullah, H. M. (2001). *Policy dialogue on quality improvement in education: A Malaysian experience*. Paper presented at the Second International Forum on Quality Education: Policy, Research and Innovative Practices in Improving Quality of Education, Beijing, China, 12–15 June.

Baker, R., & Begg, A. (2003). Change in the school curriculum: Looking to the future, in J. P. Keeves & R. Watanabe (Eds.), *International handbook of educational research in the Asia-Pacific region*. Dordrecht: Kluwer Academic Publishers, 541–554.

Bartunek, J. M., & Necochea, R. (2000). Old insights and new times. *Journal of Management Inquiry*, *9*(2), 103–113.

Beare, H., Caldwell, B. J., & Millikan, R. H. (1989). *Creating an excellent school*. London: Routledge.

Bennett, D. (2000). *The school of the future*. Nottingham: NCSL.

Blackledge, D., & Hunt, B. (1985). *Sociological interpretations of education*. Sydney: Croom Helm.

Boal, K. B., & Hooijberg, R. (2001). Strategic leadership research: Moving on. *Leadership Quarterly, 11*(4), 515–549.

Burbules, N. C., & Torres, C. A. (Eds.) (2000). *Globalization and education: Critical perspectives*. New York: Routledge.

Cheng, Y. C. (2000a). A CMI-triplization paradigm for reforming education in the new millennium. *International Journal of Educational Management, 14*(4), 156–174.

Cheng, Y. C. (2000b). Educational change and development in Hong Kong: Effectiveness, quality, and relevance. In T. Townsend & Y. C. Cheng (Eds.), *Educational change and development in the Asia-Pacific region: Challenges for the future* (pp. 17–56). The Netherlands: Swets and Zeitlinger Publisher.

Cheng, Y. C. (2001). *Towards the third wave of educational reforms in Hong Kong: Triplization in the new millennium*. Plenary speech presented at the International Forum on Educational reforms in the Asia-Pacific Region "Globalization, Localization, and Individualization for the Future," HKSAR, China.

Cheng, Y. C. (2002a). The changing context of school leadership: Implications for paradigm shift. In K. Leithwood & P. Hallinger (Eds.), *Second international handbook of educational leadership and administration*. Dordrecht: Kluwer Academic Publishers, 103–132.

Cheng, Y. C. (2002b). Leadership and strategy. In T. Bush and L. Bell (Eds.), *The principles and practice of educational management*. London: Paul Chapman, 51–69.

Cheng, Y. C. (2003). School leadership and three waves of education reforms. *Cambridge Journal of Education, 33*(3): 417–439.

Cheng, Y. C. (2005a). *New paradigm for re-engineering education: Globalization, localization and individualization*. Dordrecht: Springer.

Cheng, Y. C. (2005b). Multiple thinking and multiple creativity in action learning. *Journal of Education Research, 134* (June): 76–105.

Cheng, Y. C. (2009). Educational reforms in Hong Kong in the last decade: Reform syndrome and new developments. *International Journal of Educational Management, 23*(1): 65–86.

Cheng, Y. C. (2010). A topology of 3-wave models of strategic leadership in education. *International Studies in Educational Administration, 38*(1), 35–54.

Cheng, Y. C. & Townsend, T. (2000). Educational change and development in the Asia-Pacific region: Trends and issues. In T. Townsend & Y. C. Cheng (Eds.), *Educational change and development in the Asia-Pacific region: Challenges for the future* (pp. 317–344). Lisse, The Netherlands: Swets & Zeitlinger.

Cheng, Y. C., & Walker, J. A. (2008). When reform hits reality: The bottle-neck effect in Hong Kong primary schools. *School Leadership and Management, 28*(5): 467–483.

Collins, J. (2001). *Good to great*. London: Random House.

Coulson, A. J. (1999). *Market education: The unknown history*. New Brunswick, NJ: Transaction Publishers.

Daun, H. (2002). *Educational restructuring in the context of globalization and national policy*. New York: Routledge Falmer.

Davies, B. (2003). Rethinking strategy and strategic leadership in schools. *Education Management & Administration, 31*(3), 295–312.

Davies, B. & Davies, B. J. (2005). Strategic leadership. In B. Davies (Ed.), *The essentials of school leadership* (pp. 10–30). Thousand Oaks, CA: Corwin Press.

Davies, B., Davies, B. J., & Ellison, L. (2005). *Success and sustainability: Developing the strategically focused school*. Nottingham: National College for School Leadership.

Eacott, S. (2008a). An analysis of contemporary literature on strategy in education. *International Journal of Leadership in Education, 11*(3): 257–280.

Evans, G. R. (1999). *Calling academia to account: Rights and responsibilities*. Buckingham: Society for Research in Higher Education and Open University Press.

Farrell, A., & Hart, M (1998). What does sustainability really mean? The search for useful indicators. *Environment, 40*, 26–31.

Freedman, M. (2003). *The art and discipline of strategic leadership.* New York: McGraw-Hill.

Fullan, M. (2004). *Leadership and sustainability: System thinkers in action.* Thousand Oaks, CA: Corwin Press.

Gardner, H. (1985). *The mind's new science.* New York: Basic Books.

Goertz, M. E., & Duffy, M. C. (2001). *Assessment and accountability systems in the 50 states, 1999–2000.* Philadelphia, PA: CPRE Research Report Series.

Goldsmith, M. (1996). *Coaching for behavioral change. Leader to Leader.* San Francisco: Jossey-Bass.

Gopinathan, S., & Ho, W. K. (2000). Educational change and development in Singapore. In T. Townsend & Y. C. Cheng (Eds.), *Educational change and development in the Asia-Pacific region: Challenges for the future.* Lisse: Swets & Zeitlinger: 163–184.

Headington, R. (2000). *Monitoring, assessment, recording, reporting and accountability: Meeting the standards.* London: David Fulton.

Heck, D. J., & Weiss, I. R. (2005). *Strategic leadership for education reform: Lessons from the state-wide systemic initiatives program.* Philadelphia: Consortium for Policy Research in Education.

Heller, D. E. (Ed.) (2001). *The states and public higher education policy: Affordable, access, and accountability.* Baltimore, MD: Johns Hopkins University Press.

Hickson, D. J, Butler, R. J, Cray, D, Mallory, G. R., & Wilson, D. C. (1989). Decision and organization processes of strategic decision making and their explanation. *Public Administration, 67*(4), 373–390.

Kim, Y. H. (2000). Recent changes and developments in Korean school education. In T. Townsend & Y. C. Cheng (Eds.), *Educational change and development in the Asia-Pacific region: Challenges for the future.* Lisse: Swets & Zeitlinger: 83–106.

Koteen, J. (1989). *Strategic management in public and nonprofit organizations.* New York, N.Y: Praeger.

MacBeath, J. (2007). Improving school effectiveness: Retrospective and prospective. In T. Townsend, B. Avalos, B. Caldwell, Y. C. Cheng, B. Fleisch, L. Moos, L. Stoll, S. Stringfield, K. Sundell, W. M. Tam, N. Taylor, & C. Teddlie (Eds.), *International handbook on school effectiveness and improvement.* Dordrecht: Springer: 57–74.

Maclean, R. (2003). Secondary education reform in the Asia-Pacific region. In J. P. Keeves & R. Watanabe (Eds.), *International handbook of educational research in the Asia-Pacific region.* Dordrecht: Kluwer Academic Publishers: 73–92.

Mahony, P., & Hextall, I. (2000). *Reconstructing teaching: Standards, performance and accountability.* London: Routledge.

Mintzberg, H. (1995). Strategic thinking as seeing. In B. Garratt (Ed.), *Developing strategic thought.* London: McGraw-Hill.

Mohandas, R., Meng, H. W., & Keeves, J. P. (2003). Evaluation and accountability in Asian and Pacific countries. In J. P. Keeves & R. Watanabe (Eds.), *International handbook of educational research in the Asia-Pacific region.* Dordrecht: Kluwer Academic Publishers: 107–122.

Mok, M. M. C., Gurr, D., Izawa, E., Knipprath, H., Lee, I., Mel, M. A., Palmer, T., Shan, W., & Zhang, Y. (2003). Quality assurance and school monitoring. In J. P. Keeves & R. Watanabe (Eds.), *International handbook of educational research in the Asia-Pacific region.* Dordrecht: Kluwer Academic Publishers: 945–958.

Mukhopadhyay, M. (2001).*Total quality management in education.* New Delhi: National Institute of Educational Planning and Administration.

Novak, J. (2002). *Inviting educational leadership.* London: Pearson Education.

Pang, I., Isawa, E., Kim, A., Knipprath, H., Mel, M. A., & Palmer, T. (2003). Family and community participation in education. In J. P. Keeves & R. Watanabe (Eds.), *International handbook of educational research in the Asia-Pacific region.* Dordrecht: Kluwer Academic Publishers: 1063–1080.

Parikh, J. (1994). *Intuition—The new frontier of management*. Oxford: Blackwell.

Pefianco, E. C., Curtis, D., & Keeves, J. P. (2003). Learning across the adult lifespan. In J. P. Keeves & R. Watanabe (Eds.), *International handbook of educational research in the Asia-Pacific region*. Dordrecht: Kluwer Academic Publishers: 305–320.

Peterson, C. C. (2003). Lifespan human development. In J. P. Keeves & R. Watanabe (Eds.), *International handbook of educational research in the Asia-Pacific region*. Dordrecht: Kluwer Academic Publishers: 379–394.

Prahalad, C. K., & Hamel, G. (1990). The core competencies of the corporation. *Harvard Business Review, 68*, 79–93.

Rajput, J. S. (2001). *Reforms in school education in India*. Plenary speech presented at the International Forum on Educational reforms in the Asia-Pacific Region "Globalization, Localization, and Individualization for the Future," HKSAR, China, 14–16 February.

Ramirez, F. O., & Chan-Tiberghein, J. (2003). Globalisation and education in Asia. In J. P. Keeves & R. Watanabe (Eds.), *International handbook of educational research in the Asia-Pacific region*. Dordrecht: Kluwer Academic Publishers: 1095–1106.

Schön, D. (1987). *Educating the reflective practitioner*. San Francisco: Jossey-Bass.

Shrivastava, P., & Grant, J. (1985). Empirically derived models of strategic decision-making processes. *Strategic Management Journal, 6*, 97–113.

Stalk, G., Evans, P., & Schulman, L. (1992). Competing on capabilities: The new rules of corporate Strategy. *Harvard Business Review, 70*(2), 54.

Stromquist, N. P., & Monkman, K. (2000). *Globalization and education: Integration and contestation across cultures*. Lanham, MD: Rowman & Littlefield.

Tang, X., & Wu X. (2000). Educational change and development in the People's Republic of China: Challenges for the future. In T. Townsend & Y. C. Cheng (Eds.), *Educational change and development in the Asia-Pacific region: Challenges for the future* (pp. 133–162). Lisse, The Netherlands: Swets & Zeitlinger.

Townsend, T., Avalos, B., Caldwell, B., Cheng, Y. C., Fleisch, B., Moos, L., Stoll, L., Stringfield, S., Sundell, K., Tam, W.M., Taylor, N., & Teddlie, C. (Eds.) (2007). *International handbook on school effectiveness and improvement*. Dordrecht: Springer.

Chapter 8: Sustainable Leadership

Abrahamson, E. (2004). *Change without pain: How managers can overcome initiative overload, organizational chaos, and employee burnout*. Boston, MA: Harvard Business School Press.

Anyon, J. (2005). *Radical possibilities: Public policy, urban education, and a new social movement*. New York: Routledge.

Blackmore, J. (1996). Doing emotional labour in the education marketplace: stories from the field of women in management. *Discourse: studies in the cultural politics of education, 17*(3), 337–349.

Byrne, B. M. (1994). Burnout testing for the validity, replication, and invariance of causal structure across the elementary, intermediate, and secondary teachers. *American Educational Research Journal, 31*(3), 645–673.

Capra, F. (1997). *The web of life: A new synthesis of mind and matter*. London: Harper Collins.

Collins, J. C., & Porras, J. I. (1994). *Built to last: Successful habits of visionary companies*. London: Century.

De Holan, P. M., & Philips, N. (2004a). The dynamics of organizational forgetting. *Management Source, 50*, 1603–1613.

De Holan P. M., & Phillips N. (2004b). Remembrance of things past? The dynamics of organizational forgetting. *Management Science*, 50, 1603–1613.

Drucker, P. (2001). *Management challenges for the 21st century*. New York: Harper Collins Baumann.

Flores-Gonzalez, N. (2002). *School kids, street kids: Identity and high school completion among Latinos*. New York: Teachers College Press.

Fullan, M. (2001). *Leading in a culture of change.* San Francisco: Jossey-Bass.

Glickman, C. D. (2002). *Leadership for learning: How to help teachers succeed.* Alexandria, VA: ASCD.

Goodson, I. (2001). Social histories of educational change, *The Journal of Educational Change, 2,* 45–63.

Goodson, I., Moore, S. & Hargreaves, A. (2006). Teacher nostalgia and the sustainability of reform: The generation and degeneration of teachers' missions, memory, and meaning. *Educational Administration Quarterly, 42,* 42–61.

Hargreaves, A. (2003). *Teaching in the knowledge society: Education in the age of insecurity.* New York, NY: Teachers College Press.

Hargreaves, A. (2007). *Sustainable leadership and development in education: Creating the future, conserving the past, 42,* 2.

Hargreaves, A., & Fink, D. (2006). *Sustainable leadership.* San Francisco, CA: Jossey Bass.

Hargreaves, A., & Goodson, I. (2004). *Change over time? A report of educational change over 30 years in eight U.S. and Canadian schools.* Chicago: Spencer Foundation.

Hargreaves, A., Moore, S., Fink, D., Brayman, C., & White, R. (2003). *Succeeding leaders? A study of principal rotation and succession.* Toronto, Ontario, Canada: Ontario Principals' Council.

Harry, B., & Klingner, J. (2006). *Why are so many minority students in special education? Understanding race and disability in schools.* New York: Teachers College Press.

Louis, K. S., & Kruse, S. D. (1995). *Professionalism and community: Perspectives on reforming urban high schools.* Thousand Oaks, CA: Corwin.

MacMillan, R. B. (2000). Leadership succession: Cultures of teaching and educational change. In N. Bascia & A. Hargreaves (Eds.), *The sharp edge of educational change: Teaching, leading, and the realities of reform* (pp. 52–71). New York: Routledge/Falmer.

Marris, R. (1974). *Loss and change.* London: Routledge and Kegan Paul.

McLaughlin, M., & Talbert, J. (2001). *Professional communities and the work of high school teaching.* Chicago: University of Chicago Press.

National Center for Education Statistics (2005). 1999–2000 schools and staffing survey (SASS).

National Collaborative on Diversity in the Teaching Force (2004). *Assessment of diversity in America's teaching force: A call to action.* Washington, D.C.: Author.

Nichols, S. L., & Berliner, D. C. (2007). *Collateral damage: How high-stakes testing corrupts America's schools.* Cambridge, MA: Harvard Education Publishing Group.

Nieto, S. (2007). *The color of innovative and sustainable leadership: Learning from teacher leaders, 8,* 299–309.

Oakes, J. (2005). *Keeping track: How schools structure inequality* (2nd Ed.). New Haven, CT: Yale University Press.

Oakes, J., Quartz, K. H., & Lipton, M. (2000). *Becoming good American schools: The struggle for civic virtue in education reform.* San Francisco: Jossey-Bass.

Olsen, L. (2006). A decade of effort: Quality counts marks its 10th year in print with a comprehensive review of the nation's movement toward higher academic standards and greater accountability. *Education Week. 25*(17), pp. 8–10, 12, 14, 16, 18–21.

Orfield, G., & Lee, C. (2005). *Racial transformation and the changing nature of segregation.* Cambridge, MA: The Civil Rights Project at Harvard University.

Rothstein, R. (2004). *Class and schools: Using social, economic, and educational reform to close the black-white achievement gap.* New York: Teachers College Press, and Washington, D.C.: Economic Policy Institute.

Spillane, J. P., Halverson, R., & Drummond, J. B. (2001). Investigating school leadership practice: A distributed perspective. *Educational Researcher, 30*(3), 23–28.

Stoll, L., Fink, D., & Earl, L. (2002). *It's about learning (and it's about time).* London: Routledge.

Teachernet (2005) School workforce remodeling. Retrieved from www.teachernet.gov/uk/wholeschool/remodelling/

U.S. Census Bureau (2000a). *Profile of selected social characteristics, 2000*. Washington, D.C.: U.S. Department Of Commerce.
U.S. Census Bureau (2000b). *Statistical abstract of the United States: 2000. Based on population estimates program and population projections program*. Washington, D.C.: U.S. Department of Commerce.
U.S. Census Bureau (2004). *Ability to speak english by languages spoken at home for the population 5 years and over: 2000*. Washington, D.C.: Author.
Valenzuela, A. (1999). *Youth subtractive schooling: U.S.–Mexican and the politics of caring*. Albany: State University of New York Press.

Chapter 9: Invitational Leadership

Anderson, C. S. (1982). The search for school climate: A review of the research. *Review of Educational Research, 52*(3), 368–420.
Barth, R. S. (1991). *Improving schools from within: Teachers, parents, and principals can make the difference*. Hoboken, NJ: Jossey-Bass.
Bolman, L. G., & Deal, T. E. (1997). *Reframing organizations: Artistry, choice, and leadership* (2nd Ed.). San Francisco: Jossey-Bass.
Bolman, L. G., & Deal, T. E. (2002, February). Leading with soul and spirit: Effective leadership in challenging times boils down to qualities such as focus, passion and integrity. *School Administrator, 59*, 21.
Brookover, W., Beady, C., Flood, P., Schweitzer, J. & Wisenbaker, J. (1977). *Schools can make a difference*. Washington, DC: National Institute of Education.
Bruffee, K. A. (1999). *Collaborative learning: Higher education, interdependence, and the authority of knowledge* (2nd ed.). Baltimore, MA: The John Hopkins University Press.
Caldwell, B. & Hayward, D. (1998). *The future of schools: Lessons from the reform of public education*. London: Falmer Press.
Cleveland, H. (2002). Leadership: The get-it-all-together-profession. *The Futurist, 36*(5), 42–47.
Covey, S. R. (1989). *The 7 habits of highly effective people*. New York: Simon & Schuster.
Daft, R. L. (1999). *Leadership: Theory and practice*. New York: Dryden Press.
Davis, B. (2003). Rethinking Strategy and strategic Leadership in Schools. *Educational Management and Administration, 31*(3), 295–312.
Day, C., Harris, A., & Hadfield, M. (2001). Grounding knowledge of schools in stakeholder realities: A multi-perspective study of effective school leaders. *School Leadership & Management, 21*(1), 19–42.
Edmonds, R. (1979). Effective schools for urban poor. *Educational Leadership, 37*, 15–24.
Egley, R. (2003). Invitational leadership: Does it make a difference? *Journal of Invitational Theory and Practice, 9*, 57–70.
Farling, M. L., Stone, A. G., & Winston, B. E. (1999). *Servant leadership: Setting the stage for empirical research*, 49.
Fowler, F. C. (2004). *Policy studies for educational leaders*. Upper Saddle River, NJ: Pearson Education, Inc.
Fullan, M. G., & Miles, M. B. (1992). Getting reform right: What works and what doesn't. *Phi Delta Kappan, 73*, 745–752.
Furman, G. C. (2004). Moral leadership and the ethic of community. *Values and Ethics in Educational Administration, 2*(1), 1–8.
Gardner, J. (1990). *On leadership*. New York: Simon & Schuster.
Grogan, M., & Roland, P. (2003). A study of successful teachers preparing high school students for the standards of learning tests in Virginia. In D. Duke, M. Grogan, P. Tucker, & W. Heinecke (Eds.), *Educational leadership in an age of accountability* (pp. 114–134). Albany, NY: SUNY Press.

Hallinger, P., & Heck, R. (1999). Can leadership enhance school effectiveness? In Bush et al. (Eds.) *Educational management: Redefining theory, policy and practice*, (pp. 178–190). London: Paul Chapman Publishing.

Halpern, D. F. (2004). The development of adult cognition: Understanding constancy and change in adult learning. In Day, D. V., Zaccaro, S. J., & Halpin, S. M. (Eds.), *Leader development for transforming organizations: Growing leaders for tomorrow* (pp. 125–150). Mahwah, NJ: Lawrence Erlbaum Associates.

Halpin, D. (2003). *Hope and education: The role of the utopian imagination*. London: RoutledgeFalmer.

Hansen, J. (1998). Creating a school where people like to be. *Educational Leadership, 56*, 14–17.

Hockaday, S., Purkey, W. W., & Davis, K. M. (2001). Intentionality in helping relationships: The influence of three forms of internal cognitions on behavior. *Journal of Humanistic Counseling, Education and Development, 40*, 219–224.

Hoyle, J. R. (2002). *Leadership and the force of love: Six keys to motivating with love*. Thousand Oaks, CA: Corwin Press.

Katzenbach, J. R., & Smith, D. K. (2003). *The wisdom of teams: Creating the high performance organization*. New York: Harper Business Essentials.

Kelly, P. A., Brown, S., Butler, A., Gittens, P. (2008). A place to hang our hats. *Educational Leadership, 56*(1), 62–64.

Kouzes, J. M., & Posner, B. Z. (2003). Challenge is the opportunity for greatness. *Leader to Leader, 28*, 16–23.

Leithwood, K., & Duke D. (1999). A century's quest to understand school leadership. In J. Murphy and K. Seashore-Louis (Eds.) *Handbook of research on educational administration* (2nd edition), 45, 72.

Leithwood, K., Jantzi D., & Steinbach, R. (2000a). Changing leadership: A menu of possibilities. In *Changing leadership for changing times* (pp. 3–20). Philadelphia, PA: Open University Press.

Leithwood, K., Jantzi, D., & Steinbach, R. (2000b). Transformational leadership as a place to begin. In *Changing leadership for changing times*, (pp. 21–39). Philadelphia, PA: Open University Press.

Lencioni, P. (2002). *The five dysfunctions of a team*. San Francisco: Jossey-Bass.

Lezotte, L., Hathaway, D. V., Miller, S. K., Passalacqua, J., & Brookover, W. B. (1980). *School learning climate and student achievement: A social system approach to increased student learning*. Tallahassee: The Site Specific Technical Assistance Center.

Louis, K. S., & Murphy, J. (1994). Florida State University Foundation. The evolving role of the principal: Some concluding thoughts. In J. Murphy & K. S. Louis (Eds.), *Reshaping the principalship: Insights from transformational reform efforts* (pp. 265–281). Newbury Park, CA: Corwin Press.

McCombs, B. L., & Whisler, J. S. (1997). *The learner-centered classroom and school*. San Francisco: Jossey-Bass.

Muijs, D. and Harris, A. (2003) Teacher leadership: A review of research (Nottingham, UK: National College for School Leadership). Retrieved from www.ncsl.org.uk/mediastore/image2/randd-engaged-harris.pdf

Novak, J. M. (2009). Invitational leadership. In B. Davies (Ed.), *The essentials of school leadership*. London: Sage.

Ogawa, R. T., & Bossert, S. T. (1995). Leadership as an organizational quality. *Educational Administration Quarterly, 31*(2), 224–243.

Patton, Q. M. (1997). *Utilization focused evaluation: The new century text* (3rd ed.). London: Sage Publications.

Purkey, W. (1992). An introduction to invitational theory. *Journal of Invitational Theory and Practice, 1*(1), 5–14.

Purkey, W. W., & Novak, J. M. (1984). *Inviting school success: A self-concept approach to teaching and learning.* Belmont, CA: Wadsworth.

Purkey, W., & Novak, J. (1996). *Inviting school success: A self-concept approach to Teaching and learning* (3rd Ed.). Belmont, CA: Wadsworth.

Purkey, W., & Siegel, B. (2003). *Becoming an invitational leader: A new approach to professional and personal success.* Atlanta, GA: Humantics.

Rosener, J. (1990). Ways women lead. *Harvard Business Review*, 119–125. Routledge/Falmer.

Schein, E. H. (2000). Sense and nonsense about culture and climate. In N. M. Ashkanasy, C. P. M. Wilderom, & M. F. Peterson (Eds.), *Handbook of organizational culture & climate.* Thousand Oaks, CA: Sage Publications.

Sergiovanni, T. J. (1992). Why we should seek substitutes for leadership. *Educational Leadership*, 5, 41–45.

Sergiovanni, T. J. (2000). Leadership as stewardship: "Who's serving who?" In *Educational Leadership*, (pp. 269–286). San Francisco: Jossey-Bass.

Spears, L., & Lawrence, M. (Eds.). (2004). *Practicing servant leadership: Succeeding through trust, bravery, and forgiveness.* San Francisco: Jossey-Bass.

Stanley, P. H., Juhnke, G. A., & Purkey, W. W. (2004). Using an invitational theory of practice to create safe and successful schools. *Journal of Counseling and Development*, 82(3), 302.

Stillion, J., & Siegel, B. (2005). Expanding invitational leadership: Roles for the decathlon leader. Retrieved January 31, 2006, from www.kennesaw.edu/ilec/Journal/articles/2005/siegel_stillion/expand_leader

Stoll, L., & Fink, D. (2003). *It's about learning (and it's about time).* New York: Routledge.

Strahan, D., & Purkey, W. W. (1992). *Celebrating diversity through invitational education.* Greensboro, NC: University of North Carolina at Greensboro. The International Alliance for Invitational Education.

Strong, J. H., & Jones, C. W. (May). Middle school climate: The principal's role in influencing effectiveness. *Middle School Journal*, 5, 41–44.

Tallon, A. (1997). *Head and Heart: Affection, Cognition, Volition as Triune Consciousness.* New York: Fordham University Press. Retrieved from www.questia.com/PM.qst?a=o&d=52320252

Witcher, A. E. (1993). Assessing school climate: An important step for enhancing school quality. *NASSP Bulletin*, 77, 1–5.

Yukl, G. (2006). *Leadership in organizations* (6th Ed.). Upper Saddle River, NJ: Prentice Hall.

Chapter 10: Constructivist Leadership

Barth, R. S. (2001, February). Teacher leader. *Phi Delta Kappan*, 82(4), 34–43.

Bellah, R., Madsen, R., Sullivan,W., Swidler, A., & Tipton, S. (1985). *Habits of the heart: Individualism and commitment in American life.* New York: Harper and Row.

Bodner, G., Klobuchar, M., & Geelan, D. (2001). The many forms of constructivism. *Journal of Chemical Education*, 78(1107).

Bouck, D. H. (2004). *Striving to be a constructivist leader.* Thesis, University of Alberta, Edmonton.

Burrell, G., & Morgan, G. (1979). *Sociological paradigms and organizational analysis: Elements of the sociology of corporate life.* London: Heinemann Educational Books Ltd.

Cobern, W. W. (1993). Constructivism. *Journal of Educational and Psychological Consultation*, 4(1), 111.

Coe, J. G. (2006). *Autonomous learning and constructivist leadership: A case study in learning organizations.* Dissertation, Regent University, Virginia Beach. Gass, M. A., & Priest, S. (2006). The effectiveness of metaphoric facilitation styles in corporate adventure training (CAT) programs. *Journal of Experiential Education*, 29(1), 78–94.

DuFour, R. & Eaker, R. (1998). *Professional learning communities at work: Best practices for enhancing student achievement.* Alexandria, VA: Association for Supervision and Curriculum Development.

Freire, P. (1973). *Education for critical consciousness.* New York: Continuum.

Fullan, M. (2001). *The new meaning of educational change* (3rd ed.). New York: Teachers College Press.

Gass, M., & Priest, S. (2006). The effectiveness of metaphoric facilitation styles in corporate adventure training CAT programs. *Journal of Experiential Education, 29*(1), 78–94.

Jacobs, C. D., & Heracleous, L. T. (2006). Constructing shared understanding: The role of embodied metaphors in organizational development. *The Journal of Applied Behavioral Science, 42*(2), 207–226.

Lakoff, G., & Johnson, N. I. (1980). *Metaphors we live by.* Chicago: University of Chicago Press.

Lambert, L. (2003). *Leadership capacity for lasting school improvement.* Alexandria: Association for Supervision and Curriculum Development.

Lambert, L., & Walker, D. (1995). Learning and leading theory: A century in the making. In L. Lambert et al. (Eds.), *The constructivist leader* (pp. 1–27). New York: Teachers College Press.

Lambert, L., Walker, D., Zimmerman, D. P., Cooper, J. E., Lambert, M. D., Gardiner, M. E., et al. (2002). *The Constructivist Leader* (2nd ed.). New York: Teachers College Press.

Little, J. W. (1982). Norms of collegiality and experimentation: Workplace conditions of school success. *American Educational Research Journal, 19*(3), 325–340.

Lueddeke, G. R. (1999). Toward a constructivist framework for guiding change and innovation in higher education. *The Journal of Higher Education, 70*(3), 235–260.

Mayer, R. E. (2004). Should there be a three-strikes rule against pure discovery learning? *American Psychologist, 59*(1), 14–19.

Morgan, G. (1998). *Images of organization* (Ed.). Thousand Oaks: Sage Publications, Inc.

Northouse, P. G. (2007). *Leadership: Theory and practice* (4th ed.). Thousand Oaks: Sage Publications, Inc.

O'Loughlin, M. (1995). Daring the imagination: Unlocking voices of dissent and possibility in teaching. *Theory into Practice, 34,* 107–116.

Olsen, D. G. (1999). Constructivist principles of learning and teaching methods. *Education, 120*(2), 347–345.

Poplin, M. & Weeres, J. (1993). *Listening at the learner's level.* The Executive Educator.

Richardson, V. (1997). Constructivist teaching and teacher education: Theory and practice. In V. Richardson (Ed.), *Constructivist teacher education: Building new understandings* (pp. 3–14). Washington, DC: Falmer Press.

Senge, P., Cambron-McCabe, N. Lucas, T., Smith, B., Dutton, J. & Kleiner, A. (2000). *Schools that learn. A fifth discipline fieldbook for educators, parents, and everyone who cares about education.* New York: Doubleday/Currency

Tompkins, P., & Lawley, J. (2000). Learning metaphors. Retrieved June 16, 2007, from www.cleanlanguage.couk/LearningMetaphors.html

Trunk, Sirca, N., & Shapiro, A. (2007). Action research and constructivism: Two sides of the same coin? Or, one side? *Int. J. Management in Education, 1*(1/2), 100–107.

Vadeboncoeur, J. (1997). Child development and the purpose of education: A historical context for constructivism in teacher education. In V. Richardson (Ed.), *Constructivist teacher education: Building new understandings* (pp. 15–37). Washington, DC: Falmer Press.

Weick, K. E. (1976). Educational organizations as loosely coupled systems. *Administrative Science Quarterly, 21,* 1–19.

Weick, K. E. (1979). *The social psychology of organizing* (2nd ed.). New York: McGraw-Hill Inc.

Wheatley, M.J. (1999). *Leadership and the new science* (2nd ed.). San Francisco: Berrett-Koehler.

Wilson, B. G. (1995). Metaphors for instruction: Why we talk about learning environments. *Educational Technology, 35*(5), 25–30.

Index

An environmentally friendly book printed and bound in England by www.printondemand-worldwide.com

PEFC Certified

This product is
from sustainably
managed forests
and controlled
sources

PEFC™

www.pefc.org

PEFC/16-33-415

This book is made of chain-of-custody materials; FSC materials for the cover and PEFC materials for the text pages.

#0303 - 170516 - CO - 229/152/13 - PB - 9780415899512